THE IDEA OF CULTURE
IN THE SOCIAL SCIENCES

THE IDEA OF CULTURE
IN THE SOCIAL SCIENCES

Edited by
LOUIS SCHNEIDER
Professor of Sociology
The University of Texas at Austin

& CHARLES M. BONJEAN
Professor & Chairman of·the Department of Sociology
The University of Texas at Austin

CAMBRIDGE
AT THE UNIVERSITY PRESS 1973

Published by the Syndics of the Cambridge University Press
Bentley House, 200 Euston Road, London NW1 2DB
American Branch: 32 East 57th Street, New York, N.Y. 10022

This edition © Cambridge University Press 1973

Library of Congress Catalogue Card Number: 73-76175

ISBN: 0 512 20209 4 hardcover
      0 512 09810 6 paperback

Printed in the United States of America

CONTENTS

INTRODUCTION

The various social sciences share few concepts as pervasive and as durable as the concept of culture. It was more than a century ago that Tylor gave the concept a definition which may be regarded as the point of departure for current usages: ". . . that complex whole which includes knowledge, belief, art, morals, law, custom and any other capabilities and habits acquired by man as a member of society."[1] The rudiments of this definition have been repeatedly worked over and numerous variants of it have been proposed. The definition still presents elements that present-day social scientists apparently consider quite important. Nevertheless, much has been done since Tylor under the inspiration or at least under the rubric of his rather concise specification, as the contents of this symposium will demonstrate. The concerns here range from traditional orientations to highly innovative suggestions.

Scholars representing the disciplines of anthropology, sociology, economics, political science, history and geography, in being invited to participate in this symposium, were asked to identify the role the idea of culture plays in their respective disciplines. It was hoped that from scrutiny of their various contributions, significant convergences and divergences in usage of the idea might appear and that some important hints might emerge with regard to the unity—or lack of unity—of the social sciences. It was nevertheless recognized that each discipline would have its distinctive preoccupations and the contributors were asked to address themselves primarily to these. The present papers constitute *materials toward* the evaluation of the scope and significance of the idea of culture in the social sciences. They are not intended and never were intended as a "definitive" set of statements. The terminal essay, too, preserves a certain spirit of tentativeness to the end of the symposium and does not pretend to draw out stark and inevitable conclusions from the foregoing pieces. But the idea of culture in the social sciences, we believe, is worth consideration again and again, and the present essays are in the nature of efforts that social scientists must repeat from time to time in the hope of ever increasing insight.

The reader will find in the essays which follow discussion of a large number of issues suggested by the idea of culture and central to various social science concerns.

The anthropologist, James A. Boon of the University of Chicago, outlines a synthesis of the culture concept in his discipline through the years. Noting persistent paradoxical qualities in the concept and with an eye toward a concise comparison and review of several recent trends, he advances the notion of "cultural operators" as indicative of the way certain anthropologists have lately been approaching their problems. He loosely and initially defines such "operators" as conjunctions of elements "selected" (by the actors, the observer, or both) from different analytically posited orders of phenomena (and in perhaps more than one sense "valued"). This discussion is followed by illustrative matter drawn from opera. Finally,

---

[1] Edward B. Tylor, *Primitive Culture* (New York: Brentano's, 1924), p. 1.

aided by his historical review, his notion of "cultural operators" and his operatic example, he considers two broad areas of anthropological endeavor: approaches to "symbols" and "cultural performances" and cross-cultural comparisons of the logic of classification. His speculative, yet innovative, orientation is suggested by his title, "Further Operations of Culture in Anthropology: A Synthesis of and for Debate."

"Culture and Social System Revisited" is by Talcott Parsons, professor of sociology at Harvard University. After presenting a brief statement of the history of the relation between the two concepts of his title, he defines cultural systems and, proceeding on the view that all human societies are interpenetrated with culture, attempts a relatively systematic outline of the structure of cultural systems and of their modes of articulation in social systems. He notes the most important focus of the linkage on the cultural side lies in moral-evaluative norms and standards which may become institutionalized in the role of social values as actual parts of the structure of the social system itself. The nature of institutionalization is discussed at some length, with reference to the relations between the interests of interacting units of the social system.

Kenneth E. Boulding, professor of economics at the University of Colorado, argues that since the time of Adam Smith, economists' orientations have become progressively removed from the cultural matrix of economic phenomena. "Toward the Development of a Cultural Economics" reviews the degree to which various economic specialties have incorporated or avoided cultural analyses and then suggests problem areas where such studies might be most fruitful. Boulding indicates that there now exists in embryo form an orientation deserving of the name "cultural economics." He speculates about the future of this orientation. Much of what he sees as "cultural economics" points to content that has been in the traditional domain of the other disciplines represented in this symposium.

"Culture and Political Science: Problems in the Evaluation of the Concept of Political Culture" is by Lucian W. Pye, professor of political science at Massachusetts Institute of Technology. Pye describes the introduction, and traces the acceptance, of the concept *political culture* and warns the reader of imprecision currently associated with the concept. His central purpose is to attempt to identify why there are difficulties in conceptual precision and to suggest possible solutions. Among the matters discussed are the gap between micro and macro analysis in political science and the role that the concept of political culture has taken in attempts to reduce the gap; the effort to achieve precision in measuring culturally related phenomena, which has created new problems in conceptualization; and a number of issues associated with the testing of political culture hypotheses.

"Clio and the Culture Concept: Some Impressions of a Changing Relationship in American Historiography" is by Robert F. Berkhofer, Jr., professor of history at the University of Wisconsin. He contends that the impact of the culture concept upon the American historical profession may be discerned in the popularity of intellectual history, American studies, and the consensus interpretation of the United States past after World War II. He writes on movement toward a new definition of culture by social scientists, its coming into general scholarly usage, and the internal development of history-writing. He believes that just as the culture concept is being refined or discarded in the quest by other social scientists today for greater analytical precision, a parallel trend also appears to be starting in the history profession.

David E. Sopher, professor of geography at Syracuse University, discusses "Place and Location: Notes on the Spatial Patterning of Culture." He observes that because culture is plastic and fluid, and its areal scope variable (partly a function of ecology), the interpretation of landscape as cultural artifact and symbol is complicated. Spatial ordering of culture, related to the distance cost of circulation, is considered under several rubics: rural interaction fields, circulation dynamics of culture regions, social significance of location, and the effect of modern communications technology.

The symposium concludes with a set of "Critical and Supplementary Observations" by Louis Schneider, professor of sociology at the University of Texas at Austin. His essay is designed to have both organizing and provocative functions. Selected materials in the preceding papers are juxtaposed and an effort is made to point up some of the inevitable limitations and omissions of the other essays in such fashion that scholars interested in coming to grips with "the idea of culture in the social sciences" in the future may conceivably obtain some profit from the whole of the present endeavor.

We are of course aware of the relative brevity of this symposium. That brevity was intended from the beginning and we felt that there might be advantages in it. Reference to a few matters omitted, however, may not be amiss. There is a tradition of theorizing or speculating about large cultural "types," some of it rooting in Nietzsche, to which attention might have been given. Representative of this tradition are Ruth Benedict's semi-popular work, *Patterns of Culture,* Spengler's *Decline of the West* and Sorokin's massive *Social and Cultural Dynamics.* Nikolai Danilewski's old and crotchety but still curiously provocative *Russland und Europa* may certainly also be said to stand within this tradition. (Benedict, Spengler and Sorokin are only glancingly referred to in the pages that follow.) Echoes of the tradition live on in the suggestion that Appollonian moderation and Dionysian excess may have some bearing on the contrast between "parental culture" and "youth culture" in the present day. In a larger symposium it might have been well to call upon experts in social philosophy, intellectual history and art history to discuss various intriguing issues hereby suggested.

Further, there has recently been a lively exchange among scholars with regard to the utility of the concept of culture especially with reference to poverty. That the poor share distinctive patterns of value and belief and broadly exhibit a style of life that departs significantly from that of the rest of society—that there is a culture or "subculture" of poverty—is an idea which has generated great disagreement but at the same time may be said to have demonstrated the relevance of the culture concept to some currently pressing questions of public policy. This has not been taken up in these pages. Again: Boulding is well aware of institutionalism in economics, yet could hardly consider that movement in detail. In the work of Commons and others there is evident a certain obtrusion of "extra-economic," cultural (for example, legal) factors into the economic sphere that might repay closer scrutiny than it could be given here. In his terminal observations, Schneider contends that the notion of culture, although well worked into political science, is "given no special articulation or theoretical development in that discipline." This does not mean that "interesting" work pertaining to culture is altogether lacking in political science, or would not have been worthy of consideration here.

But this is surely enough, lest we verge on saying more about things omitted than about things not omitted. Now we must ask the reader to consider, simply, that this symposium has had a double object. One has been to effect as suggestive and illuminating a reconsideration of the idea of culture in the social sciences as could be managed within brief compass. The other and closely related object has been to be stimulating enough so that there may be some hope that others will be tempted to efforts that may soon supersede the present one. If this endeavor does prove stimulating and prompts to the consideration of wider concerns or issues than could be touched upon here, yet within some such context as is here evident, we shall not be discontented with having worked, ourselves, within the limits to which we have felt it necessary to hold.

Six of the articles appearing in this symposium were originally solicited for the September, 1972 issue of the *Social Science Quarterly*. They are reprinted here by permission of the authors and publisher. The above introduction by the editors of this volume and the concluding chapter by Schneider are revised and expanded from materials originally appearing in that issue.

In addition to the authors who graciously consented to the republication of their essays, we are indebted to Jan Hullum Edwards and Cynthia Gardner for editorial assistance.

LOUIS SCHNEIDER

CHARLES M. BONJEAN

FURTHER OPERATIONS OF "CULTURE" IN ANTHROPOLOGY: A SYNTHESIS OF AND FOR DEBATE[1]

JAMES A. BOON
University of Chicago

EVERY DISCIPLINE—A COMMUNITY OF DIALOGUE AND DEBATE—REQUIRES a fruitful paradox; in anthropology it is "culture." As true today as yesterday is Kroeber's patent assertion that "the anthropologist..., if he wishes to remain such, has necessarily to concern himself first of all with that aspect and product of human behavior—and reinfluence upon it —which is usually called 'culture'."[2] For the concept of culture allows anthropologists to deal with human phenomena in a way that is at once (ideally) descriptive, holistic, and comparative. As a concept it is both complex and ephemeral, therefore continuously controversial, yet tenacious to a degree which suggests it is indispensable. For all these reasons "culture" is difficult to talk about and impossible to agree upon, which is as it should be. There are, of course, frequent lamentations of this state of affairs as symptomatic of the pre-scientific "paradigm" woes of current socio-cultural anthropology. Yet whether or not anthropology is a "science," it is, to start with, a discipline, integrated to a large extent by comparing results of empirical investigations into the phenomenal paradox of "culture." That much at least can hardly be debated.

The present paper is offered in the spirit of such healthy controversy, as much in its opening historical review as in the somewhat brash analytic strategy it coins as a mark of recent anthropological thinking; the same spirit continues even more so in the concrete example portrayed and on into its discussion of work on "symbols," "cultural performances," and cross-cultural approaches to classificatory systems. Following a summary, debate, it is to be hoped, wages on.

---

[1] Since everything written in anthropology bears somehow on "culture," it is difficult to write, and especially selectively to document, a short paper on it. My strategy in writing has thus been to describe one modern, yet somewhat traditional, way of investigating "culture"; my strategy in documentation has been to minimize it. Apart from direct sources, I cite only various seminal volumes and debate-fostering collections which carefully work out the ideas discussed, often in a format that suggests why these ideas have been at issue in recent anthropology.

Thanks to David Schneider and Milton Singer for extensive comments on earlier drafts of the paper. Thanks also to Bob Conkling, Paul Friedrich, Clifford Geertz, Bess Keller, Martin Silverman, Sam Stanley, William Sturtevant, Hervé Varenne, and Oswald Werner for stimulating chats relevant to its topic; and thanks to my wife for her help.

[2] A. L. Kroeber, *The Nature of Culture* (Chicago: University of Chicago Press, 1952), p. 104.

THE "CULTURE" CONCEPT THROUGH THE YEARS: A DEBATABLE
SYNTHESIS IN FOUR PARTS

I. The "culture" concept has most basically assumed that there is some
sort of orderly significance in all human phenomena, from the most trivial
and everyday to the most grandiose and far-reaching. Optional sorts of
orderly significance proposed have included: (a) that one set of human
phenomena is qualitatively (or morally) inferior to another set and that
there is movement through time from one set to another in one direction or
another; (b) that some set of phenomena is more adaptive than another
set to certain non-cultural parameters; (c) that different sets of similar
phenomena are generically related; (d) that very different phenomena in
one "group" are mutually reinforcing; (e) that some set of phenomena is
more adaptive to some principle of consistency or conceptual harmony or
solidarity and reciprocity; (f) that one set of phenomena is like another
seemingly unlike set in certain ways, or that two seemingly like sets of
phenomena are unlike in certain ways, with one set of phenomena advanced as determinant; (g) that all of some kinds of human phenomena
are variations on a theme (such as a human "need") or on a dimension
(such as social differentiation); (h) that all of some kinds of human phenomena occur according to some set of principles (limits) not directly observable in the phenomena themselves, etc.[3] The concept of "culture"
has been variously equated with the order among phenomena itself or with
the characteristics of human behavior, such as "learned," "shared," "institutionalized," which help establish and reinforce such orderly significance.

II. "Culture" has had a history—part of the recent history being the discovery of this history—which reflects its essential nature of fruitful paradox
in a "(professional) tribe."[4] In its earlier history an implicit question was
"What does *everyone* have?" (only later to be refined to "By what means
does everyone communicate?"). The answer was "culture," which suggested the question "What is culture," with answers over time ranging
from "shared *things*" to "communication *processes*." The concept was traditionally regarded as the child of a single founding father (E. B. Tylor in
1871), emblazoned along with "Civilization" as ". . . that complex whole
which includes knowledge, belief, art, morals, law, custom, and any other
capabilities and habits acquired by man as a member of society."[5] It was
subsequently developed and/or obscured and misunderstood.

The American developments were synthesized and illumined by the
tribal giants Kroeber and Kluckhohn in *Culture: A Critical Review of Con-*

[3] One might match to this incomplete list general "schools" of anthropology, such as:
(a) evolutionary theory (b) culture history and cultural materialism (c) diffusionism
(d) functionalism (e) French *sociologie* (f) British "social structuralism" (g) psychological anthropology (h) French structuralism, etc.

[4] Dell H. Hymes, "On Studying the History of Anthropology," *Kroeber Anthropological Society Papers*, 26 (Spring, 1962), pp. 81–86.

[5] E. B. Tylor, *Primitive Culture: Researches into the Development of Mythology,
Philosophy, Religion, Language, Art, and Custom* (New York: Brentano's, 1924), p. 1.

cepts and Definitions, which saw culture as value-laden, transmitted patterns selected from tradition, which "may on the one hand be considered as products of action, on the other as conditioning elements of further action."[6] A decade after this tenuous consensus there ensued extensive revaluations of the legitimacy of the concept's founding father, with Stocking advancing Matthew Arnold as the more rightful claimant in the history of the profession as such, and others tracing threads of the concept to various distant sources. We should note what these reassessments see as indicative of a true "culture" concept. Stocking states that Arnold's culture was "both for the individual and for society, an organic, integrative, holistic phenomenon"; moreover, "Arnold's culture, like that of most modern anthropologists, was an inward ideational phenomenon."[7] Rowe proclaims the Renaissance as "origin of the comparative point of view of anthropology" because it "created a 'perspective distance' at which antiquity or any more recent culture might be seen whole and observed with a respect that would make it an acceptable object of study."[8] In his history of theories of culture Harris submits that "all that is new in anthropological theory begins with the Enlightenment," since, among other reasons, "the mechanisms responsible for sociocultural transformation were now regarded as purely natural expressions of cause and effect relations."[9] Lévi-Strauss lauds Rousseau as the initiator of a proper Nature/Culture dichotomy and appreciates his sensitivity to the challenge facing the philosopher-comparativist, whereby "man must first come to know himself as 'another' before he can hope to think in terms of himself."[10] Finally Stocking credits Boas with perfecting a modern culture concept stemming from the ethnographer's critique of evolutionalist ethnology:

> Underlying this critique was a holistic and historicist point of view that came in part from Boas' training in geography and that tied him to the German romantic tradition. This historicism provided a somewhat discordant counterpoint to the positivist materialistic orientation that he associated with his training in physics. The former drove him always to the detailed consideration of the individual cultural phenomenon in its actual historical context. . . .
>
> Almost unnoticed, the idea of culture, which once connoted all that freed men from the blind weight of tradition, [this idea persists as the highbrow's concept of "culture"], was now identified with that very burden,

[6] A. L. Kroeber and Clyde Kluckhohn, *Culture: A Critical Review of Concepts and Definitions* (Cambridge: Harvard University Peabody Museum of American Archeology and Ethnology Papers, 1952), vol. 47, no. 1, p. 181.

[7] George W. Stocking, "Matthew Arnold, E. B. Tylor, and the Uses of Invention," *American Anthropologist*, 65 (Aug., 1963), p. 795.

[8] John Howland Rowe, "The Renaissance Foundations of Anthropology," *American Anthropologist*, 67 (Feb., 1965), pp. 1, 14.

[9] Marvin Harris, *The Rise of Anthropological Theory* (New York: Crowell, 1968), pp. 9, 26.

[10] Claude Lévi-Strauss, "Rousseau, Father of Anthropology," UNESCO *Courier*, 16 (no. 3, 1963), p. 13.

and that burden was seen as functional to the continuous daily existence of individuals in any culture.[11]

III. The concept relates to diverse philosophical and scientific schools and tendencies. "Culture" has been influenced by and has influenced traditions as different as German idealism, French intellectualism, British empiricism, and American pragmatism, resulting in sometimes curious hybrids (and always hybrids) of approaches to what is divergent and what is general in human action. The concept fundamentally embraces differences among peoples, while insisting on commonality. Various practitioners from the different schools of inquiry have each been prevented by their sense of "culture" from degenerating into their schools' characteristic oversimplifications, which from "culture's" point of view would be pathological. The German Romantic view that ideas and ideals determine actions—especially as characteristic of German historicism—was tempered and brought nearer to "culture" through Weber's "ideal type" formulation, which, while essentially a device for formulating generalizations, emphasized value-free scrutiny of total historical contexts.[12] French intellectualism, firmly rooted in a positive, rationalist mode of thinking in oppositions and striving toward schematic harmony, was saved from metaphysics and salvaged for "culture" by Durkheim's empirically-oriented notion of *représentations* of *conscience collective*.[13] British empiricism, gaining easy access

[11] G. W. Stocking, "Franz Boas and the Culture Concept in Historical Perspective," *American Anthropologist,* 68 (Aug., 1966), pp. 871, 878. See also his *Race, Culture, and Evolution: Essays in the History of Anthropology* (New York: The Free Press, 1968).

[12] Likewise crucial to strengthening "culture"-like conceptualizing was Weber's recognition that certain promising sociological "theories" have been misinterpreted by their proponents as "a desideratum [*Sollen*]—as an ideal valid in the sphere of values, instead of as an ideal type useful in this empirical investigation of the existential [*Seiend*]," cited in Ernst Topitsch, "Max Weber and Sociology Today" in Otto Stammer, ed., *Max Weber and Sociology Today* (Oxford: Basil Blackwell, 1971), p. 12. Yet, that such theories were perhaps elaborated out of misguided, less than value-free, motives did not altogether preclude their proper use as ideal types. As Topitsch observes: ". . . according to Weber's conviction, pure economic theory has proved so effective as a methodological tool for research into the actual, that despite the danger of misinterpretation as *Sollen* or ideal—or we might prefer to call it a misapplication as an ideology of economic liberalism—it deserves a place in the behavioral theory of the economic sciences" (*ibid.*). See also in the same volume Talcott Parsons, "Value-freedom and Objectivity."

[13] Paul Bohannan, in his *"Conscience Collective* and Culture" in Kurt H. Wolff, ed. *Essays on Sociology and Philosophy by Emile Durkheim, et al.* (New York: Harper Torchbooks, 1960), pp. 77–96, discusses the exact relationship between Durkheim's concepts and "culture" as an analytic construct. At one point he succinctly contrasts the viewpoints of Durkheim and Robert Redfield: "Whereas Durkheim postulates a *conscience collective* as the organization of collective representations as they are manifested in social relationships, Redfield postulates a culture as an organization of conventional understandings manifested in act and artifact. The difference between social and cultural anthropology could not be more starkly exposed" (p. 88). While this is true, it should be noted that a Durkheimian social relationship *as represented* (in some collective representation) is not at all unlike an artifact. Thus, those works by Durk-

to a wealth of data throughout the empire and able to find a common ground of common (utilitarian) sense in the most esoteric phenomena, was called back to the comparativist rudiments of "culture" by the indirect means of concepts of "social structure."[14] Lastly, "culture," while being refined in America, allowed scholars there to be pragmatic (would-be philosophical neutrals) and open to various modes of generalization, although psychological ones often took precedence; most importantly it ultimately kept us beyond reach of the clutches of behaviorism. In other words "culture" has been dialectical from the start. It has bridged materialist and idealist interpretations for observed behavior as distinctly as the Marx-versus-Hegel controversy has for history. "Culture" remains situated between materials and ideas; between unconscious and/or conscious motives and clearly conscious rationalizations; between indigenous categories and analytic constructs (both indigenous constructs and outsiders' constructs); between little actors and "great traditions"; between statistics and norms; between fundamental "religious" *values* of existential commitment and seemingly trivial *values* of taste and propriety; between anthropology's humanistic respect for particularistic fieldwork and its scientific will toward general propositions—a source of "somewhat discordant counterpoint" for Boas, and a source of paradox (and polemic) for all.

IV. The concept has been extensively developed along two different, yet related, lines of conceptualization: (1) "culture" as but one of several members in a set of analytic constructs and (2) "culture" as totalistically opposed to not-culture, as A is to not-A.

Viewpoint (1) has been most thoroughly elaborated by the sociological school of Talcott Parsons, which poses as a minimal analytic framework the composite of human "action" out of which can be abstracted "biology" as the organism-requirement pattern, "psychology" as the individual-needs pattern, "society" as the institutional pattern, and "culture" as the values pattern.[15] Complete analyses of any "action" must take into account all abstractable levels in a grand concatenation of inter-determinisms. Viewpoint

heim—especially with Marcel Mauss, *Primitive Classification*, R. Needham, trans., (Chicago: University of Chicago Press, 1963)—prefiguring what Bohannan calls the "Neo-Durkheimian science of representations" (p. 94) are perhaps more a forerunner of current cultural anthropology than of social anthropology.

[14] To trace these subtle developments in British anthropology, see Milton Singer, "The Concept of Culture," under "Culture" in the *International Encyclopedia of the Social Sciences*, vol. 3 (New York: Macmillan and The Free Press, 1968), pp. 527–543.

[15] This inadequate allusion to Parsonian theory should be taken as simply that, and the same holds for the subsequent allusion to Lévi-Straussian theory (although his methodology will later be further considered). The sole point here concerns a basic contrast at a particular level. The Parsonians' major contributions in advancing a total theory of action (and of "culture" as one of its components) are not broached in this paper, since our aim is eventually to view three trends in anthropology as variations on a lower level analytic strategy, with any full-fledged theories of culture they ultimately advance remaining in the distant background and in fact, as will be suggested, somewhat conflicting.

(2) has been most recently revived and expounded in the works of Claude Lévi-Strauss, who conceives of "culture" most generally as that peculiar, orderly selectivity which is characteristic of all human (as opposed to natural) phenomena. Natural elements are viewed as the material for "culture," this problematic human capacity which has differentially left its mark on (i.e. has selectively reduced and arranged) everything from biological sexual processes to astrological physical conditions. Of far less importance in viewpoint (2) than in viewpoint (1) is the notion of "*a* culture" as a systematically integrated space-time isolate.

To most succintly characterize "culture" in this two-fold conceptualization, we might consider an approach which purposefully bridges the above two viewpoints—Schneider's notion of "culture" as outlined in his *American Kinship*. Taking off from Parsons, Schneider sees "culture" as a system of definitions and values. The definitions (implicit and explicit) he loosely calls "units":

> A unit in a particular culture is simply anything that is culturally defined and distinguished as an entity. It may be a person, place, thing, feeling, state of affairs, sense of foreboding, fantasy, hallucination, hope, or idea.[16]

Most critically, a cultural unit is not coterminous with a specific *term for* the unit (if there is one), nor are units consisting in *definitions* of persons coterminous with persons as actors. In short, Schneider radically isolates ideals—ideal definitions (= cultural nits) ideally interrelated (= values). A theory of description (ethnography) is then advanced wherein one treats culture as "a symbolic system purely in its own terms rather than by systematically relating the symbols to the social and psychological systems, and to the problems of articulating them within the framework of the problems of social action." Implicit in the theory of description are the makings of a theory of comparison (ethnology) which would interrelate multiple symbolic systems so isolated.

Thus, "culture" plays a dual analytic role in Schneider's work. First, as a member in a set of conceivable analytic constructs (in a sort of heuristic contrast with other constructs), it enables him to zero in on patterns of ideals as expressed through symbols. However, subsequently "culture" turns the tables on the other constructs, since it comes to employ them as mere sources of material for expressing the values comprising itself. For example, in Schneider's analysis the "biological" stuff of sex affords "culture" potential diacriticals for establishing valued meaning. "Culture" uses "biology" as material, but any direct relationship between the biological (and by extension the social and psychological) and the cultural is problematic at best. Thus, this approach is like the Parsonian viewpoint insofar as

---

[16] This and the following quotation are from David M. Schneider, *American Kinship: A Cultural Account* (Englewood Cliffs: Prentice-Hall, 1968), pp. 2, 1n. See also his "What is Kinship All About," in Priscilla Reining, ed., *Morgan Centennial Volume* (Washington Anthropological Society, 1971), a more recent effort to isolate a "pure cultural" level of analysis.

it stresses the systematic quality of "culture," especially of *a* "culture system." Yet it is also like the above viewpoint (2) of Culture-versus-Nature, since "culture" looms as an independent variable, which only requires "biology," "psychology" and "sociology" as sources of material *for* establishing systems of definitions and values in any particular time and space.

Even this rapid perusal of "culture's" minimal assumptions, history, related philosophical frameworks, and two major analytic roles suggests it is less paradigm than paradox. "Culture" has generally served not so much as a model or theory allowing anthropology to progress to the right analysis of human phenomena, but as a more or less articulate sense of dilemma which helps prevent anthropologists from committing inadequate reductionisms when confronted with radically complex, and always colorful and intriguing, data. If one were obliged to report on the current state of the paradox, he might controversially observe: By the 1950's those paradoxical qualities of "culture" early appreciated by Sapir (especially insofar as they echo qualities of "language") and most tirelessly stressed by Kroeber were well established in the minds of anthropologists.[17] Always maintaining a subsidiary awareness of the "culture" paradox (and profiting from international developments in linguistics and interdisciplinary work on various sorts of communication theory), researchers concentrated on refining their *methodologies* in order to better clarify whatever "culture" was or, more precisely, however it worked. Common to many such refinements has been extensive re-thinking concerning both the locus of the integration of meaning and value expected in "culture" and the level at which it can be approached. As we proceed to synthesize a practical analytic strategy symptomatic of several recent trends in anthropology—each attempting still to bridge the heady theoretical problems of "how man communicates" and the pedestrian fieldwork difficulties of "communicating with men" (these two sides of the same anthropological reality)—the rationale behind the rethinking should become clear.

PRIVILEGED OPERATIONAL ZONES OF CULTURE

"Culture" pertains to operations which render complex human phenomena communicable. Any set of human phenomena—whether an abstracted type of phenomena such as "language," or a provisionally isolated complex "event" or "situation," or a larger scale isolate in time and place such as "a society"—can be *described*, although not necessarily exhaustively, as a juncture of analytically separable orders of elements. What we might call the experience-as-conceived (or let us simply say the communication) of those phenomena is achieved by some sort of selection (implies reduction) and emphasis of some of the elements from each of the orders adduced. And these elements are themselves *connected* in a more or per-

[17] Most of Sapir's views are in *Selected Writings of Edward Sapir in Language, Culture, and Personality*, David G. Mandelbaum, ed. (Berkeley: University of California Press, 1963), and in *Language* (New York: Harcourt, Brace, 1921): Kroeber, *The Nature of Culture, passim.*

haps in a less traditional arrangement—i.e. in an arrangement which implicitly refers back to tradition either by being like it or unlike it. Most generally, *some sort* of selection of elements from posited orders which are evidenced in the phenomena, communicates the phenomena (or in effect *is* the communication of the phenomena) in complex conscious and/or unconscious ways to those persons enacting the phenomena themselves. (This communication pertains to general conceiving of experience—i.e. perception and cognition.) *Some sort of* selection communicates the phenomena to an indigenous novice, enabling him to approach *sharing* them. (This communication pertains to "culture" insofar as it can be transmitted.) Similarly, *some sort of* selection (not necessarily the same sort) communicates the phenomena to an outside observer, enabling him to approach *understanding* them. (This communication pertains to "culture" insofar as it can be analyzed.) The nature of all these sorts of communication through selection is a matter of current and hot debate; yet all such differential (which is as much as to say weighted or valued) selection is at the crux of "culture."[18] In sum, communicable experience is achieved through the process of selecting and interrelating sets of elements from various orders of phenomena (e.g. in Saussurian linguistics the order of sound-image and the order of concept). This process we might call simply the *operation* of the analytically posited orders. And the result of such operation is *some sort of* communication such as those just mentioned.

In light of the above framework it is useful to formulate a notion of "privileged operational zones of culture," to be understood simply as those human situations and contexts in which the observer can more directly observe cultural *operation* going on. Note that nothing here is being said about the best way to isolate whatever the orders operated might be. In anthropological parlance we are opting neither for an emic approach (which would stress the primacy of so-called native categories) nor for an etic approach (which would stress the primacy of cross-cultural compar-

---

[18] It is obvious that these issues recall the Kroeber and Kluckhohn emphasis on "culture" as patterns *of* and *for* action. It is perhaps less obvious that they also recall the insistence by phenomenologists (not to mention gestaltists) that percepts and concepts cannot be patly distinguished; as well as Saussure's implication that *connections between* posited orders must be positively accepted as axiomatic, since without such connections between orders there could be no orders detectable to be connected—and therefore, we can add, no perception or cognition (see below).

The general thrust of this discussion is in a word to view culture as "code." And while encoding, recoding, and decoding are three distinct kinds of communication through "selection," we are here stressing processes common to all three. Moreover, while any code—even "culture" as a meta-code including "language," "technology," "social structure," etc.—is at some level perfectly systematic and "closed" (although mutable), the point is that the encoding, recoding, and decoding all occur with less than perfect mastery of the hypothetical total code in question. Thus, the fieldworker, for example, can proceed to study cultural phenomena with a hope in ultimately perfect "code" and the conviction that there are areas of social life which more directly render that code accessible to persons not fully proficient in it (such as any individual indigenous actor; as well as novices and outsiders), in order for actors to be mindful of their "culture," and in order for novices to learn it and for outsiders to analyze it.

ability), nor for first one and then the other. Rather it is simply suggested that, minimally, somehow from somewhere at some point a set of orders must be (perhaps vaguely) isolated. Yet once this is done, what is most pertinent to "culture" is not how each order is bound, or how each order is itself interiorly organized, or by what criteria the analyzer selected these orders—although each of these questions is important in other respects. Rather, of greatest pertinence are the connections among different orders, the patterns by which elements from ostensibly or hypothetically different "spheres" of experience are related. Without assuming that any particular order is necessarily more thoroughly intra-organized—e.g. "kinship" for everyone, or plant-lore for gardeners—the observer can view zones which most readily present themselves as multiple orders of selectively contrasted and connected elements. These are not only the standard "cognitive map" zones or explicit native classifications, but also zones of inter-media productions and of complex "framed" activities.

To study such privileged operational zones is to focus on the short circuits between the posited orders, whether sensory orders, orders suggested by the natives, orders suggested by the analyzer.[19] For example, there are situations where one can more readily see standard verbalizations, gestures, attitudes, affects, etc. being selected and interrelated. One obvious situation is the acquisition of cultural forms—language, bodily comportment, reading (if present), music, dance, and so forth. Since any learning process presents an automatic contrast set of the versed versus the unversed members of that culture, such a process can be described (with no need for an analytic construct like "personality") as the acquisition by the unversed of selections of elements from some orders keyed to selections of elements from other orders—all aimed more or less toward the model of the versed. In other words the operations characteristic of the versed and those of the unversed are somehow similar, but very different; therefore the two sets of operations are contrastive and comparable (as opposed to identical). For any one group the observer can describe contrasts between the versed set of operations and the unversed set and later try to delineate patterns of how the unversed set is transformed into the versed. Or he can compare the range of orders selected and the operations effected across groups.

Another crucial aspect of cultural operators is this: When some systematic arrangement of elements from different orders appears to be *necessary* (or to be thought necessary) to the group in question, the observer can hypothesize that at some level at some time an operator (to reify the

---

[19] Note at once that even this apparently innocuous and casual typology of three varieties of orders overlooks important concerns in recent anthropology. Harold C. Conklin's milestone article on color classification in "Hanunoo Color Categories," *Southwestern Journal of Anthropology*, 11 (Winter, 1955), pp. 339–344, had such resounding effects in the discipline because he demonstrated how the supposedly safest "natural" etic of color perception (sensory categories) was subject to rules of an emic grid ("native" categories).

concept of "cultural operations") has been present which effected the connection of that selection of elements from orders in that way. The term "effected" is vague, even ambiguous. Possibly there is no discernible operator, whether there simply is not one present or the one that was present has "fallen into disuse." ("Language" has been deemed "arbitrary" in Saussurian linguistics precisely because no "motivated" operators for the connections are evident.) Some operators are more obscure and there is *always* the danger that we are reading operators into the complex event at hand. But all such difficulties notwithstanding, if such an operator, such a succinctly formed connection between elements selected from multiple orders, can be discovered and articulated, then the observer has a tool for arguing various points, such as "why" that systematic arrangement "works" (or indeed what makes the arrangement *systematic*); or if the operator is witnessed in action, why the event has an effect on the actors; or if the operator is abstracted from textual material, what it is that makes some assortment of texts a "corpus." Moreover, he has a privileged instance of "culture."

In brief, then, a cultural operator can be defined as a succinct and orderly conjunction of elements from what appear to the analyzer, to the actors, or to both, as diverse orders. The operator is involved in acquiring the orders-so-related and perhaps too in reinforcing, or in manipulating and altering, the orders-so-related later on.[20] Some sorts of viable operations are signaled by emotive responses by those involved, such as laughter, tears, sighs. Operations are most "cultural" when they recall the genesis of signification, as when a baby matches the right phones from his language system to the right portions of his context system, or when within the universe of some theatrical production or film a particular leitmotif eventually comes to evoke a certain character or mood. In a broad sense these two phenomena are the same sorts of occurrence: a pattern of elements from one order is conjoined to a pattern of elements from another order, and if the prerequisites of any codes involved are met, the *fact* that they are so-conjoined attains the aura of necessity, of being "how it should be"; the conjunction becomes a value. But it can be a value in two ways: the conjunction can be a "value" in and of the fact that elements from more than one order are conjoined (the prime example of this is the "arbitrary" value of Saussurian linguistics); let us call this "selection-value." The conjunction can also be involved at what we might vaguely call an "action-value" level (or perhaps a normative level); while there are many ways of supporting an argument that a given conjunction of

[20] In our general framework any definition of "symbols" would be characterized by some additional criterion—e.g., in Freudian terms "condensation," in Durkheimian terms "objectification," etc. However, Charles Pierce's "symbol" relates more directly to our concerns (see note 21). All discussion of Saussure is based on Ferdinand de Saussure, *Course in General Linguistics*, W. Baskin, trans. (New York: McGraw-Hill, 1966).

elements reflects certain action-values, perhaps the simplest way is to re-port the responses of those involved when that conjunction is denied.[21]

A somewhat technical digression is necessary, since the distinction we are drawing cuts across Saussure's distinction between "arbitary" and "motivated." What is here being called a selection-value follows Saus-sure's notion of the purely conventional *value* of a linguistic sign: the sound-image (*signifiant*) "sheep" is connected to the concept (*signifié*) "sheep" by simple convention; the connection just sits there—two syste-matically interrelated slots in the two component orders of "language"—having no consequences in any other phenomenal order as abstractable from experience (e.g. the sound-image is itself not "wooly"). On the other hand what is here being designated "action-value" differs from such a simple selection-value in two ways: (1) some other abstractable orders are involved, for example the imitation of nature in an onomatopoeia (in Saussure's thinking this is a "motivated" or "non-arbitrary" sign); *and* (2) the fact that other orders are involved has consequences in still other orders at observable behavioral levels; the consequences thus serve to signal when *values* are being operated. A standard example should clarify the matter. Take any word which appears to exemplify an "arbitrary" se-lection value. Suppose then that the analyzer discovers a natural sound that apparently, in Saussure's terms, "motivates" that word (making it a so-called onomatopoeia). In our usage any such *value* that can be argued by the analyzer to be "motivated" may or may not be an action-value. For example, an onomatopoeia which has been routinized, which is no longer sensed as such by speakers, is not an action-value. (One might say that it is still "motivated" in Saussure's analytic sense, but it is "unmotivated" in a pragmatic, psychological sense.) But if the onomatopoeia provokes a smile or a child's sparkle of recognition (kindled by his awareness that disparate orders are being connected) then it involves action-values. In the latter case the selection-values comprising the onomatopoeia have conse-quences in other orders, and the consequences provoke an observable re-sponse: a smile, a sparkle.[22] The pragmatist would show interest in this

---

[21] For example, for complex reasons stemming from the systematic nature of "language," a baby must make correct verbal-scene connections; if "wrong" verbal-scene connections are made (which would contradict the language's selection-values), the connections are corrected or at least not reinforced (such responses comprise the related action-values of competent speakers). Or in American films a passionate em-brace may not be accompanied by a boogie-woogie; rather some variation on gradually surging strings is in order (unless comedy, especially parody, is the film's game—which would play on the action-values emoted from an audience whose selection-value expec-tations have been thwarted).

[22] There is something like an action-value component in Charles Pierce's concept of "symbol" as a class of signs with creative power: "Thus the mode of being of the symbol is different from that of the icon and from that of the index. An icon has such being as belongs to past experience. It exists only as an image in the mind. An index has the being of present experience. The being of a symbol consists in the real fact that something surely will be experienced if certain conditions be satisfied. Namely, it will

response as a point of psychological (or cultural) "reality"; the rationalist would show interest in this response as a point of intersection of multiple mappable orders.

Thus, we have on the one hand simple Saussurian "arbitrary" values and what one might think of as compounded values (Saussure's "motivated," but with the corrective that there is an "arbitrary" element in the way a natural sound, for example, is limited in a so-called "motivated" onomatopoeia)—both of which we call selection-values. We have on the other hand selection-values that activate an observable response in behavior— and these we call action-values. Of course, any hard distinction between selection-values and action-values is by analytic fiat. Whether or not there can indeed be an "arbitrary" selection-value—i.e. a connection between two orders which is unrelated to any other orders—is a matter of current debate even in linguistics.[23] In other words any *value* might when fully understood reveal both selection and action aspects. But the point remains that an outside observer witnesses many operations in another culture which appear to be either "arbitrary" or (in Saussure's analytic sense) "motivated" selections, only some of which are clearly action-value tinged, e.g. conducive to "instrumental action," inducive of emotional response, etc. In short, and debatably, much anthropological work continues to be essentially a description of a particular array of selection-values, often coupled with the will toward isolating related action-values—both being germane to "culture."

A CONTROVERSIAL CONCRETE EXAMPLE

It usually seems vacuous, or at least bland, to discuss "culture" in the absence of concrete examples (which is why philosophy is often bland and why anthropology, which is first and foremost concrete, fails sufficiently to ponder its intellectual paradoxes). Most cultural examples would have to be too long for this paper. Thus, there follows something like a "cultural" example, but shorter. Operations similar to those we are calling "cultural" are perhaps most familiar in the area of synthetic arts and spectator situations. To take a personal favorite: Verdi's *La Traviata*. The complex of human phenomena that is *La Traviata* can be described as a set of various orders (e.g., orchestral score, vocal score, lyrics, plot, love theme, act divisions, etc.); all of which might be divided into a myriad of sub-orders

---

influence the thought and conduct of its interpreter," cited in Roman Jakobson, "Quest for the Essence of Language," *Diogenes,* 51 (Fall, 1965), pp. 36–37.

    [23] On these general issues in approaches to semiotics, see Paul Friedrich, "The Lexical Symbol and its Non-arbitrariness," paper presented at the annual meeting of the American Anthropological Association, 1971. For an exemplary anthropological study concerning whether the simplest kind of selection in perception or cognition (e.g. selecting one side of a binary opposition) does not entail an implicit "action-value" commitment, see E. R. Leach, "Anthropological Aspects of Language: Animal Categories and Verbal Abuse," in Eric H. Lenneberg, ed., *New Directions in the Study of Language* (Cambridge: M. I. T. Press, 1964).

(e.g., treble/base, melodic motifs, verbal images, sub-plot, father-love sub-theme, shifting tableaux, etc.). Some of the orders are unconscious components of all human phenomena; some are conscious components peculiar to musical phenomena; some are directly signaled within the opera; some are adduced through critical interpretation. The opera is about a moribund woman in love who manages to survive long enough to sing the opera. And at one profound, penultimate instant all the orders are marvelously conjoined in a way, it could be argued, that achieves the work's theme. This comes when the heroine is on the verge of the most prosaic of death-rattles, which in its depth hits a register of breathiness that (apparently automatically) launches her back up several octaves to the peak of the love aria. In this acoustically sublime instant the groan of death *becomes* the full-voice of romantic enthusiasm. It is one of the most scintillating *operators* I know. Whether consciously intended by the singer or composer or not, we can call it an operator because thanks to this connection between the very disparate sets of elements from different orders—a visceral, plot-line near-grunt of death, and the lofty, thematic melody of Verdi's aria—the many components of the opera retrospectively fall together in complementarity. There is resolution; we sense "why" the opera's orders (thematic ones as well as acoustical ones) have been being interrelated as they have been being interrelated. *During* the opera the operator effects the "symbolic action" of the experience of the performance. *After* the opera the operator serves as a tool with which to describe and interpret the orders involved.

Note that it might be misleading to call this acoustical groan/melody operator a "symbol." It is not at all visual and far from explicit and not in any clear sense "grounded" in nature (as opposed to conventional). It is covert, easily escapes articulation, and is not necessarily intended by anyone. Yet the operator is there, as evidenced, for example, by the simultaneous sigh of several thousand spectators, who felt its effect (sensed it as action-value) or as critically evidenced by the way it makes all the orders tie in together (at the level of selection-values). Moreover, no more than a "symbol" could I call it an "opposition" in Lévi-Strauss' precise sense, at least not without extensive explanations as to the nature of the two sets involved that should stand in total contrast. We can think of operators as the minimal class, of which both "symbols" and "oppositions" are varieties or particular methodological slants. An operator is more vaguely a cluster (a nexus) of diverse components which, when so juxtaposed (whether in analogy or in contrast) provide the potential of effecting a burst of cross-referencing significance. And on the stage "meaning," and in social life "culture" is born.

This opera example is true, but also contrived. Opera is a straw man example for demonstrating the detection of operators. It is easier to talk about opera as complexes of more or less interrelated orders, because the explicit history of opera as a genre concerns the development of the distinct orders—sometimes independent of each other—and the changing

degrees of their interrelation. At some point in history plot is added to
voice and orchestra; at some point the relative disjunction between aria
and instrumental segments is surmounted, as vocal line(s) and orchestral
lines approach equal status, complete inter-articulation; finally in Wagner's music dramas the aim is to embrace all possible orders—the gamut
of which now includes poetic text, national mythological traditions, stage
setting, and complete music hall control—in a new plenitude of operations.
Opera, perhaps more than any other synthetic art (although film runs it a
close second) lends itself to being described in these terms: there is some
ideal total array of *orders* of elements at the ideal creator's disposal. He
can select some set of the orders from tradition, while creatively altering
certain aspects, as long as he still "communicates." He may then draw on
each of the orders to license or justify ("motivate") the selection of various
features in the other orders: e.g. the hero must have a particular voice
type because he is accompanied by a particular instrument. (The audience in its turn re-selects and connects orders—perhaps from a different
"pool" of orders—and dialectically relates them to the creator's orders—
with the result being interpretation, which implies experience, of the
work.) Essentially then, we are viewing *La Traviata* as an array of selection-values—some "arbitrary" or purely conventional (e.g. "do" and the
first position on the scale), some "motivated" in the sense of compoundly
selected (e.g. a baritone accompanied by a cello)—one set of which (those
in the groan/aria moment) becomes an action-value. We can support the
contention that this operatic moment reflects an action-value by citing the
audience's sigh, by administering psychological tests, by asking people,
by defining relevancy in terms of interpretive power (thus making action-
values subordinate to selection-values), etc. We need not support contentions concerning selection-values in this way, but only clarify how they are
possibly relevant interconnections across orders, as suggested by our background in various contextual matters, such as the history of opera, the
musical career of Verdi, the phenomenology of music-hall participation,
dynamics of vocal music and so forth.[24]

But what has the above to do with a real culture (if we can accept such
a construct) which is on the ground rather than a stage? Other human
phenomena, when placed in the full perspective of cross-cultural relativ-
ity, can be *described* in a like fashion—in short described (and implicitly

[24] We have treated this set of human phenomena independently of any social context,
biological parameters, or personality factors. This is not to imply that an opera must be
talked about in this way (any more than "a culture" must be), but only that it *can* be.
There are no doubt, for example, sociological dimensions to *La Traviata*. Verdi's
acoustical instant of death/romance *might* point to features of general American society;
La Traviata is after all presented in America more often with higher attendance than
many other operas—in this sense it is doubly selected. It much more probably relates
to something American opera-goers, and doubtless more still to nineteenth
century Italian opera-goers. In other words the same significant forms can operate
differently for different folk, and art, although it might afford convenient clues to "culture," does not in any direct way "reflect" a society's interests and needs.

contrasted) as "cultures." This is not to say that every set of human phenomena could be equally as readily described as a complex of interrelated orders. But it never hurts to try. Moreover wherever one finds orders being interrelated, he will not necessarily find so complex an operator of both selection- and action-values as the example from *La Traviata* (this work of art more intensely integrated than "life itself," which, as art, can be expected to employ artful devices to direct, or at least limit, the spectators' responses). But again, it never hurts to try. And the argument here is simply that much work in recent anthropology has been trying just this: to locate privileged operational zones of culture (i.e. both kinds of value) in sets of human phenomena, and more problematically and spectacularly to detect universal operators employed by "culture" itself (to reify a bit), as it articulates on-going experience, just as Verdi's sublime acoustical instance articulates an on-going opera. .

"SYMBOLS" AND "CULTURAL PERFORMANCES"

It has long been observed by anthropologists that examples of what we have glossed as "cultural operations" tend to become objectified and rigidified. What result—we can think of them as little "culture crystals"—are often designated "symbols."[25] In his extensive works on Ndembu rituals, Turner specifies that which appears to him the "basic unit or 'molecule' of human ritual behavior, which contains both verbal and non-verbal constituents":

> Such a molecule, or smallest portion to which a ritual sequence or dynamic total can be reduced by subdivision without losing its semantic structural identity, is the ritual *symbol*. A multivocal symbol, in so far as it is a *symbol*, is a thing (object, event, person, relationship, activity, place, period of time, etc.) regarded . . . by general consent . . . as "naturally" typifying or representing something by possession of analogous qualities or by association in fact or thought.
>
> The great rituals of mankind are emitting information in the veiled and disguised forms of multivocal symbols. . . .[26]

[25] A major effort to derive an anthropological perspective from the vast international and interdisciplinary literature on "symbols" and symbolic systems is found in several articles by Clifford Geertz, "Ethos, World-View and the Analysis of Sacred Symbols," *Antioch Review*, 17 (Winter, 1957–58), pp. 421–437; "Ideology as a Cultural System," in D. Apter, ed., *Ideology of Discontent* (New York: Free Press, 1964); "Religion as a Cultural System," in Michael Banton, ed., *Anthropological Approaches to the Study of Religion* (London: Tavistock, 1966). See also his "Deep Play: Notes on the Balinese Cockfight," *Daedalus*, 101 (Winter, 1972). Two other favorite examples from the literature are Suzanne Langer, *Feeling and Form* (New York: Scribner's, 1953), and Maurice Merleau-Ponty, *Signs*, R. C. McCleary, trans. (Evanston: Northwestern University Press, 1964).

[26] Victor W. Turner's works on the Ndembu include *The Forest of Symbols: Aspects of Ndembu Ritual* (Ithaca: Cornell University Press, 1967); *The Drums of Affliction: A Study of Religious Processes Among the Ndembu of Zambia* (Oxford: Clarendon, 1968); and *The Ritual Process: Structure and Anti-Structure* (Chicago: Aldine, 1969). The quotation is from his introduction to "Forms of Symbolic Action," *Proceedings of*

If *La Traviata's* groan/aria had been patently and indisputably "objecti-fied," then it would no doubt qualify as an exemplary multivocal symbol. That it was not illustrates the danger in assuming that things like cultural operations are necessarily well-articulated or at any level distinctly set off and bound. In short all "symbols" are operators, but not the contrary. Minimally, an anthropological investigation into "culture" concentrates first on the inter-connection of different orders (which, we suggest, remains the crux of any definition of "symbol") without generalizing as to some ultimate nature of a higher level unit. Minimally a focus on privileged operational zones seeks to open vistas onto cultural symbols and connec-tions among them, while lessening the risks of prematurely forcing the data into cut-and-dried, crystallized mega-symbols. For the dangerous tendency in studies of significant forms and in seeing "culture" as holistic significant form is to "over-literarize" the facts at hand. The investigator, attracted by bound, multivocal, sensory-rich productions, only derives full satisfacton if he can finally abstract and completely interrelate the total range of components. However, that critical satisfaction most readily obtained from analyzing individually created, closed aesthetic productions (often produced with this sort of satisfaction in mind) is difficult to attain from observing cultural micro-processes that extend through macro-time.

A complicating factor is that different societies might reduce and inter-relate their constituent orders into symbol-prone wholes to differing de-grees. Mary Douglas has recently implied that for every ritually multi-vocal group anthropology discloses, there might be another one that is ritually impoverished.[27] Such a group's order and affect—for we assume that all groups have order and affect—is manifested elsewhere or perhaps hoarded individualistically. Moreover, in any "society" some segments might be highly prone to complex ritual and symbolic programs (e.g., a priestly class with its indigenous hermeneuticists), while other groups de-monstrate that shoulder-shrugging, un*engagé*, patently indifferent attitude to, in this case, ritualized operations. In short it is the plight of anthropolo-gists—as interpreters of the values which render intelligible cultural proc-esses—generally to fall short of perfect "poetic closure."

The above plight—a bane for investigators with the traditional Malin-owskian drive toward total explication of a supposed primitive, slice-of-time isolate—has been more realistically dealt with in approaches to liter-ate civilizations. In a recent reevaluation of such studies, Hsu notes:

> When anthropologists finally turned to literate civilization, their research usually assumed one of three forms: (1) investigation of a single aspect of a literate civilization, (2) investigation of a single community within a literate civilization, or (3) a broadly psychologcal approach to the literate civilization as a whole.

the 1969 *Meeting of the American Ethnological Society* (University of Washington, 1969), a useful, debate-provoking volume.

[27] Mary Douglas, *Natural Symbols: Explorations in Cosmology* (New York: Pan-theon, 1970).

The third group emphasized the shared patterns between the written literature, novels, movies, myths, folktales, the sacred books, traditional philosophies, and such, and the values, feelings and preoccupations of the common peoples as expressed through their activities, problems, and utterances. Since these anthropologists are most often psychologically oriented, they attempt to assess common psychological patterns which underlie and unite the disparate aspects of each civilization.[28]

This later emphasis on expressive idioms reflects an early rejection of the idea that the whole of whatever was being investigated could be encompassed within the cover of one monograph or even a series. The major constructs employed—"civilization" or "nation," as opposed to some ideal tribal isolate—were exceedingly problematic. And since the whole was clearly beyond grasp, things not unlike "symbols" of the whole were sought. Yet there were shortcomings in such studies, most obviously the rush to various reductionisms, especially Freudian ones. Often, as soon as a pattern was discerned in the interesting zone of real individuals interrelating their corporeal selves in everyday ways, that pattern was prematurely plugged into Freudian syndrome X, with abundant parallel patterns never wanting, and a national, "explanatory" neurosis was born.[29] Another shortcoming lay in the studies' emphasis on *contents* of behavior and textual materials. They sought thematic and plot-line parallels between the ways people lived and their expressive forms; and again, if any contradictions in the contents were discerned, premature Freudian explanation was handy. The analyzers always assumed they were being misled, that the distortions of these cultural *projections* had to be corrected. They committed the same sort of error (from the viewpoint of information theory) as Lévi-Strauss

[28] Francis L. K. Hsu, *The Study of Literate Civilizations* (New York: Holt, Rinehart and Winston, 1969), p. 3.

[29] See, for example, Nur Yalman, "On the Purity of Women in the Castes of Ceylon and Malabar," *Journal of the Royal Anthropological Institute,* 93 (Part 1, 1963), pp. 25–58, with its criticism of Kathleen Gough's use of the "Oedipus complex" to explain Nayar female puberty rites. Such debates are part of the general turn toward more "structural" (versus "sentimental") methods of explanation, on which see Rodney Needham, *Structure and Sentiment: A Test Case in Social Anthropology* (Chicago: University of Chicago Press, 1962).
Especially instructive in earlier "character"-type studies is Margaret Mead's work, and especially, since we are discussing literate civilization, in Bali. Mead and Bateson's classic portrait of *Balinese Character* (New York Academy of Sciences, 1942) is peppered with dead-end observations on Freudian topics, as in discussing Balinese "defense of the mouth" where "we find a development of unresponsiveness which is commonly expressed by plugging the mouth or by tight closure of lips. Both plugging and tight closure are modes with anal as well as oral significance" (p. 108). Yet Mead has long been striving toward a broader basis for learning theory in non-Western cultures. Her *Growth and Culture,* with Frances Macgregor (New York: Putnam, 1951) is an explicit inter-disciplinary attempt to delineate gestalt learning patterns in Bali. However, again there is the application of too rigid a Western laboratory framework. As Mead, in her *Continuities in Cultural Evolution* (New Haven: Yale University Press, 1964), later reflected back over her own work: "The most immediate lack is on pattern or gestalt learning, which is exceedingly important but not yet documented by the order of fieldwork on which I am drawing here" (p. xvii).

has noted among scholars studying tribal myth, who felt that some historical and ethnographic reality deviously camouflaged by the myths was
their objective. Investigators were interested primarily in *what really*
happened, and only secondarily in how the people in question thought of
whatever happened. (These priorities have in much more recent anthropological work been reversed.) The immediate materials at hand were
treated as much as obstacles as they were clues to this "reality." The bias
can be traced to Boas; witness his views on biographies and autobio-
graphies of (in this case tribal) informants:

> . . . they are not facts but memories and memories distorted by the wishes
> and thoughts of the moment. The interests of the present determine the
> selection of data and color the interpretation of the past.
>   In (the informants') records personal likes and dislikes may also affect
> the presentation of events, inclusion or omissions of pertinent data. In short
> the tricks that memory plays on us are too important to allow us to accept
> autobiographies as reliable factual data.[30]

With a concept like "cultural operators" in mind, rather than placing
hopes in "reliable factual data," one welcomes any such "tricks that memory
plays" as clues to differential ways in which significant items from ongoing
experiences are selected and ordered in retrospect. Somewhat in the spirit
of good New Criticism, an emphasis on operations first accepts any textual
material for what it is, without rushing to explain why it is that, by means
of a reductionist construct such as "personality of the actors," "real drives
behind the epiphenomenal matrix of idioms," and so forth. A description
of operations does not necessarily discount such explanation, but it would
wait a very long time before trying it—perhaps until the investigators knew
at least as much about the investigated as about themselves. Finally any
such approach denies the primacy (but not the relevance) of theme and
contents.

Just what aspects of a literate civilization are amenable to "cultural"
interpretations persists as a vital issue in anthropology. Of particular interest to culture theory have been developments of approaches to "cultural
performances."[31] These zones of operations enable the observer to focus

---

[30] Boas cited in L. L. Langness, *The Life History in Anthropological Science* (New
York: Holt, Rinehart and Winston, 1965).

[31] Milton Singer's "The Cultural Pattern of Indian Civilization," *Far Eastern Quarterly*, 15 (Nov., 1955) outlines an approach to South Asian "cultural performances"
which include "plays, music concerts and lectures . . . prayers, ritual readings and
recitations, rites and ceremonies, festivals . . . ," whose performers thought of "their
culture as encapsulated in these discrete performances which they could exhibit to
visitors and to themselves" (p. 37). See also M. Singer, ed., *Krishna: Myths, Rites, and
Attitudes* (Honolulu: East-West Center Press, 1966) for concerted philological, sociological, and cultural approaches to different aspects of certain performances.
  To see very different current concepts of "civilization integration" at work, compare
the synthesis of South Asian "ideology" in Louis Dumont, *Homo Hierarchicus: An
Essay on the Caste System*, M. Saintsbury, trans. (Chicago: University of Chicago
Press, 1970), with the panorama of South Asian "society" in David G. Mandelbaum,

at once on both of Redfield's classic divisions of the great tradition (i.e. high, literate culture) and the little tradition (grass-roots culture) and on changes affecting how any tradition is actually tapped and activated in "action." Singer has advanced this approach to performances in moderniz-ing India, where "there is no sharp dividing line between religion and culture and the traditional culture media not only continue to survive in the city but have also been incorporated in novel ways into an emerging popular and classical culture."[32] One important point is that the "great tradition" and the "little tradition" are themselves abstracted and ordered constructs, assembled by different observers for different ends. The great tradition is sometimes something of a normative theory of society advanced by powerful literati; while the little tradition is sometimes a theory of society (often normative as well) advanced by outside observers (e.g., anthropologists) as a partial corrective to inadequacies noted in the great tradition theory.

Our present concern though, is the implicit operational basis for any approach to "cultural performances." In general, whenever a multiplicity of media is brought together and each used to reinforce the others' com-ponents in some sort of production (rite, "show," etc.), operators abound. For the potential redundancy stemming from the sensory superabundance inherent in the situation sets the stage for generating productive equiva-lences and contrasts in the "messages" of the constituent orders. While possibly containing obvious "tags," such as clear-cut didactic messages, these events are best described as irreducibly complex systems of more or less contrived effects, directed sensations and guided responses. Yet although "irreducible," the productions should reveal operations—and ideally even a *La Traviata*-type "super-operator"—that render them in-telligible. While it is doubtful that such complex programs directly "reveal" the culture in question, they do afford direct views of the way the culture *is presented* by and to its participants. And such "self presentation" by and to some group is, we recall, the sort of paradox that "culture" is all about.

With regard to social action, whenever even a figurative curtain is raised on some program of events, the participants witness the genesis of opera-ations, insofar as elements are immediately selected from several orders and conjoined. And at least as long as this program of events is our uni-verse-of-concern, that conjunction is somehow normative. The conjunction persists, whether for that performance alone, or over some specific series of performances. It persists and can be manipulated—e.g., reiterated and echoed, or contradicted and denied, or perhaps most modernly ignored.

Society in India (Berkeley: University of California Press, 1970). For an idea of the issues currently in dispute, see the two reviews of Dumont by McKim Marriott, *Ameri-can Anthropologist*, 71 (Dec., 1969), p. 1165; and Nur Yalman, "De Tocqueville in India," *Man*, 4 (March, 1969), pp. 123–131.

[32] M. Singer, "The Great Tradition in a Metropolitan Center: Madras," in M. Singer, ed., *Traditional India: Structure and Change* (Philadelphia: The American Folklore Society, 1959), p. 173.

Yet, whether repeated, contraried, or subversively "forgotten," the conjunction remains an ordering principle behind the universe-of-concerns,
an operator which steers the recognition, the surprise, the discomfort, the
joy, the dismay of those affected, at least temporarily.

Peacock has studied Javanese proletarian drama as such a "cultural performance" (or more exactly a "socio-cultural performance"). He outlines
a narrative approach to social action in literate civilizations, derived in
part from the dramatistic view of Kenneth Burke.
The approach

> treats behaviors as if they were organized "aesthetically" as in a play that
> arranges its scenes poetically and climactically to evoke appreciative and
> cathartic responses from an audience. The task of the investigator is to show
> how forms, climaxes, settings focus around evoking such response from
> some audience.[33]

(Our privileged operational zones can be seen as a set of guidelines direct-
ing observation towards the areas of activity where such dramatistic tactics
might predominate). While Peacock's societal narrative is a telling instance of cultural operations achieved through symbolic action during
performances, the particular case of Javanese *ludruk* also points up the
central difficulty in interpreting any such event. In the case of *ludruk*
Peacock can state confidently:

> Narrative is thus seen as providing both a way in and a way out, as
> beginning by seducing participants into involvement with its form and as
> concluding by propelling the now-transformed participants out into life.[34]

Doubtless, some narrative forms and their contexts do straightforwardly
"direct" their participants' action-values in the fuller range of social life.
But often, perhaps usually, the effects of performances, while intense at
the time and place of their production, fade with disconcerting celerity as
soon as the participants leave the "theatre." The forms seem of little direct
consequence in subsequent general action. While we need to document
the *ludruks* of this world which "mirror" social change and somehow condition those affected, anthropologists must also consider significant forms
which, if they relate to general action, do so in much more obscure (devi-
ous?) fashion. It is the classic problem illustrated by Flaubert's *Madame
Bovary*: Emma reads a book and immediately rushes out to *do* what it is
about—she is almost literally seduced by action-value involvement with
its form. More "sophisticated" enthusiasts of literature can open the book,
read it, and close it to go about their merry, disturbingly independent, way:
unalloyed selection-value prevails. Any outside observer faces the problem

---

[33] James L. Peacock, "Society as Narrative" in Turner, *Forms of Symbolic Action*,
pp. 167–177. See also J. L. Peacock, *Rites of Modernization* (Chicago: University of
Chicago Press, 1968). Kenneth Burke summarizes his own "dramatism," under "Interaction" in the *International Encyclopedia of the Social Sciences* (New York: Macmillan
and The Free Press, 1968), vol. 7, pp. 445–453.

[34] Peacock, "Society as Narrative."

of whether the sophisticate-pattern or the *ludruk*-pattern predominates among the different members of any groups involved in a given ritual process or audience spectacle.

Recalling that groups might be more or less prone to rich instances of manifest "cultural operation," and now noting that any operation possibly sits more lightly on those involved that the observer might wish, we can attempt to characterize certain limits of approaches to "symbols" and "performances." All "cultures" possess relatively intense zones of symbolic action and content, but these zones can be more or less routinized and popularized. Any culture requires some specialists in symbolic action. Such specialists—most simply the shaman and/or chief, most expansively Madison Avenue, Washington politicians, Hollywood, etc.—articulate and utilize multivocal forms and ritual contexts. They are socially licensed to control the principles of symbolic forms and action (although such controllers are not to be mistaken for the authoritative experts on the meaning of the forms they direct.) Perhaps the bulk of the populace relates only "spuriously" (as Sapir would put it) to these, in the sense that ordinary folk cannot articulate the forms and are relatively subject to them (or at the extreme even enslaved by them).[35] The general populace need not "understand" the programs for symbols or performances. It perhaps need only be aware that there is some such significant zone ("Religion," "State," "Ancestral sphere," etc.,) that, in Geertz's well-known terms

> acts to establish powerful, pervasive, and long-lasting moods and motivations in men for formulating conceptions of a general order of existence and clothing these conceptions with such an aura of factuality that the moods and motivations seem uniquely realistic.[36]

Folk trust that there is such a zone; perhaps a select few vitally *sense* that zone; while knowing *about* the zone is left to institutionalized specialists. However, specialists and populace alike would be expected at least occasionally to feel some emotive effects of their symbol-rich significant forms (whether or not in different ways,) unless certain specialists have taken upon themselves the role of Grand Inquisitor.

In other words analyzing ritual and symbolic behavior does not necessarily reveal the specific "needs" of the participants. They might just generally need "to get away from it all" or to feel near the "source" of it all (c.f. Durkheim's "sacred"), whatever *it* is—vague "action-values" indeed! It is difficult to be sure if participants are in fact infused with meaning at such times. But we can analyze their forms to detect what sorts of meanings they might be infused with, if they were.[37] It is, then, always problematic just how ideationally and affectively efficacious symbols in

---

[35] The term is from Sapir's "Culture, Genuine and Spurious," in Sapir, *Selected Writings*.

[36] Geertz, "Religion as a Cultural System," p. 4.

[37] Note that this last point would lead us to take a selection-value view of action-values, which is generally just what anthropology does.

society are. This issue remains one of the critical problems in the study of "symbols" and "cultural performances." Doubtless anthropologists want "culture" as conveyed by symbols to be pregnant with meaning and vital to its actors. Sapir wanted "culture" to be genuine, not spurious. This is understandable, since it is more difficult to explain patterns of culture steeped in an ethos of "I can take it or leave it" rather than "do or die."[38] Perhaps the fact of the matter is that only a minimal subsidiary awareness by actors of their symbolic systems is critical to maintaining motivation, without necessarily entailing that the symbols themselves be genuinely "interiorized." This at least is a possibility anthropologists must face. But by concentrating on operations at work in the privileged zones of "symbols" and of "cultural performances," the observer can at least witness a partial set of selection-values at work and perhaps glimpse a few action-values being operated as well. It never hurts to try.

CROSS-CULTURAL COMPARISON OF THE LOGIC OF CLASSIFICATION

For all that it can be described essentially as operations among selected elements across various orders, the La Traviata performance as depicted earlier could not properly be submitted to a latter day Lévi-Straussian analysis of covert classifications.[39] This is because that example depicts what is (1) a *single* performance, (2) *directly* witnessed, (3) which is the product of an *individual* genius (however much drawing on social artistic conventions), (4) many elements of which are interrelated in a *conscious* fashion. Lévi-Strauss on the other hand studies myth, which he defines as (1) complex texts found in *multiple* versions across different groups and

[38] In "Religion as a Cultural System," p. 43, Geertz notes: "But if the anthropological study of religious commitment is underdeveloped, the anthropological study of religious non-commitment is non-existent." This point helps us frame the issues here more adequately. Take any cultural "symbol" or "performance." Its actors can be committed to it dutifully and consciously (which implies an awareness of denied alternatives), and/or infused by it (which implies more or less blind acceptance). Or its actors can be committedly non-committed (cf. Nietzsche and the Church), or perhaps most difficult of all to study, they can be indifferent and unaffected. All such responses fall under our gloss of "action-values." Moreover, all these possibilities are no doubt crucial to the operation of "culture" as a whole.

[39] By latter-day Lévi-Strauss I intend his work evoked in Tristes Tropiques, J. Russell, trans. (New York: Atheneum, 1961); prefigured by "The Structural Study of Myth," in Structural Anthropology, C. Jacobson and B. Grundfest Schoepf, trans. (New York: Basic Books, 1963); launched by Totemism, R. Needham, trans. (Boston: Beacon, 1963) and The Savage Mind (Chicago: University of Chicago Press, 1966); and fulfilled in the four volumes of Mythologiques: The Raw and the Cooked, J. and D. Weightman, trans. (New York: Harper, 1969); Du Miel aux cendres (Paris: Plon, 1966); L'Origine des manières de table (Paris: Plon, 1968); and L'Homme nu (Paris: Plon, 1971). For a full treatment of the views that follow, see my From Symbolism to Structuralism: Lévi-Strauss in a Literary Tradition (Oxford: Basil Blackwell; and New York: Harper and Row, 1972) and its references. The term "communal censorship" is from Roman Jakobson's chapter on "Linguistics" in International Study on the Main Trends of Research in the Social and Human Sciences, vol. 1 (The Hague: Mouton, 1970). On pensée sauvage as "analogical thought," see especially The Savage Mind, p. 263.

languages, (2) as evidenced *indirectly* by the translations of oral performances recorded by fieldworkers. (3) developed by and for members of the
whole *society* (as is possible in small preliterate groups with their "communal censorship" of expressive forms), (4) at a more or less *unconscious*
level of selection and interrelation of distinctive features from fragments
of the groups' experience—which selection is influenced by, but in no
simple and direct relationship with, the ethnographic context. In brief
Mythologiques studies a particular human capacity—the analogical capacity (first sketched as *la pensée sauvage,* which is defined as "analogical
thought"). *Mythologiques* studies that capacity by concentrating on human phenomena which seem most confined to it, namely preliterate texts
of the sort defined above.

Lévi-Strauss analyzes at a distance the mythic motifs that have been
differentially exchanged among groups with different social organizations
and languages or maintained by two once identical groups as their social
organizations and languages diverge (or, if we follow his implications to
the limit, perhaps social organization and languages have been exchanged
across myths). He maps the consistent patterns of principles that seem to
have directed differences the myths assume, such as one variant presenting
a set of elements related in an inverse fashion to the relation among the
same set of elements in another variant. He calls what he maps "structure."
Lévi-Strauss' "structures" are similar to what we have glossed as "cultural
operations" but at a different locus. Briefly, we can see "structure" as the
result of *operations.* As some portion of a myth is borrowed by one group
from another, operations of transformation occur; or if a group splits, its
once co-terminous mythic corpus is differentially operated in dialectic with
the now different ethnographic conditions and historical events. In his
comparativist study of *mythologiques,* the "structures" Lévi-Strauss derives can be seen as directions for how to *undo* various operations that
the evidence (mythic texts plus ethnographic reports) suggests have been
done. (Note that this is not the same as deriving directions which presume
to show how to reproduce the operations that have been done.) He uses
the analytic device of binary opposition to detect possible operations that
are evidenced in compounded fashion throughout some mythic corpus
found across New World tribal peoples.(He also uses the broad "structures" detected to delineate a "corpus.") In sum, the structures he derives
are retrospective representations *of* paths followed by various operations,
especially those operations involved in cross-cultural borrowing (*exchange*
of mythic motifs) across different language groups. The structures are a
comparative gloss of the selection-values encoded by the texts studied.
Some of the selection-values might have been tapped as vital action-values
by some groups now and then, here and there, but none need necessarily
have been.

What Lévi-Strauss discovers in examining structural limits of the operation of myths across groups is of great consequence to general culture
theory, particularly in his insistence that

matter is the instrument, not the object of signification. In order that it yield to this role, it is first necessary to impoverish it: retaining from it only a small number of elements suitable for expressing contrasts and for forming pairs of oppositions.[40]

His vast empirical demonstrations of how the seemingly concrete things of social experience are better seen as potential idioms for orderly signification complement and document general theories of the "logico-aesthetic" integration characteristics of "culture." Lévi-Strauss is most interested in the myths' detailed elaboration of valued customs, which often appear at first glance absurdly epiphenomenal. He proposes that myths indirectly record the systematic abstraction and interrelationship of elements from freshly isolated orders of social experience—as when myths depict the dawns of cooking and dining customs viewed normatively, or when new conceptualizations of cyclic time are coded by cross-referencing selected aspects of female biological cycles to likewise selected aspects of solar phenomena.[41] In short he detects various cultural operations indirectly attested in records of oral expressive genres of various groups. This allows different groups to be "culturally" contrasted according to the different orders selected, much in the way *La Traviata* (as a text independent of any actual performance) might be contrasted to some other oral music text which does not select and activate the potenial plot-line orders, or which has different elements from different musical orders connected in different ways with internal musical "development" of a different kind.

Yet while in these respects Lévi-Strauss' portrayal of "structure" complements traditional theories of "culture," in other ways it implicitly challenges them. For Lévi-Strauss invites us to consider the whole of New World Indians as participants in a single semantic environment:

---

[40] Lévi-Strauss, *Le Cru et le cuit* (*The Raw and the Cooked*) (Paris: Plon, 1964), pp. 346–347; my translation.
As an example of how men use matter from their experience to establish significative contrasts, consider this summary of Lévi-Strauss' interpretation of a South American mythic variant, whose contrasts have been set in relief by comparing it to other similar variants: "A violation of the bonds of marriage (the murder of the incestuous wife, which deprives a child of his mother), aggravated by a sacriligious act—another form of excess—(the interment of the woman, thus denying her an aquatic burial, the precondition of reincarnation) leads to the disjunction of the two poles: heaven (child) and earth (father). The agent, whose double misdeed banishes him from the society of men (which is an "aquatic" society, like the society of souls whose name it bears), re-establishes communication between heaven and earth by creating water; and having established his abode in the land of souls (since he and his companion became the heroes Bakororo and Itubore, the chiefs of the two villages of the beyond), he re-establishes communication between the dead and the living by making the latter acquainted with bodily ornaments and adornments, which are both emblems of the society of men and spiritual flesh in the community of souls" (*The Raw and the Cooked*, pp. 58–59).
[41] This aspect of *Mythologiques* comes out clearest in vol. 3 (*L'Origine des manières*) where the mythic texts reveal a new concern with temporal principles of order; see this author's "Lévi-Strauss and Narrative," *Man*, 5 (Dec., 1970), pp. 702–703.

From the start then, I ask the historian to look upon Indian America as a kind of Middle Ages which lacked a Rome: a confused mass that emerged from a long-established, doubtless very loosely textured syncretism, which for many centuries had contained at one and the same time centers of advanced civilization and savage peoples, centralizing tendencies and disruptive forces. . . . [The set of myths], such as the one studied here, owes its character to the fact that in a sense it became crystallized in an already established semantic environment, whose elements had been used in all kinds of combinations—not so much, I suppose, in a spirit of imitation but rather to allow small but numerous communities to express their different originalities by manipulating the resources of a dialectical system of contrasts and correlations within the framework of a common conception of the world.[42]

With this in mind he proceeds to detect the limits of what would have been a "great cultural" tradition, had it ever been summarily formulated. But since, as far as we know, there was no such great tradition, then the limits discovered would seem to reveal the nature of the processes by which mythic formulations evolved among and across groups. Vastly diverse myths are clearly related, but not necessarily *for* those who possess them. Native populations seem perfectly capable of articulating their concepts and percepts by means of mere fragments of an intercontinental mythic corpus which can only be seen in its true nature of a "corpus" from a distant, analytic, cross-cultural perspective. Thus, the sort of holistic integration of ideas and values that grander concepts of "culture" posit *for* each and every group is here nowhere in sight at this particular level of analysis. Through structural relations between mythic texts, Lévi-Strauss demonstrates that groups are playing out principles of human expressions which are of a greater order than anything about the groups themselves. This is why detailed studies of the operation of myths-as-performed by actual members of actual groups in actual instances—while relevant—cannot afford a full understanding of the operation of myth (now seen as something of a near-independent human capacity) as it occurs outside of conscious awareness in preliterate populations. Only by moving across groups and languages, as the myths themselves have, can we discern the principles of order which constrain the different sets of conceptual selection-values that set groups apart from each other, while leaving them interrelatable. As Lévi-Strauss has most recently put it:

Rarely seized upon at their origin and in a state of vitality, these relationships of opposition between myths emerge vigorously from a comparative analysis. If thus the philological study of myths does not constitute an indispensable preliminary approach, the reason for this lies in what one might call myths' diacritical nature. Each of the myths' transformations results from a dialectical opposition to another transformation, and their essence resides in the irreducible fact of translation *by* and *for* opposition. Considered from an empirical point of view, every myth is at once pristine

[42] Lévi-Strauss, *The Raw and the Cooked*, p. 8.

(*primitif*) in relation to itself, and derived in relation to other myths; it is situated not *in* a language and *in* a culture or sub-culture, but at the point of articulation of cultures with other languages and other cultures. Myth is thus never in its language (*de sa langue*), it is a perspective on *another language....*[43]

The goal of Lévi-Strauss' science is to map the human universe of selection-values, totally reduced and arranged through comparison, yet always capable of new operations (within limits).

In *Mythologiques* Lévi-Strauss studies the manifest constraints in implicit classifications from translations of direct (i.e., not artificially elicited) textual material from many groups. Another area of endeavor in recent anthropology has been designated variously as the "new ethnography," "ethnosemantics" and "ethnoscience."[44] It studies more explicit classifications, or tries to evoke responses from informants to make more explicit their implicit classifications, concerning that group's variation on areas of general human perception and conceptualization (e.g., "color") or on a particular concern for that particular people (e.g., "firewood" or "hamburgers and hotdogs"). The so-called new ethnographers have sought to improve the reliability, validity, and thoroughness of fine-grain ethnographic inquiries (1) by alerting anthropologists to subtle points in the logic of classifications, points most often taken over from linguistics, requiring careful use of concepts such as "sets and contrast sets," "taxonomies," "paradigms," "componential analysis," etc., and (2) by applying various formal and mathematical apparatuses to certain "domains" of ethnographic data. It is generally agreed that any particular logic of classification as well as any particular apparatus should ideally correspond to either an unconscious operation (read "ground rule") or a conscious operation (read "strategy rule") of the natives themselves. (And even more ideally any logic or apparatus should also be a universally cross-culturally applicable one, i.e. a true "etic.") Conklin has emphasized "the importance of distinguishing those conceptual principles which generate systems of obligatory categories—and upon which there is unanimous agreement—from those principles and resulting categories which are less obligatory, or optional, or *irrelevant*."[45] Or, as Sturtevant has summarized the matter: "Since the ethnoscientific method aims at discovering culturally relevant discriminations and categorizations, it is esssential that the discovery

---

[43] Lévi-Strauss, *L'Homme nu*, p. 577; my translation.

[44] Important works in this trend include Dell Hymes, ed., *Language in Culture and Society* (New York: Harper and Row, 1964); John J. Gumperz and Dell Hymes, eds., "The Ethnography of Communication," *American Anthropologist*, 66 (Dec., 1964); A. K. Romney and R. G. D'Andrade, eds., "Transcultural Studies of Cognition," *American Anthropologist*, 66 (June, 1964); E. A. Hammel, ed., "Formal Semantic Analysis," *American Anthropologist*, 67 (Oct., 1965); Stephen A. Tyler, ed., *Cognitive Anthropology* (New York: Holt, Rinehart and Winston, 1969).

[45] H. C. Conklin, "Comment" on Charles O. Frake, "The Ethnographic Study of Cognitive Systems," both in T. Gladwin and W. C. Sturtevant, eds., *Anthropology and Human Behavior* (Anthropological Society of Washington, 1962), pp. 72–92.

procedures themselves be relevant to the culture under investigation."[46]

What is still being investigated, only with increasing methodological rigor, is "culture"; and what remains at issue is how to isolate privileged areas to trace the value-laden patterning of native categories. One issue concerns the criteria by which we can designate a discrimination or categorization "relevant to the culture under investigation." Is it relevant if psychologically "real," and if so how does one test for it? Is the categorization relevant if it helps the analyzer account for more data in a more parsimonious fashion? Is a category most relevant to the culture (in an action-value sense) if its members would die for it, or wage war to maintain it? Is a cultural "domain" more relevant if it is more completely overtly particularized (e.g. the Eskimo "snow" straw man) or if it is more covertly obscured by some sort of cultural trappings?[47] A related issue centers on how to bound a domain, how to justify approaching some selection of items—e.g., an assortment of kinship terms—as a closed set. The main difficulty lies in establishing systematic criteria for excluding items from the set which, if admitted, would compromise its orderliness.[48]

Invoking once again "privileged operational zones of culture," a provisional solution appears. One admits that cultural categories might be inherently flexible, not rigorously bound, and perhaps relevant in different ways to different members of a group at different times. Suspecting that this might all be crucial to their "operability" in experience, one relaxes his "scientific" tendency to define, isolate, and bound specific domains, and opts instead for a vaguer notion of the prevalence of "categoriness" or orderliness plus a concentration on connections among *apparently* differ-

[46] William C. Sturtevant, "Studies in Ethnoscience," in Romney and D'Andrade, *Transcultural Studies of Cognition*, p. 111.

[47] The latter possibility which recalls—at a lexical level—Whorf's notion of "covert class"—see Benjamin Lee Whorf, *Language, Thought and Reality*, J. B. Carroll, ed. (New York: Wiley, 1956), pp. 65–86—is seldom discussed, except perhaps in terms of "taboo." I have in mind George Devereux, "Art and Mythology: A General Theory," in B. Kaplan, ed., *Studying Personality Cross-Culturally* (New York: Harper and Row, 1961), which argues that artistic form functions to insulate and obscure "dangerously" relevant ideas and categories and feelings. Or we can ask ourselves if the paucity of overt lexemes referring to matters of "sex" in the language usage of various puritanical groups proves the category is irrelevant. If not, then we are left with "relevance" being equally well signaled by presence (e.g. Eskimo "snow") and absence (e.g. Puritan "sex") of verbal markers—not very sound criteria.

[48] For a review of literature on these matters see Dell Hymes, "Linguistic Method in Ethnography: Its Development in the United States," in P. L. Garvin, ed., *Method and Theory in Linguistics* (The Hague; Mouton, 1970), pp. 249–325, especially the comments on Schneider's and Tyler's criticisms of componential analysis and on the promising developments in sociolinguistics. An over-simplified example should illustrate the problem of bounding a domain: In *La Traviata* it would seem indisputable that one domain is the "orchestra"—a bound set of instrument-types in a taxonomic arrangement (even laid out in space). Problems would arise, however, if in some production a moog synthesizer were added, which, informants might insist, is part of the "orchestra"; but how, the observer would beseech, does it fit into that once elegant taxonomy. The issue comes down, as usual, to one between formal elegance and native response.

ent orders or categories (not of course reducing his awareness of sophisticated logics and formal apparatuses that *might* pertain to the categories).
In fact one could so opt even if it necessitated employing a bit of intuition
and empathetic note of the actors' emotive responses—both of which are
viable strategems, if they pay off in analytic results. The scientific value of
replicability does not exclude using one's imagination in dreaming up varieties of experiment. This view conflicts somewhat with the new ethnographers' "quest for formal elegance" (attributed to them by Harris) and
their "demonstration of the *need* for nonintuitive . . . procedures."[49] Having once shifted out of an overdrive for formal elegance, one might more
readily rely on the emotions as clues to areas of "relevant" categorization.
For example, following Mary Douglas, building on Bergson and Freud, an
informant's laughter would be taken as a possible index that one scale of
order has suddenly imposed itself where another scale is normally expected.[50] Using affect in this way would in no way compromise the rigor of
the analytic procedures then employed, but might point one more directly
toward "relevant," not so perfectly bound and less than overtly proclaimed,
domains.

The main debates in new ethnographic pursuits have centered on issues
such as bounding a domain, formalized techniques, and various problems
in semantics—the anthropological (as opposed to linguistic) forebearer of
such issues being the locus of "models" in formulating generalizations from
social experience.[51] Yet there are other problems touched on in this approach which, from a viewpoint of privileged operational zones of culture,
merit fuller consideration. Some studies, for example, have shown a
healthy, if preliminary, inclination to reassess the true nature of what
anthropologists tend casually to gloss as "data."[52] An approach through
"cultural operators" would stress awareness that the raw data of anthropology are not objective facts of observable behavior, but imperfect communications between sender and receiver. What the outside observer frequently confronts are responses of some well-versed member of the culture

---

[49] Harris, *The Rise of Anthropological Theory*, chap. 20; and Conklin, "Comment,"
pp. 86–92.

[50] Mary Douglas, "Social Control of Cognition: Factors in Joke Perception," *Man*, 3
(Sept., 1968), pp. 361–367.

[51] On the locus of models of social structures see Sol Tax, ed., *An Appraisal of Anthropology Today* (Chicago: University of Chicago Press, 1953); and the recent review of
the issues in I. R. Buchler and H. A. Selby, *Kinship and Social Organization* (New
York: Macmillan, 1968; see also Ward H. Goodenough, *Description and Comparison
in Cultural Anthropology* (Chicago: Aldine, 1970). For a recent review of the literature on approaches to kinship terminologies see Robert McKinley, "A Critique of the
Reflectionist Theory of Kinship Terminologies: The Crow/Omaha Case," *Man*, 6
(June, 1971), pp. 228–247.

[52] See, for example, C. O. Frake, "How to ask for a Drink in Subanun," in Gumperz
and Hymes, *The Ethnography of Communication*, pp. 127–132; and Stephen A. Tyler's
use of sociolinguistics as a corrective for overly rigid approaches to terminological systems in "Context and Variation in Koya Kinship Terminology," *American Anthropologist*, 68 (June, 1966), pp. 693–707.

to some inarticulate, unversed interrogator. Examples of the latter are (if the observer is focusing on the acquisition of cultural forms) children in that culture and (regardless of what he is focusing on) himself.[53] The answers of the well-versed indigenous adult when responding to unversed interrogation should not necessarily be treated as factual information about how things are. The responses should rather be viewed more realistically as either reduced and highlighted or over-elaborated, perhaps condescending, either lightly amused or pompous, perhaps image laden and concretized for the children, perhaps uncommonly intellectualized for the observer (perhaps vice versa[54]); all because something that should be obvious is being inquired about by someone lacking the fully "rational" common sense of the ideal peer. However, such distortion gives no cause to disparage the responses as *information*. Rather the observer immediately seeks out a contrast set, in order to delineate patterns in the reductions, contrived emphasis, and tendencies to concretize or intellectualize. This contrast set might be derived from some ideal full panorama of how the informant *might* have responded, or from observing normal information exchange between two well-versed actors. But the contrast set is not derived in order to correct the slant of the original responses. It is derived to set in relief the patterns in the original responses which can be taken as modes of transmitting that "culture." For once again we are not looking for "culture" as it *is*, rather as it is *received*. Thus, the original slanted (e.g., overtly-concrete, overly-abstract) information is most valuable, if only we can discern how that slant is being operated.

Another area requiring further consideration is the refinement of less formalizable "zones" for witnessing cultural operations. For example, drawing on Frake's influential approach to a set of religious categories and Geertz's more recent work on person concepts, one might advance as a possibly viable cross-cultural privileged zone something like "narrative

---

[53] We should note that any acquisition of culture forms, whether by an indigenous novice or an outside observer, is a two-way affair. It is not just a matter of children or foreigners gradually mastering various codes; the competent actor also masters certain sets of special codes (and acquires them as the child is acquiring his?) to facilitate the other's process of gaining competence. For example, in English language acquisition the adult's baby talk pattern possibly relates to what linguists have described as the infant's "pivot grammar." In such a dialectic of acquisition both the versed and the unversed employ special sets of significant forms. As recently stressed in Charles A. Ferguson, "Absence of Copula and the Notion of Simplicity: A Study of Normal Speech, Baby Talk, Foreigner Talk, and Pidgin," in Dell Hymes, ed., *Pidginization and Creolization of Languages* (Cambridge: The University Press, 1971), the same sorts of special codes characterize phenomena not only of baby talk, but also of foreigner talk.

[54] This is not a mere parenthetical sophism; see for example, Margaret Mead's ingenious 1933 article which refutes theories of animism as a trait *natural* to primitives with a demonstration that "animism" is learned, since Manus children explain unfamiliar events to an outsider more "rationally" than do their animistic-sounding parents: "An Investigation of the Thought of Primitive Children, with Special Reference to Animism," reprinted in Robert Hunt, ed., *Personalities and Cultures* (Garden City: Natural History Press, 1967).

accounts of personal duration."[55] The simple field strategy would be to invite informants to relate their life history. Steadfastly non-Boasian from the start, we stipulate that possibly no native informant in any kind of culture tells what has *really* happened to himself. Rather he reduces and orders a selection of features (sometimes "accurate," sometimes not) retrospectively; and his operations achieve significance out of meaningless continuity. Focusing on the zone of personal self-histories constructed by actors would likely point toward matters often covered in studies of "religion," much of which involves normative patterns of remembrance and value-laden notions of time (as in the Frake study mentioned). But as a field tactic such a focus (if the group studied responded in manageable ways) would afford a convenient means of approaching "religion" without having to rely solely on the opinions of local specialists. For actors definitely (phenomenologically) exist in duration; the question becomes: how will they communicate that fact, if prodded. Indeed, in light of Geertz's study, do they themselves normally select the verbalized recollection of personal duration as a basis for the establishment of significant forms at all; and if not, what do they select?

As a final example of what a "new ethnographic" inquiry with less tendency to formalize and bound domains might look like, let us consider "reading." Reading is a complex human phenomenon involving various combinations of numerous cultural orders (and thus a classification of sorts). There are necessarily an order of graphics and some order of mental-image which is derived from language and related to the graphics. But there are also less obvious orders. For example, American advocates of speed reading point out orders of vocalization or sub-vocalization. The test for this is to subvocalize a pattern of sounds (e.g., "a-b-c") while reading; the result is usually a failure to "comprehend" the material read. Practice overcomes the sub-vocalizing tendency, which speed reading enthusiasts consider an impairment, since completely "silent" reading permits faster "comprehension." Or there is a variety of reading described by Marcel Proust (actually induced by reading his work) which includes an additional order of programmed recollection.[56] This reading phenomenon involves a page of printed language, plus a light "comprehension" of the page's contents, plus a range of subsidiary associations suggested partly by those contents and partly by the context in which the reading takes place. Or in Bali one finds that "Archipelago Sanskrit" oral reading by Hinduized priests which includes these interarticulated orders: a written text of patterned significative syllables, accompanying prescribed vocalizations

[55] C. O. Frake, "A Structural Description of Subanun 'Religious Behavior'," in W. Goodenough, ed., *Explorations in Cultural Anthropology* (New York: McGraw-Hill, 1964); C. Geertz, *Person, Time and Conduct in Bali: An Essay in Cultural Analysis* (New Haven: Yale University Southeast Asia Studies, no. 14, 1966).

[56] Proust's views on reading are scattered throughout his vast works; see however the new volume: Marcel Proust, *On Reading*, J. Autret and W. Burford, trans. (New York: Macmillan, 1971).

of the syllables, accompanying prescribed bodily gestures for the syllables, accompanying prescribed visual images to have "in mind" during the syllables.[57] The priest-reader is thus a pre-programmed sensory-intellect quartet conducted by a written text (I suppose that affect too is programmed). Or, we all know that our personal "silent reading" phenomena vary. Sometimes we read critically, analytically, at a distance—reducing and piecing together *enroute*. Sometimes we read more emphatically, keying the order of ourselves directly to some prose rendition of another self. (This perhaps very "Western" type of reading again characterizes Flaubert's Madame Bovary, who cannot divorce her own experience from that read about in novels.)

Thus, as many philosophers, creative authors, and educationalists have observed, there are variable orders involved in "reading."[58] The teaching of reading can in turn stress different conjunctions of elements from these orders, in short employ various operators. Again, certain speed reading courses illustrate this fact when the teachers attempt to eliminate the order of vocalization and activate an order of mental visualization, with the instructions: "Mumble 'a-b-c' as you read, and 'picture' the contents of the page." Acquisition of reading, then, entails operations between the medium of graphics and various orders. To better appreciate the force of certain issues related to this fact, consider something somewhat like "reading," but somewhat different: "reading music" (in the West). Imagine a beginner before his piece at the piano, whose teacher simply inquires: "What's the first *note*?" The question precipitates a dilemma: is he to hit a key, point to the notational device on the sheet of music which corresponds to it, or announce the letter that corresponds to both (or if the pupil is prematurely programmatically inclined, he might even name an image the note evokes)? It is more than a terminological problem, for each of these—key, notational device, letter—represents the note in some sense. Moreover, the music may be "read" either intellectually by (theoretically) "thinking" it, orally by "lettering" it, or gesturally by "playing" it. What a concatenation of cultural *operations*, and how complex is their acquisition! It is this sort of complexity, although perhaps on a lesser scale, that is involved in any "reading" (a viable action-value in most societies) with its variable orders. Yet one need not carefully circumscribe the bounds of "reading" as a classification in action, since there is a single diagnostic trait—i.e., a written text being responded to as a set of coded information—which when found serves to focus the investigation. (The trait is all the more interesting since many preliterate human groups are known to exist without it.) Thus, by loosely viewing "reading" as a privileged operational zone of "culture," a genuinely cross-cultural comparison of certain im-

[57] See C. Hooykaas, *Surya-Sevana, the Way to God of a Balinese Siva Priest* (Amsterdam: Noord-Hollandsche U.M., 1966).

[58] A slight interest in reading-as-action, although writing-as-artifact is the primary concern, is shown by some anthropologists in J. R. Goody, ed., *Literacy in Traditional Societies* (Cambridge: University Press, 1968).

portant classifications—the explicit goal of "ethnoscience"—could be achieved.

SUMMARY

To condense much recent anthropology into variations on a single quest for privileged operational zones of "culture" is at worst brazen and at best argumentative. More disputatious still has been the suggestion that anthropology's characteristic dilemma consists in determining whether a given conjunction of heterogeneous elements from orders of human phenomena (i.e., a possible *operator*)—as set into relief by a cross-cultural perspective —displays simple or compounded selection-values and/or action-values (and values *of* what and *for* whom), and the further suggestion that this dilemma can be effectively taken by its horns thanks to the fruitfully paradoxical concept of "culture," which serves not only to interrelate disparate phenomena of social life, but also as we have tried to show, to interrelate disparate endeavors of social anthropology. Yet, to stress a common (somewhat traditional) minimal analytic in symbolic anthropology, Lévi-Straussian structuralism, and new ethnography is not to deny their marked differences. Indeed, we have seen that in the long run at least, approaches to "symbols" and "cultural performances" side with the pragmatist goal to isolate action-values; Lévi-Strauss and his followers take the rationalist option of mapping totalized selection-values, systematically compared; and new ethnography (especially in light of the "psychological reality" of analyses controversy) sits peculiarly in the middle, flirting with various formalisms in its pursuit of a viable etic. Yet, such endeavors as these cannot be completely at cross-purposes; for if that were the case, "culture" would no longer be debatable; it would simply be wrong.

CULTURE AND SOCIAL SYSTEM REVISITED

TALCOTT PARSONS
Harvard University

A S ONE OF THE MORE SENIOR SOCIOLOGISTS STILL EXTANT, I HAVE LIVED through a considerable gamut of discussions of the concept of culture and its relations to various of the social science disciplines. In particular, I was involved for a good many years in the venture at Harvard called a department of social relations which attempted to bring together social anthropology and sociology along with parts of psychology and, naturally, in the relations of the sociologists to the anthropologists the problem of culture was very central. Indeed, one has had the phenomenon that certain anthropologists called themselves cultural anthropologists and others social anthropologists and at least a mild amount of conflict developed between these two groups.

A very high point for me in these matters was a series of discussions I had the good fortune to have with the late Alfred L. Kroeber during the year 1957–58 which I spent at the Center for Advanced Study in the Behavioral Sciences at Stanford, California. It was a great satisfaction to me when Professor Kroeber, who surely was the dean of American anthropologists at that time, proposed that he and I should make a joint statement, the main purport of which would be to emphasize the importance of the distinction between cultural and social systems as concepts and to attempt to clarify their respective natures and relations to each other.[1] I think it perhaps can be said that the position which Kroeber and I took was far from being generally accepted at the time on either side of the disciplinary line. I think, however, that it has made substantial progress in this direction in the intervening years. On the anthropological side, for example, I cite the extremely interesting, though far from identical developments, in the recent work of such authors as Clifford Geertz and David Schneider, both of whom, of course, were trained in the Harvard Department of Social Relations.

In my own work as both a sociologist and a theorist working at the level of the general theory of action I have found this distinction to be completely indispensable. Moreover, I do not think it is too much to say that the main lines of the distinction have become quite sufficiently clarified to be serviceable for most working purposes, though of course major theoretical conceptualization is unlikely to remain completely stable over very long periods, and hence revisions in both concepts and the way of relating them to each other are to be anticipated.

Perhaps it is best to begin a more detailed statement by interweaving the concepts of cultural and of social system. I assume that man as the

---

[1] A. L. Kroeber and Talcott Parsons, "The Concepts of Culture and of Social System," *American Sociological Review*, 23 (Oct., 1958), pp. 582–583.

symbol-using animal as it is sometimes put is always a "culture bearer." There is no human society known, for example, without a fully developed language which is a medium of expression and communication very specifically at *symbolic* levels expressed in the language, for example, both in beliefs and sentiments and in various modes of overt action. There is always a comprehensive system of modes and aspects of the meaning of speech acts, ritual acts, and various other kinds of acts. This system of meaning is the focus of what I mean by a cultural system, but within the framework of orientation to and by meanings and of man as a behaving biological species of organism, I conceive of the social system as the system generated by the fact of the *interaction* of a plurality of human beings with each other. The master example of the social system in turn is the society. This is constituted by a plurality of interacting individuals, usually a substantial number, who act within the meaning-framework of a common culture and who also maintain an identity as a system transcending the life span of the particular human individual. A society, that is to say, is at least in large part, though by no means necessarily exclusively, recruited through processes of biological reproduction.

In my theoretical conception of a society I have come increasingly to follow the lines of analysis put forward by Durkheim. Relative to non-members, which category may be very important in its environment, a society exhibits the property Durkheim called *solidarity*. This may be characterized at the level of what one might call collective identity as above all expressed through the collective pronoun "we." A good example is Raymond Firth's monograph title, "We, The Tikopia."[2] We might, however, extend it to such expressions as "we Americans" or "we Japanese." Readiness to use the concept "we" seems to indicate both that the collectivity referred to has some kind of relatively definite identity and that the individual participant has a sense of "belonging" to it, that is, of membership. This in turn leads to the question of the nature and strength of the "bonds" by which he is in fact attached to such a collectivity, that is, that has the status of member. Here we may speak of loyalty.

Of course, societies are internally differentiated and, therefore, the individual persons who are members of a given society are at the same time members of a variety of subcollectivities of which the society is at one level "composed." One major reference, of course, is kinship, but in modern societies, there are also occupation in employing organizations, local or residential communities, religious groups, political associations, and many others. Here it is a cardinal proposition of contemporary sociology first that no individual is a member only of one solidary collectivity, but of a plurality. Even within such a small unit as a nuclear family, husband and wife constitute a subcollectivity distinguishable from that of their children and of the nuclear family as a whole. Moreover, it is fundamental that in a pluralistic society, persons who are members of the same collectivity in

[2] Raymond Firth, *We, The Tikopia: A Sociological Study of Kinship in Primitive Polynesia* (New York: American Book Co., 1936).

one reference do not necessarily share the same memberships in other collectivities. Thus the occupational involvements of husband and wife, supposing both are "gainfully employed," need not be in the same employing organization and certainly not necessarily in the same status within that organization.

Another essential point is that there are many collectivities which cut across two or more societies. When I identify myself occupationally as a sociologist, for some purposes it is necessary to qualify that by saying I am an American sociologist because there are many sociologists who are citizens of other national societies. International sociology is in some respects an effectively organized collectivity, the members of which are in other capacities citizens of many different nations. If in the modern world we consider the "nation" to be the prototypical society, then of course there are limits to the levels of loyalty to transnational collectivities which are compatible with continuing membership in a national society. Those the functions of which are relatively specialized are apt to cause little difficulty, though, for example, in a more totalitarian type of society, such as those of the Communist world, the problem of the status of a sociologist who is a Soviet national, for example, but also a member of the international sociological group, may be a source of greater strains than it would be in the so-called "free world."

TRANSITION TO A FULLER DISCUSSION OF CULTURE

It should be evident from the above that what at the human level we call social systems and societies, that is, systems of action in the technical sense I and many associates have used, society is not understandable apart from its relations to a cultural system. This is to say that the actions of individual persons in their capacities as members of a social system must be oriented in terms of the meanings of cultural symbol systems, of what is sometimes called patterns of culture. Furthermore, the society itself and various other social systems as object of orientation must also have meanings defined in cultural terms. Moreover, the two sets of meanings, that is, from the point of view of actors as components of their orientation patterns and of the objects to which they are oriented, must to some degree be integrated with each other at the cultural level.

Cultural systems, however, are by no means fully integrated but may be regarded as varying from a pole of virtually complete integration to one of a nearly random assortment of meaning components. Furthermore, the actual behavior of individuals, their symbolically oriented action, may be to a widely varying degree congruent with the meanings of the cultural system. This applies, of course, as well to those aspects of meaning which we speak of as being institutionalized to constitute aspects of the actual structure of a social system and those which we speak of as being internalized to constitute actual components of the structure of personality systems.

The above qualifications are necessitated by a cardinal consideration about culture. This is that the meaning of cultural patterns seen in the context of their relation to action is *always* in some degree and respect normative. This I take to be implicit in the concept pattern which has been so widely used by anthropologists in this connection. There is, that is to say, always some range of variation from "correct" or otherwise acceptable action in relation to a cultural pattern or complex of patterns and varying modes and degrees of "incorrect" or unacceptable modes of action. This is nearly obvious in cases where the cultural pattern lays down explicit norms for behavior. It is less obvious in such cases as language where there is, however, a fundamental line of distinction between correct and incorrect usage of the language according to rules of choice of vocabulary, grammar, and syntax. The normative character of the language itself may be quite different from other norms imposed in the same culture with respect, for example, to the contracting of marriage relationships. But this is not to say that it is in any general sense non-normative. Another very important example is from the cognitive field. There may be a high degree of normative neutrality with respect to motives for attempting to acquire knowledge or for the use of knowledge once commanded. However, with respect to the content of knowledge itself, there are always explicit or implicit norms which I have lately been referring to as those of cognitive validity and significance. As a category of cultural object, knowledge cannot be oriented to without a relevant normative dimension.

We consider a cultural system itself to be complex and internally differentiated. According to the paradigm of the four primary functional divisions of any system of action, we have analyzed it respectively into the four categories of cognitive symbolization, moral-evaluative symbolization, expressive symbolization, and constitutive symbolization.

By contrast with the cultural system, which is specifically concerned with systems of meaning, the social system is a way of organizing human action which is concerned with linking meaning to the conditions of concrete behavior in the environmentally given world. This is a world which must be classified as constituting on the one hand the environment outside the social system of reference, an environment which includes personalities of individual participants, and the social system itself conceived as an environment relative to which the action of participants must be understood.[3] In this connection the most crucially important part of a cultural system for social systems is the moral-evaluative aspect. This concerns norms or complexes of norms which define rights and obligations and more concretely expectations in the relations of social interaction itself on the part of those who constitute a social system.

We can, therefore, speak of the moral-evaluative aspect of a cultural system interpenetrating with the actual structure of the social system through the status which we call institutionalization. This is to say that the normative cultural meanings defining desirable patterns of social interaction come to be regarded as the standards by which unit action shall be

[3] Talcott Parsons, *The System of Modern Societies* (Englewood Cliffs, N.J.: Prentice-Hall, 1971).

evaluated. There are two crucial corollaries of this statement to be considered before we enter into a fuller discussion of the nature of institutionalization: (1) It is a criterion of institutionalization that what may be called "socialized" individual participants can on the statistical average be considered to have a personal psychological interest in acting in accord with the normative standards in question. (2) The normative system will constitute the primary axis for the organization of sanctions, that is, of rewards and deprivations which may be expected to follow upon the range of concrete actions as evaluated relative to the institutionalized normative framework. Such normative patterns, insofar as they become actual parts of a social system through institutionalization, are in the first instance what we call institutionalized values. They constitute relatively generalized patterns of orientation which, to use cybernetic terminology, define programs for the operation of the social system of reference. It is important to interpret the program component which applies to the social system as a whole at a sufficiently high level of generality. Only in a limiting case does a social system, most especially a society, have one particular goal which would be defined as a specific mode of relationship between the system and its significant environment. More general value patterns define *directions* of orientation, including either the exclusion or the downplaying of alternatives to the principal direction. It requires much greater specification before the level of particular goals is reached. Even here, however, there are goals for the social system as a whole, but subsidiary to these are both lower order value patterns for subsystems and subcollectivities and particular goals for each of these.

What characterizes a social system in this respect is not "a value" but a value *system*. Insofar as such a value system can be regarded as relatively integrated, it will be characterized by a dominant pattern defining directionality in the sense just noted. It will, however, also include specifications to lower levels of generality and also to differentiated functions within the system. Thus, for a modern, large-scale society there may be an overall general value pattern, and subsidiary to this there may be societal goals. Insofar as a society as a whole is involved in goal attainment activity, it has to be primarily through the agency we call government. Complex modern societies, however, are differentiated into many different collectivities at many different levels. Therefore, the subvalues of business firms, universities, and political parties, to select three subtypes, though articulated and in some sense congruent with the more general value patterns, are not identical with them because of the combination of the lower level of generality and the functional differentiatedness of the subsystems to which they apply. For example, in a forthcoming manuscript we have argued strenuously that a university should *not* be conceived as a microcosm of a society; on the contrary, it should be conceived as a functionally specialized subsystem.[4]

Values in this sense focus on the normative regulation of social relation-

[4] Talcott Parsons and Gerald M. Platt, *The American University* (Cambridge: Harvard University Press, forthcoming).

ships. Indeed, the term institution seems to me to be more properly applied to this focus of normative regulation rather than to collectivities as is so frequently the case in sociological usage. Thus the institution of property and the institution of authority cannot conceivably be defined as collectivities but rather as complexes of norms regulating behavior in certain functional areas of the nexus of social relationships. It is particularly important in this connection to emphasize that a value defines a relational complex which includes acting units of the social system, not only as such, but in relation to objects. Typically, every "social object" is at the same time also an acting unit. The concept, value, therefore is a way of linking the actor-object modalities of the same concrete units in a social system precisely because at certain concrete levels of action there are many potential conflicts between the "role" of actor and the "role" of the object of action by others. It is important that there should be outside leverage with regulatory functions, that is to say, leverage grounded in cultural meanings rather than only in the exigencies of social interaction as such.

We may now pursue the ramifications of the normative complex in social systems in two different directions. One of these involves the interpenetration in social systems of aspects of the cultural system other than that of moral-evaluative culture. The second involves the stages of institutionalization of interpenetrating culture from values through norms to the structure of collectivities and roles. A brief sketch of each of these two contexts will be necessary.

NON-EVALUATIVE CULTURE IN SOCIETY

We consider values to be one of four primary subsectors of the cultural system. They are, as we have suggested, the sector most intimately involved in interpenetration with social systems, but the other three should not be neglected. There will not, however, be space for more than a few brief comments. First, historically there would probably be rather little argument about the salient importance of religion in the more general matrix of cultural meanings which bear on the functioning of social systems. At one level the classic modern statement in this area was made by Max Weber in his analysis of what he called the "problems of meaning" in a religious setting and their consequences for the formulation of values for his particular interests, especially in the economic sphere.

Durkheim's equally classic statement in *The Elementary Forms of the Religious Life*[5] was made from a somewhat different perspective. He chose to analyze a particularly primitive religion explicitly defining primitive in an evolutionary sense. The implication of this was that religion was not specifically differentiated from other components of the action system at either the cultural or the social levels. The relations between what we have come to call myth as an aspect of Durkheim's belief systems and the

[5] Emile Durkheim, *The Elementary Forms of the Religious Life*, trans. by Joseph Ward Swain (Glencoe, Ill.: The Free Press, 1954).

symbolism involved in ritual actions constitutes the religious framework within which the value system of the Australian Aborigines becomes in a certain sense meaningful. Durkheim did not work out a Weberian analysis of the various steps between religious commitment and obligations in the field of social action, especially in what he called the profane sphere, but the congruence with Weber's analysis is quite clear.

I think we may speak of a revived interest in and sensitivity to this level of problems of what we have called constitutive symbolism in the subtle interrelations between society and culture. There is a sense in which the movements by virtue of which many of our older established traditions have come into flux have inevitably raised problems in this area. In what is sometimes called the counter-culture of our time there are unquestionably religious undertones which link up, for example, with some of the Oriental religious traditions.

All we want to suggest at the moment is that this level of cultural symbolization is always implicit, if not explicit, in the cultural grounding of any major social system, certainly of any society.

Different, though closely related in many respects, is the problem of the relation of cognitive culture to the social system. Like any other branch of culture, it must be articulated in the value system the relevant aspect of which we have called the values of cognitive rationality (see my forthcoming book). As an aspect of culture, however, it is primarily of adaptive significance to human action, not of moral-evaluative significance. But in the course of socio-cultural evolution this aspect has, as is well-known, come to be of increasingly salient importance. On the purely cultural side, we have the impressive development, definitely cumulative since the 17th century, of what are often called the intellectual disciplines, most particularly the sciences, and on the side of social organization what I have been calling the educational revolution as a major phenomenon of social change, the apex of which is the institutionalization of mass higher education and high quality professionalism in the field of cognitive competence and research.[6] This is an area in which the concrete phenomena which are very salient in our time simply cannot be understood without an attempt to articulate the cultural level of analysis with that of the social system. The intellectual disciplines are cultural phenomena, though very salient ones at this juncture. The university, however, with the rest of the educational system, is an integral part of modern society, precisely in the analytical sense as social system. At the cultural levels this cognitive complex, as we have been calling it, must articulate with the other aspects of culture, notably the moral-evaluative and the religiously constitutive, but also the expressive. At the social system level it must, like values, be institutional-

---

[6] Talcott Parsons, "Unity and Diversity in the Modern Intellectual Disciplines: The Role of the Social Sciences," *Daedalus*, 94 (Winter, 1965), pp. 31–65. Christopher Jencks and David Riesman, *The Academic Revolution* (Garden City, N.Y.: Doubleday & Co., 1968).

ized if it is to be the focus of the performance of highly important societal functions, as it undoubtedly has come to be.

Finally, a few words should be said about the fourth primary functional category which we have called expressive symbolization. Its most important, relatively formalized organization is to be found in the areas which we call those of the arts. These, as is well-known, have become over a long course of social development progressively further differentiated from other cultural components, notably religious and moral. However, as Durkheim's analysis of the religious ritual of the Australians made clear, there is in many cases a very prominent expressive component in the overt action patterns of many social situations. This expressive component at the level of cultural meanings ramifies into and interpenetrates with all of the other three. There is, for example, in the cognitive field a component that is sometimes referred to as intellectual "elegance," which is perhaps particularly highly valued in mathematics. There are certainly very intimate relations between religious commitments and expressive "acting out" of the implications of these commitments and there are perhaps less obvious connections between the moral and the aesthetic. In this case the two seem quite frequently to stand in conflict with each other as alternative cultural emphases.

With respect to the expressive aspect, as well as the rest of the cultural aspects, one important general point ought to be made. This is perhaps most familiar in the cognitive field. Since Kant I think it is fair to say that the overwhelmingly dominant epistomological opinion has been that knowledge could not be interpreted simply as the intrusion into the human mind of "raw" data coming from the external world, on the assumption that the mind was some kind of a purely passive photographic plate on which information from outside was automatically registered. Knowledge, on the contrary, is the product of the combination of an input of what traditionally had been called "sense data" with cultural components, in Kantian terms, the categories, and certainly requiring the active agency of a knowing personality. We suggest that the broad pattern must be similar for expressive symbolization. The parallel to sense data from the external environment in this case is "subjective" experience, but this does not constitute an organized output until it has been combined with cultural components through the active agency of personalities in society. That is to say, there is a cultural framework sometimes called that of "style" within which "raw" experience is organized and given meanings that definitely transcend the immediacy and particularity of the specific experience itself. At high levels of organization these patterns of style become organized into what is sometimes called myths of the type illuminatingly discussed by Northrop Frye.[7] We should contend that just as in the other cases of the other aspects of a cultural system, the involvement with processes of social action is essential in this case. There have to be social analogs to uni-

[7] Northrop Frye, "The Critical Path: An Essay on the Social Context of Literary Criticism," *Daedalus*, 99 (Spring, 1970), pp. 268–342.

versities and colleges as modes of social organization favoring learning and the production of knowledge if sufficiently high-level and "relevant" forms of expressive symbolization are also to be produced. The great periods in the history of art give ready illustrations of the relevant kind of social situation.

COMPONENTS OF INSTITUTIONALIZATION

After this very cursory review of the main components of cultural systems, we may return to the social system. We have already stated above that values constitute the most important zone of interpenetration between the cultural and the social systems. We stress the idea of a zone because the more complex a social system is, the more it is characterized not by a single *pattern* of values, but by a value-*system*. The existence of an identifiable common pattern is one major characteristic of a value system. But as a system it must be conceived to be differentiated in two main respects. The first of these concerns levels of generality which follow the line of the differentiation of concrete social systems which is usually called segmentation. A segment of a larger system, for example, involving a small fraction of the geographical area of relevance to a total society, can be adequately "controlled" by values stated at a rather low level of generality. Contrariwise, one that must cover the conflicts and exigencies which arise in a much larger scale and more complex social system must be couched at a much higher level of generality.

The second basis of differentiation is that of the functions of the subsystems in which the relevant subvalues are institutionalized. Thus we consider the educational system generally and the university in particular to be a functionally differentiated subsystem of a modern society, and the paramount values in this subsystem—notably those of cognitive rationality—we consider not to constitute, as it were, a random sample of the value components of the total societal value system. Similar things would be true of the governmental system as differentiated in relation to political function or the economy differentiated with reference to the function of economic production, the economy or an industry or business firm as a subsector of the economy.

The general principle is that every subsystem of a society is itself a social system. As such it must have its own values, but the values of the subsystem must somehow be understood to be articulated with those of the society as a whole and, of course, beyond that, those of the particular society with still larger systems of societies.

We have stated above the general theorem of institutionalization, namely, that the interests of participating units, that is, what they desire, should be considered to be in conformity with the standards of desirability which are involved in the value patterns. If this theorem is correct, it is so under certain extremely important conditions. The very first of these is that in the process of social interaction by and large sanctions contingently administered by others should reinforce the direction of interest of acting participants, whether these participants be individual or collective units. This set of conditions has been classically formulated in those branches of economic theory that define the conditions of a competitive market system where it is said to be in fact to the interest of participating firms to conform with the "rules of the game."[8] Since, however, political power in the analytical sense is cybernetically higher than economic interest, the crux of the interest problem and the integration of interest with the institutionalization of values lies at the level of the political interest structure.

It has for very long been the contention of what might be called the dissident schools of social theory in modern society that integration on this level was not possible except under the conditions of a drastic revolutionary overturn. This is to say it is contended that under modern conditions there will necessarily be drastic differences of political power which in turn are in varying ways functions of economic differences, especially with respect to control of productive resources. It is then further contended that such differences of power will always and inherently be used exploitatively—that is, on the part of the more powerful to repress or "oppress" the less powerful. We may raise some points of skepticism with respect to the inevitability of what from the point of view of interests of "social justice" might be called the abuse of power, but even where the contention that this will indeed occur is justified, there is also ground for skepticism that the revolutionary overturn which is so frequently advocated will lead to the automatic installation of a regime of perfect social justice.

There seems to be at least the theoretical possibility that value systems with sufficiently strong emphasis on patterns of equality on the one hand, certain types of freedom on the other, can at least substantially mitigate these pessimistically diagnosed consequences of the undoubted empirical importance of political power and its inequalities in human society. That such values have indeed characterized American society has been very widely contended by a great diversity of observers. In certain respects, they were written into the founding documents of the Republic, notably by Thomas Jefferson. But a particularly impressive witness was Tocqueville[9] and such relatively recent observers as Lipset and Smelser have reinforced this pattern.[10]

All of these observers I think agree that equality is cross-cut by a value-pattern which is often formulated as that of achievement, that is, the expectation that social system units will contribute to the best of their capacities to valued outputs for the system as a whole. Since it cannot be assumed that capacities are equally distributed, though efforts to equalize

---

[8] Frank H. Knight, *The Ethics of Competition and Other Essays* (New Jersey: Augustus M. Kelley, 1951).

[9] Alexis de Tocqueville, *Democracy in America*, trans. by George Lawrence, ed. by J. P. Mayer (Garden City, N.Y.: Doubleday & Co., Anchor Books, 1969).

[10] Seymour Martin Lipset, *The First New Nation* (New York: Basic Books, 1963). Neil J. Smelser, ed., *Public Higher Education in California—Growth, Structural Change and Conflict* (Forthcoming).

them are certainly possible, the outcome of the achievement emphasis certainly tends to produce what is felt to be relatively justified inequality. The main focus of the attempt to integrate these two patterns lies in the concept of equality of opportunity, which is a very central one in Western society generally and that of the United States in particular.

VALUES AND NORMS

There is a certain tendency to assume that the category of values exhausts the relevant normative components which are institutionalized in social systems and which must be classified as cultural. To me, however, it has seemed increasingly important to make a definite analytical distinction between values and what in a more technical sense I have called norms.[11] "Norms," as the term itself suggests, is not a category of interests or desires, but a category of what in some sense is desirable. Unlike values, however, we conceive of norms as relatively specifically situation-linked. A fairly closely synonymous term is rules and an obvious field of relevance is the legal. One way of putting the distinction is to say that values serve to *legitimize* modes of more concrete action, whereas norms serve to *justify* them.[12]

We may think of the enunciation and establishment of norms as above all a mechanism through which a kind of pragmatic consistency in the implementation of values can be approximated. The major premises of a normative complex may be held to lie at the level of values, but these values alone do not determine the more detailed and circumstantial content. This is a function of exigencies of more particular situations. In particular the development of norms is a way in which the relevance of values to classes of interest such as those in rights of possession in the property sense or of rights of authority in the collective decision-making sense can be established across different categories of particular situations and collectivities.

In particular the primary concrete sanctions that impinge on the interests of acting units are those prescribed in the structure of norms rather than values as such. Values, that is to say, carry much more moral authority in Durkheim's sense and much less "teeth" in the sense of relatively specific situational sanctions. As such, we consider norms to be an indispensable bridge between the value level of the institutionalization of normative culture and the interest level of the impetus to concrete action.

A particularly important point is that in reference to objects, including modes of overt action, values and norms do not coincide but cross-cut each other. This is a consequence of the fact that, though both are cultural and

[11] Talcott Parsons, "General Introduction," in Talcott Parsons, Edward Shils, Kaspar D. Naegele, and Jesse R. Pitts, eds., *Theories of Society* (New York: The Free Press, 1961), pp. 3–79.

[12] Talcott Parsons, "Equality and Inequality in Modern Society; or, Social Stratification Revisited," *Sociological Inquiry*, 40 (Spring, 1970), see the technical note, pp. 56–69.

both institutionalized as part of the structure of social systems, in the latter capacity they subserve *different* functions. When we have spoken of values as "a directional component" in the structure of the social system, we have tended to imply a certain primacy of the cultural emphasis. One way of saying this is that values are a mode or mechanism of maintaining the cultural integrity of orientation within the exigencies of the actual functioning of social life. Norms, on the other hand, may be understood to have in a corresponding sense a societal primacy. They constitute normative mechanisms which operate to adjust and adapt the requirements of value integrity on the one hand to the exigencies of going social life and its interest structure on the other.

The distinction, I think, is clearly marked in the structure of the American legal system. Though what exactly constitutes statements of them is difficult to pin down, what are usually referred to as "constitutional principles" may be said to lie predominantly at the value level. On the other hand, the vast body of legal precepts, whether they have entered the law by judicial decision or by legislation or indeed by administrative ruling, would be classed as norms. These fall into such familiar classificatory rubrics as those of property, contract, authority, and the like. It is important to note here that every going social organization has "problems" in each of these spheres, regardless of the respects in which its larger functions are differentiated according to the dominant subvalues to which it is committed. Thus, though a business firm is concerned with economic production and the imperative of solvency, whereas a university is primarily concerned with cognitive rationality and the imperatives of cognitive validity and significance, as ongoing social organizations each has to handle property interests and each has internal structures of authority. The norms regulating these in the two cases are more likely to be similar than they are to be different. The values, however, are more likely to be different than they are to be similar.

CONCLUSION

The above is an exceedingly sketchy outline of some highlights of the relations between social and cultural systems. It can be seen that I have interpreted my mandate to discuss the relations of culture to sociology broadly to cover the concern of the student of social systems with problems of culture. Looking back, I think it can be said that in recent years very substantial progress has been made in clarifying this range of extremely vital problems of theory and orientation in social science. I am inclined to think, for example, that it is legitimate to compare what has happened in the last generation in social science with what happened approximately a generation earlier in the biological fields. There an immense amount of time and intellectual energy was taken up with arguments which often became extremely heated as to the relative priorities and importance of heredity and environment, with a strong tendency for the discussants to polarize over the question of heredity versus environment. This type of argument has almost disappeared from the biological literature. The main reason, I think, is that the relations of heredity and environment are now so much better understood than they were that it is meaningless to state significant problems in the old form.

Though social scientists use the old biological formulae of heredity and environment, the argument more specific to them was over the materialistic interpretation of history; whether "in the last analysis" the course of social change was determined by what in Germany were called the *Realfaktoren* or the *Idealfaktoren*. This argument revolved particularly about the Marxian scheme but was in fact much more general than the intellectual impact of Marxism alone would suggest. The tendency was to relegate anyone who, like Max Weber, became concerned with the importance and specific role of cultural factors like religious beliefs and values in historic social process to the "idealistic" school of the philosophy of history and to accuse him of being "in the last analysis" one of the tender-minded rather than the tough-minded type of intellectuals. Indeed, Weber probably did more than any other single individual to break out of this dilemma and to make it clear, though many of his subsequent critics have failed to get the point, that it was a false dilemma.[13]

Long before the argument could have been said to be resolved within the social sciences on their own grounds, however, a remarkable development took place. This was what amounts to a revolution in general science theory, one with a number of different facets, the best-known of which is the cybernetic idea. By virtue of this mode of thinking it could be respectable for biologists, for example, to treat the genetic constitution of organisms as a set of information-bearing mechanisms which did not constitute the primary energy systems of the particular organism or species, but yet could be the primary determinants of pattern and form. The parallel for the human sciences dealing with cultural matters could not for very long be missed, especially with the grand-scale application of cybernetic and information theory in computer technology. Another very important line of development, however, was that of the science of linguistics, with its particularly close relations to anthropology, specifically as a discipline concerned with culture. Linguistics, fortunately, originated as a "tough-minded" discipline and fell very readily into the general cybernetic pattern of analysis and thinking. It seems to me particularly significant that a "tough-minded" anthropologist like the late Clyde Kluckhohn, who was very much concerned with linguistics, but also had for a good many years a long-standing interest in values, came to look at the end of his life to linguistics as providing the most important theoretical models for the analysis not only of values but of culture more generally.

It is my strong feeling that, looking back from the vantage point of the year 2000, historians of the intellectual disciplines in our own time will

[13] S. N. Eisenstadt, ed., *The Protestant Ethic and Modernization: A Comparative View* (New York: Basic Books, 1968); David Little, *Religion, Order, and Law* (New York: Harper Torch Books, 1969).

evaluate what has happened in the last 10 to 15 years in these respects as constituting a genuinely new phase of theoretical advance in these disciplines and that the capacity to integrate the analysis of culture as symbolic systems, and therefore very specifically concerned with information, with the older traditional modes of analysis of social phenomena especially in economic and political contexts will prove to have been one of the most important achievements of this generation in social science.

TOWARD THE DEVELOPMENT OF
A CULTURAL ECONOMICS

KENNETH E. BOULDING
University of Colorado

T HE FOUNDING FATHER OF ECONOMICS, ADAM SMITH, HAD A STRONG SENSE
of the cultural matrix of economic phenomena. One of the most interesting of the unasked questions of intellectual history is how the
science of economics should have lost this sense and become an abstract
discipline void almost of any cultural context. The loss of interest within
the economics profession in the cultural matrix of its own discipline is a
fairly continuous process, almost from the days of Adam Smith. David
Ricardo, perhaps, was one of the first culprits in the process of reducing
economics to a culturally free abstraction. By contrast, his great contemporary, T. R. Malthus, had a very strong feeling for the significance of
culture, especially as it affected the dynamics of population. Successive
editions of his great *Essay on the Principle of Population* elaborated and
diversified the cultural theme. Even his much more abstract *Principles of
Political Economy* (1836), a work which foreshadowed the work of John
Maynard Keynes a hundred years later, was also significant in attributing
to the larger cultural matrix of economic life many of the characteristics
which would lead towards development or stagnation.

The work of John Stuart Mill, while in many respects it follows the abstract model of Ricardo and is not as rich as Adam Smith in its observations
of economic culture, is nevertheless far from being pure abstraction, and
gives a strong sense of the importance of the political and social matrix of
economic life and institutions. Alfred Marshall's *Principles of Economics*,
closer still to pure mechanical abstraction, represents a further movement
away from the richness of Adam Smith, but its sequel, *Industry and Trade*,
has a strong institutional flavor and indicates that he was well aware of
the complex cultural reality that lay beneath the abstractions of demand
and supply.

The marginalist school, from its very beginnings in Stanley Jevons,
Principles of Political Economy and Auguste Walras, *Principes d'Economie
Pure*, both in 1870, found the mathematics of the differential calculus and
simultaneous equations highly acceptable in the push towards abstraction,
and removed economics even further from its cultural matrix. The abstractions become more and more rarified as we move toward the beginnings of econometrics in the 1920's and the 1930's, where economics is reduced to equations and parameters, time series and regressions. Even
Ricardo at least talked about real commodities—about corn, wine, and
cloth, about employers and laborers. In modern economics these have become x's and y's. There is no sense of the corniness of corn or the clothiness
of cloth, or of any qualitative richness and variety, even in the world of
commodities, and still less in the world of man.

John Maynard Keynes stands a little aside from this movement towards abstraction. He made a very important contribution in the development of abstract models, but even his models had to be straightened out by his followers. His sense of the real world, at least of the speculators and financiers which he knew so well, probably hindered him in the development of pure models, but it gives his works something of the richness of cultural detail that one feels in Adam Smith, even though in a more limited range of culture. Keynes I suspect has no real conception of what it was like to be either poor or working class. His own cultural setting was very much that of upper middle class dons in Cambridge.

In the present generation, as far as economic theory is concerned, abstraction has completely conquered the field. One can look in vain, for instance, through issue after issue of the *American Economic Review* to try to find anything which even remotely suggests a cultural context. The computer, if anything, has accentuated this trend. It has enabled economists to put a lot more variables together and to develop more complex models with larger numbers of equations. But it has not, on the whole, encouraged the search for new data. It has increased the quick payoffs from the analysis of old data, and by this very fact, has distracted economists from the crucial first stage of the knowledge process, which is the stage from the real world to the data. One gets a depressing feeling that the typical Ph.D. dissertation these days is done by grabbing a fist full of somebody else's data and putting it through an elaborate statistical analysis on the computer. The culmination of this movement, of course, is the use of imaginary data, which is increasingly popular. This consists of the simulation of more and more complex models, using arbitrary or even randomly generated data. In the Monte Carlo method, indeed, the table of random numbers becomes the principal source of inputs into the system. How far from the real world can one get?

A very interesting and puzzling question of intellectual history is why the American institutionalists, especially the three great names of John R. Commons, Thorstein Veblen, and Wesley Mitchell, and their later descendants, such as Clarence Ayres, failed to affect the mainstream of economic thought in the United States, when a great deal of what they were saying seems to foreshadow the cultural economics for which I am arguing in this paper. The problem is not confined to the United States, for what might be called the "European Institutionalists"—Max Weber, Sidney and Beatrice Webb, and the English Fabians—likewise failed to affect the mainstream of economic thought, although they had a profound effect on social policy and political history. As one reflects also that the New Deal of the 1930's in the United States was largely an accomplishment of the pupils of John R. Commons, the paradox of apparent political success and apparent intellectual failure becomes even more striking. One can point, of course, to certain intellectual deficiences in institutionalist writers —Commons, for instance, was certainly deficient in literary competence, but this could not be said of Veblen, who perhaps was too competent, so that his work was admired but subconsciously dismissed as being merely aphoristic and entertaining. Mitchell, while he made enormous contributions in developing the empirical basis of subsequent economics at the National Bureau of Research, devoted his life to following a Newtonian will-o'-the-wisp in the business cycle, and never himself developed adequate theoretical models. When all this is said, however, the puzzle still remains and the answer has to lie deep in the sociology of the professions.

When one looks at the particular fields of economics, the situation seems, in places, a little better. The field which is perhaps the closest to an interest in the cultural matrix is labor economics and industrial relations, where the emphasis for a long time has been descriptive and empirical rather than analytical. There is a long tradition in labor economics in the study of the culture of the factory, of the collective bargaining processes, of the trade union organization and so on. This indeed is perhaps the greatest contribution of the institutional economists in the United States and their counterparts in Europe. Thus, the classic studies of John R. Commons in the American labor movement and of Beatrice and Sidney Webb in many aspects of English life, with their rich documentation of cultural backgrounds are perhaps the classic expression of what might be called "cultural economics." Unfortunately, the almost complete divorce between "analytical economics" and "cultural economics" is reflected in these authors. The theoretical and analytical foundations of their work are not really adequate. Neither John R. Commons nor the Webbs really understood the processes of inflation and deflation, and this failure to appreciate larger analytical models of the economy rendered their work inadequate beyond what might be called the "micro level." At this level, however, the study of what actually goes on in the field and the factory, around the bargaining table and in union meetings, has hardly been bettered since.

Next to labor economics, the field which comes closest to cultural economics is a rather loosely defined area which might almost be called "legal economics," covered by such titles as industrial organization, government regulation of business, and various subfields such as marketing, transportation and so on, many of which are more apt to be found in schools of business than they are in departments of economics. Such topics as the interaction of regulatory commissions with the activities which they are supposed to regulate, and the interactions of firms with each other and with the antitrust division of the Department of Justice, all reflect at least awareness that economic transactions take place in a legal and cultural setting. Even here, however, the emphasis has been on the legal rather than the cultural, on cases, judicial precedents, and the details and minutiae of the law, rather than on the behavioral component of the problem and the interaction of legal regulations with decisions at different levels and in different organizations.

There is one pioneering attempt by Cyert and March[1] to develop a be-

---

[1] Richard M. Cyert and J. G. March, *Behavioral Theory of the Firm* (Englewood Cliffs, N.J.: Prentice-Hall, 1963).

havioral theory of the firm, which was based on some empirical study of an almost complete lack of interest on the part of all the disciplines in the learning process in the behavior of business decision-makers. This study does not seem to have been followed up. It can certainly be regarded as a pioneering work in the cultural economics of the firm, but it does not seem to have produced any descendants.

Agricultural economics has had some tradition of studying the interaction between farmers and the institutions around them, but even this in these days seems largely to have run off in the direction of abstract econometrics, and there does not seem to be the cooperation between the agricultural economists and the rural sociologists which one would hope for.

As we move towards the fields of money and banking and public finance, we find an increasing reliance on rather formalistic mechanical models and an almost complete lack of interest on the part of all the disciplines in the cultural matrix within which the institutions of money and finance operate. I have argued for years that bankers were a savage tribe who should be studied by the anthropologists rather than by the economists, and I once tried to persuade Margaret Mead to do a book on "Coming of Age in the Federal Reserve," with, I regret to say, no response at all! The culture of bankers, indeed, is more mysterious than that of the Dobuans or the Chuk-Chuks. The Navaho indeed may have a Harvard anthropologist in every family, but the Federal Reserve Board has, to my knowledge, never allowed a single one to attend the ceremonials in its marble hogan. Nobody really knows what bankers are like, what kinds of images of the world they have, what they talk about, what kind of gossip they follow, what taboos they have, and how their decisions are made. The economics of money and banking is almost entirely a matter of the analysis of published statistics and the attempt to find correlations among them. It is pure "black box" analysis with practically no attempt to pry off the lid to see what are the actual processes which produce the often very peculiar outputs.

Another area where the expansion of cultural economics might be highly useful is in the relation of government to the economy. This is an enormous field and different parts of it tend to be cultivated with rather different instruments. Public finance, for instance, the study of government taxation, revenues, and expenditures—is frequently discussed in a rather mechanical way in terms of the impact of taxation and expenditure on the output of various commodities, on employment, on distribution of income, and so on. There is some justification for a mechanical approach here, as a good deal of the impact of public finance is in fact mechanical. The culture of the tax collector may make some difference to the efficiency with which taxes are collected, but this difference is likely to be somewhat peripheral to the major impacts of the tax and expenditure system. The anthropology of the tax collector might be just as interesting as the anthropology of bankers, but it might not be so significant in regard to its total impact on society. Where a cultural approach might be helpful would be in a study of the acceptance or legitimacy of taxation, and the study of tax resistance or tax acceptance. Societies differ widely in this regard. In the United States, for instance, taxes are paid with quite astonishing fidelity, and the system relies to a very large extent on the individual honesty of the tax-payer, though the efficiency of the Internal Revenue Service in unmasking tax evaders unquestionably has some impact. There are other societies, however, in which tax evasion is so widespread and so universal that no system of policing could possibly induce the mass of individuals to pay their legal taxes. This is really a cultural phenomenon, but as far as I know it has been very little studied.

A point at which cultural studies would be of great interest (and are somewhat neglected) is in the political decision-making process by which taxes are in fact passed into law. The actual legal tax system emerges as a result of the interaction of a number of different governmental subcultures, that, for instance, of the Treasury and Civil Service, which brings a technical point of view and a long memory of previous administrative problems to the task of formulating the details of tax administration. There is also in the United States the President and the Executive branch which makes proposals to Congress, and there is Congress itself, which is the ultimate source of fiscal authority. The actual tax system emerges as a result of a long historical process, involving especially the changing culture of Congress, and this in turn reflects the changing culture of its constituencies. The processes of logrolling and political bargaining are fairly familiar. Not so familiar are the processes by which certain ideas become fashionable or unfashionable, and even certain interests become fashionable or unfashionable.

The idea that political decisions are made by the raw conflict of interests involved in the bargaining process is certainly inadequate. Interests, indeed, are often extremely hard to determine. It is extremely hard to estimate, for instance, what would be the effect on the overall distribution of income or wealth of any particular tax proposal. Any decision, even of private persons, will divide the human population into three possible groups—those who are favorably affected by it, those who are adversely affected by it, and those who are unaffected by it. In the case of the small decisions of private and unpowerful people, the third category is overwhelmingly the largest. In the case of decisions by powerful people, the power of the decision-maker could well be measured hypothetically by the size of the first two segments of the population. In most cases, however, these three boxes are empty. It is very hard to tell even how many people fall into one box or the other, and still harder to tell who these people are. It is the perception of interests, not the realities (whatever this may mean), which really affects behavior, and the perception of interest is very much a function of the culture within which the perceiver is embedded. Therefore, the way in which the culture of government changes as mistakes are made and lessons are learned, as information flows in, creating new ideas, new concepts, and new values, is of great importance in the study of the process by which decisions are actually made. A good example of a study of this kind is Herbert Stein's work on *The Fiscal Revolution in America* (1969), which shows how a combination of the failure of existing policies, and the perception of that failure, coupled with ideas about alternative policies coming in largely from the academic profession, transformed what might be called the "conventional wisdom" of American government in the space of a little over 30 years, from Herbert Hoover's tax increase in the middle of the Depression in 1932 to the Kennedy-inspired tax cut in 1964. This book indeed is one of the best examples of "cultural economics" that has been produced in this generation.

Another aspect of government interaction with the economy is regulation of private economic activity by legal prohibitions and government regulating agencies. There is a large amount of this kind of activity, ranging from regulation of labor relations by the National Labor Relations Board and similar agencies in certain specific industries, to regulatory agencies like the Interstate Commerce Commission, the Federal Communications Commission, the Securities and Exchange Commission, on to the rather looser activities of the antitrust division of the Department of Justice. Most of these agencies are concerned with the enforcement of prohibitions of various kinds. Thus, the law defines as illegal, certain "unfair labor practices" on the part of both employees and unions. It defines certain collusive practices as illegal under the antitrust laws. By licensing it makes such practices as running a radio station legal for some people and illegal for others. The whole problem of the cultural interaction between the regulating commissions and authorities of different kinds and the regulated is an extremely interesting subject which has not been studied as much as one would wish. Each of the commissions and agencies develops a subculture of its own which is transmitted to each new generation of role occupants in ways that are not wholly dissimilar from the way in which a doctor transmits his culture to his successors.

It is clear that there is something, which now exists perhaps only in embryo, which deserves the name of "cultural economics." Because it has not yet taken an unambiguous form, it is obviously hard to describe it. Nevertheless, it is at least interesting to speculate what the embryo might look like if it ever lived to grow up. It may, of course, be just a mythical beast, and the fact that several promising starts seem to have come to very little suggests that it may have some genetic deficiencies which interfere with its growth in the harsh milieu of the academic community. Nevertheless, even the sketchiest attempt to describe this mythical beast portrays such a gentle and useful animal that it seems a pity not to try to bring it into the world.

Being economics, it would have to start with the phenomenon of exchange, beginning with the exchange of goods, a "good" being something that somebody wants and which has a positive marginal utility, that is, he wants more of it. There is nothing wrong with the pure economic theory of exchange as an abstract model, and indeed some anthropologists have failed to understand certain aspects of the economics of primitive societies because they have not seen that exchange was a universal phenomenon, which might be overlaid with all sorts of custom, ritual, and conventional behavior, but which nevertheless always involved some kinds of "terms of trade" or exchange ratios, which were relevant to the satisfaction of the participants and to their continued behavior in the role of exchangers. The failure to recognize the significance of the phenomenon of terms of trade is by no means confined to anthropologists. I recall once being on a committee which was considering the question of a university program in industrial relations, with a psychiatrist who was convinced that industrial conflicts could be wholly described in terms of the love life of the foreman or the frustrated sexuality of the workers, and could not be persuaded that wages had anything to do with industrial conflict. The economist, as economist, therefore, has a professional duty to point out the importance of terms of trade and, indeed, the whole structure of terms of trade that comprise the price system. This is an integral part of any set of cultural relations. Furthermore, man's experience with various terms of trade is a great cultural teacher. Even though it is a very fundamental principle of economics that no uncoerced exchange takes place without both parties believing that they benefited at the time, this leaves plenty of room for deception and regret, concepts that have very little place in formal economics. Deception, when it is found out, however, and regret, when the right lessons are drawn from it, are both very important teachers. It can hardly be said too often that we learn new things only from failure, never from success, and we learn a great deal from our failures in exchange. We buy a certain brand, and we don't like it, so we do not buy it again. We take a job, don't like it, and quit.

An enormous learning process goes on within the individual as he encounters the market, makes exchanges, whether in the labor market (where he takes a job) or in the commodity markets (where he buys things) or in capital markets (where he borrows or invests). In any of these experiences, disappointment is likely to lead to some sort of learning. The emphasis on learning is perhaps the crucial difference between mechanistic economics and cultural economics. Mechanistic economics tends to take preferences and even skills and techniques for granted, as the data or ultimate determinants of the economic process. Cultural economics must look upon both preferences, skills, and techniques as essentially learned in the great processes of cultural transmission. It may well be that one of the things which holds us up in cultural economics is the absence of any satisfactory abstract models of learning in the way, for instance, that we have abstract models of decision-making or maximizing behavior. Nevertheless, even though the models may be crude, the phenomenon is fundamental. Social learning, indeed, is the central concept of culture.

Economics has tended to restrict itself to the exchange of goods and to regard other forms of dyadic relationships, such as what I have called the "grant," that is, the one-way transfer of an exchangeable, as something a little outside the main focus of interest of economics.[2] Cultural economics, however, would have to include all these dyadic relationships which involve exchangeables or goods, whether they conform to the traditional form of exchange or not. There are, indeed, two major forms of the one-way transfer, each of which is the door to a very large world of social organization and human relationships. One is the *gift*, which is the expression of an integrative relationship, that is, identification of the giver with the welfare of the recipient. The other is *tribute*, that is, a one-way transfer made in response to threat, a threat being a conditional undertaking to produce a negative commodity, or a bad. In its illegitimate form this is the bandit; in its legitimate form, the tax collector. I must confess that I pay my taxes mainly because, if I did not, something unpleasant would happen to me and I reckon the loss entailed by paying the taxes is less than the loss that would be entailed by suffering the sanctions of the law if I did not pay them. The threat system has a vast culture of its own which we cannot go into here. It impinges significantly on economics, for instance, in the legal sanctions which seem to be necessary to induce people to make provision for public goods. And cultural economics will certainly recognize the complexity of the culture which surrounds the various threat relations.

The dynamics of the integrative system, which produces gifts, likewise has an interesting cultural context. Why, for instance, do we support children within the family, and, in many cultures, old people as well? These patterns of behavior are clearly learned, and arise out of the culture. In the process of the development of culture itself, however, great importance has to be assigned to *reciprocity*. This often looks very much like exchange, but it is actually something rather different. Exchange is conditional. If I give you A, will you give me B? Reciprocity is at least hypothetically unconditional, that is, I give you something out of the sheer goodness of my heart and you give me something out of the sheer goodness of yours. Reciprocity does, of course, tend to slip over into exchange and very frequently is formalized as exchange, in which case it often loses its integrative aspect. The transmission of culture depends a great deal on serial reciprocity, that is, A gives something to B, which creates a sense of obligation on B's part, which he releases by giving something not to A, but to C. We make grants to our children because we received grants from our parents. We make sacrifices for posterity because our ancestors made sacrifices for us. The only answer to the famous question, "What has posterity ever done for me?" indeed, is that our ancestors, ourselves and our descendants are all part of a larger community of the imagination extending over time and space.

One of the most interesting questions in cultural economics is the extent to which any particular system of economic institutions will survive or fail to survive because of changes in the cultural matrix which the economic

[2] K. E. Boulding, *The Economy of Love and Fear* (Belmont, Calif.: Wadsworth, 1972).

institutions produce. A related question is that of changes which spontaneous changes in the cultural institutions may produce in the economic order. We think of the time structure of society as a series of "layers" of somewhat independent systems, involving, for instance, an economic dynamic, a political dynamic, a religious dynamic, an intellectual dynamic, an artistic dynamic and so on. Each layer has a certain independence and coherence in its own movements, but also interacts strongly at times with other layers. This contrasts with what might be called the "monodynamic" view of society, in which one of the layers, such as, for instance, the economic system, is regarded as dominant with an inherent dynamic of its own, which is not much affected by influences from outside and which, as it were, carries all the other processes of society along with it. The Marxist interpretation of history tends to be "monodynamic" in this sense. My own view is "polydynamic," in the sense that I doubt whether there is any single system which at all times dominates the others, though if there were such a system I would nominate the dynamics of the integrative system of legitimacy and community rather than the dynamics of wealth and power, for without legitimacy neither wealth nor power can be preserved.

Examples of this "polydynamic" approach would be Max Weber's theories of the impact of Protestantism in the transformation of late feudal and early capitalist society, and the views of Schumpeter regarding the instability of late capitalism and its tendency to slip over into socialism because of the inability of exchange institutions to develop an integrative matrix in terms of legitimacy, trust, acceptance, and so on, without which they cannot really function. The trouble with capitalism isn't so much that it doesn't work, as that nobody loves it! It is unloved because it depends so heavily on exchange as its social organizer, and neither merchants nor banks are capable of attracting much affection. It is reciprocity rather than exchange which creates legitimacy and community. Reciprocity, however, itself tends to be unstable and is formalized into exchange. A general theory of the interaction of the dynamic sectors of society, however, has not yet been developed and remains as a task for the future.

Perhaps the most significant attribute of a cultural economics is that it must be evolutionary. Mechanistic economics can be dynamic in the sense that it can produce models of time sequences of variables. Indeed, I would argue that dynamic mechanistic economics, as reflected, for instance, in difference equation theory, has made a small but important contribution to the development of a general social science. Mechanical dynamics, however, has sharp limitations. It depends for its predictive power on the discovery of stable parameters for its difference or differential equations. Unfortunately, in real social systems these parameters are very rarely stable. Thus, even demography, which is perhaps the most successful of mechanical dynamics systems, has been disastrously unsuccessful in its predictions. National income economics is not much better. We have tried to solve this problem by "Ptolemization," that is, the development of increasing numbers of "epicycles" through the addition of new variables, new parameters, and new equations to our models. Unfortunately, there is not much evidence that this increase in the complexity of models has increased their predictive power, and we may be looking for the famous black cat in the dark room that isn't there. It may be, that is, that there are no stable parameters in social systems. We then have to fall back on evolutionary theory, that is, mutation and selection. There is no doubt that this is a useful, descriptive paradigm of the dynamics of society as well as the dynamics of biological evolution. In social systems the mutations consist of new ideas, new inventions (both mechanical, biological and social), new organizations, especially new species of organizations, new patterns of behavior that can be imitated by others and so on. Selection occurs in the process of total social interaction and learning. Some mutations are eliminated by bankruptcy, by conquest, by death, by the loss of legitimacy, and other selective forces. As a result of this vast melée of selective forces some things survive and some do not.

Social evolution is a good deal more complex than biological evolution. It is harder to define social species, as we do not have the delightful simplicity of biological mating. Automobiles are not produced by other automobiles as horses are produced by other horses, but by other forms of social organization, such as automobile firms. As a result of this complexity, mutation can take place at several levels. We can, for instance, have mutation which will change the rate of mutation itself, and we can have mutations which profoundly affect the selective processes. Thus, social evolution may be more Lamarckian than it is Darwinian, if only in the sense that it is harder to distinguish the genotypes from the phenotypes. There is not the nice, clear distinction between mutation in the genotype and selection in the phenotype that we have in Darwinian evolution. In social evolution, the genetic and the selective processes are much more closely interwoven than they are in biological evolution.

A good illustration of the complexity of these processes is found in the theory and history of invention, which is almost the same thing as social mutation. Inventions are clearly not "random" in the sense that all inventions have equal probability of being discovered at any time. In any particular state of the social system, some new inventions are much more probable than others, if only in the sense that a perceived "hole" in the social system is likely to be filled. In regard to invention the problem of the "levels of mutations" becomes extremely important. Thus, inventions which reduce uncertainty are likely to increase the subsequent rate of invention. We see this in the processes of economic development, where the unwillingness of people to change their ways is often closely related to a quite realistic appraisal of the uncertainties involved in so doing. Reduction of uncertainty, such as took place in American agriculture, following the development of price supports in the 1930's, may easily set in motion a large process of technical improvement and increasing productivity, as indeed in the above case it did.

The success of revolutionary movements often depends on the fact that they create uncertainties in the society which is being challenged, and hence prevent that society from making the changes which would lead to its development. The stagnation and failure of the old society then feeds the fires of revolution. Once the revolution has been accomplished, however, the success of the regime depends a great deal on its capacity to diminish the uncertainties of the society and so permit evolutionary change again.

It is highly significant that the current descendants of the American institutionalists have formed a society which they call The Association for Evolutionary Economics. The institutionalists' main criticism of traditional mechanistic economics was on the grounds that it was not evolutionary. One recalls Veblen's famous article on "Why is Economics Not an Evolutionary Science?"[3] The criticism basically is that mechanistic economics assumes that there is an equilibrium price structure, that is, an equilibrium set of all prices and money wages, in terms of trade, which is determined on the one hand by the structure of production functions, that is, what inputs produce what outputs, and on the other by the structure of preference functions, that is, what combinations of commodities are preferred to what. The demonstration, indeed, that corresponding to every set of these determinants there is only one set, or at most only a very limited number of sets, of equilibrium prices, is a beautiful piece of logic and is developed at great length and with much affection in all standard textbooks. The critical question, however, is what happens if there is a divergence between the equilibrium price set and the actual price set at which exchanges are currently taking place? Mechanistic economics assumes that under these circumstances pressures will be set up to change the price set towards the equilibrium, though there are still quite serious unsolved problems as to the actual machinery of this process, whether it operates, for instance, through excess demands and supplies or through excess profits or losses. The exact conditions under which a determinant solution will be reached are extremely complex and are still not wholly spelled out.

The critical question for evolutionary economics, however, is whether a disequilibrium, that is, a divergence between the actual price set and the equilibrium price set, will work back on the supposed determinants of the equilibrium as well as work on moving the actual price set towards the equilibrium. Thus, if the actual price set is not the same as the equilibrium set, this may have an effect on preferences, according to the famous "sour grapes" principle, for instance, according to which if you can't get something, you decide you don't want it. It may also affect the production functions, in the sense that if there is a commodity in excess demand, resources within the industry will be diverted away from sales towards the improvement of production and productivity; whereas if there is a commodity in

[3] In Joseph Dorfman, ed., *The Place of Science in Modern Civilization* (New York: Viking Press, 1919).

excess supply, there is very little incentive to improve productivity and most of the activity will be centered on sales and marketing.

This is, indeed, a special case of a general question in the evolutionary theory which as far as I know has never been satisfactorily answered. Evolution takes place by ecological succession, that is, by irreversible changes in the determinants of the equilibrium of an ecological system. These changes may simply be irreversible physical changes, like the filling up of a pond, or they may be changes in the genetic structure through mutation. The general assumption of ecological theory is very similar to that of orthodox mechanistic economics; that if there is a divergence between the actual structure of populations of different species in an ecosystem and the equilibrium structure, those populations which are "too large" by this criterion will decline, those which are "too small" will increase, and the movements of the populations will be towards equilibrium. The critical question now, of course, is what changes the equilibrium itself, and particularly whether the existence of a disequilibrium has any impact in changing the equilibrium itself. Ecological theory seems to be in much the same state as orthodox mechanistic economics. It may well be, therefore, that the reason why evolutionary economics has been somewhat disappointing (one has to confess, it has not presented up to now a challenge to mechanistic economics which could really unseat it) is that evolutionary theory itself is in a very unsatisfactory state, and that the questions which the evolutionary economists are trying to raise are themselves still unanswered by evolutionary theory in general.

What one looks for, therefore, is a general evolutionary theory which can illuminate not only biological evolution, but cultural evolution, linguistic evolution, economic evolution, religious evolution, class evolution, family evolution, sexual evolution—anything that we would like to mention. The general outlines for such a theory, indeed, are fairly clear. It can be expressed, indeed, in three sentences: (1) The dynamic processes of any existing system will produce strain; (2) once strain increases beyond a certain threshold something will give, that is, there will be change in the parameters in the system; (3) a system gives at its weakest point, that is, what adjusts is the most easily adjustable. Any specific adjustment, however, creates further strain in other parts of the system, so the process starts all over again.

The first part of this theory is perhaps the easiest epistemologically, in the sense that it is fairly easy to detect the on-going, regular processes of a system, and even to perceive that the strain is being increased. The second process, that of the system giving under the strain, is much harder to predict, much harder to find out about, simply because the weaknesses of the system are frequently only revealed after the event, that is, after the adjustment has been made, and are not necessarily revealed by those ongoing processes of the system which can be easily observed. The difficulty here is that what we are observing is a "threshold" phenomenon. It is often extremely difficult to find out where a threshold is until we have reached it, after which it is frequently too late. When the strain does not reach the threshold, nothing happens and it is extremely hard to observe nothing, although what does not happen is often a great deal more interesting and significant than what does. The inventions that were not made, the wars that did not happen, the revolutions that never took place, the depressions that never materialized, the crises that were avoided—these are the things that will tell us most about the social system and yet these are precisely the things which never get into the history books.

The same problem exists in biological evolution: all we know about are the mutations that were successful, at least successful enough to leave a record. There must have been thousands, perhaps millions as many times the number of mutations that were immediately unsuccessful, and these leave no record. Consequently, it is quite impossible to estimate even the probability of things turning out the way they actually did, and we tend to have an illusion that the evolutionary record, as we find it on our own planet, had a kind of necessity about it, simply because it existed; whereas, in fact, it may have been the result of a series of extraordinarily improbable accidents. Some astronomers to the contrary, we really have no way of estimating the probability of life in other parts of the universe, simply because we have no way of estimating the probability of its having developed on our own planet. We face very much the same problem in human history. Was it, for instance, just a succession of lucky accidents that turned the dynamics of European society into science, with such incalculable consequences for all the rest of mankind?

The great weakness of evolutionary theory is illustrated by the fact that it is quite impossible to detect evolutionary potential at the time when it occurs. In evolution we can be wise only very long after the event. Why did the evolution of the vertebrates, for instance, proceed so much further than that, shall we say, of the octupus, who really seems to have so many advantages? Why should man have emerged out of the anthropoids rather than out of the felines, who again seem to have so many advantages? And who could have predicted at the time the enormous significance in cultural evolution of Moses or Jesus or Mohammed, or even Karl Marx? For all we know, the evolutionary potential of the twenty-fourth century is now being created in an obscure valley in the Andes and nobody will find out about it for at least a hundred years. Are the hippies an evolutionary potential which will create vast changes in life styles and demands for commodities in the next hundred years? Or are they just an unsuccessful mutation, a flash in the pan, which will produce only a little dust on shelves of the libraries, while the Mormons or Jehovah's Witnesses go on to conquer the world? It is not perhaps, therefore, too surprising that so far, at any rate, evolutionary economics has made little theoretical impact, simply because while it has a good deal to propose, it does not really have very much to say. The great English economist Alfred Marshall, who was by no means unaware of these problems, headed his great *Principles of Economics* off with Volume One; Volume Two, alas, which should have been evolutionary economics, was never written, and I think one has to confess, it is still not written, although it is still in prospect.

In a remarkable new book, *The Entropy Law and the Economic Process*,[4] one of the most erudite and imaginative of the modern economists, Nicholas Georgescu-Roegen, has raised the question aṣ to whether the entropy concept cannot be brought in to give economics a dynamic and a sense of direction, indeed a "time's arrow." The idea is very suggestive. Economic processes, like evolutionary processes, again, are anti-entropic in the sense that they use free energy to create structures in the way of commodities and organizations, roles, professions, and so on, of increasing complexity and improbability. Evolution is the segregation of entropy, the building of little islands of low entropy and high order in the form of living organisms, artifacts, and social organizations, at the cost of creating more disorder elsewhere. It is quite tempting, therefore, to try to formulate an "entropy theory of value" in which value is identified in some sense with negentropy or order and the loss of value with the increase in entropy or disorder. This would certainly seem to make more sense than the labor theory of value, which is essentially circular; labor being defined as activity which produces value, without defining what the activity consists of.

Nevertheless, in spite of the monumental and suggestive work of Georgescu-Roegen, it seems to me that the attempt to construct an economics or any social science on the basis of the entropy concept has not so far been successful. There may be a very good reason for this lack of success. The difficulty with the entropy concept is that it is essentially negative, that is, it is a measure of disorder and the significance of the concept depends on the kind of order that is diminishing. In thermodynamics the kind of order which is diminishing is a very simple kind of order and could easily be defined, so that the entropy concept is at least moderately clear, though as Georgescu-Roegen points out, it is by no means clear that we can equate entropy, as Boltzman did, with a probabilistic-mechanistic system.

A good deal of excitement was aroused in the early days of information theory by the fact that the information measure as developed by Shannon and Weaver[5] was formally identical with the Boltzman measure for entropy, or rather for negentropy, as information is a measure of order rather than disorder. Here again, however, the kind of order which is being measured is a very simple kind of order, very useful for Bell Telephone, for whom the conversations of a teenager and of the President of the United States over the "hot line" represent exactly the same technical problem. The concept, however, has not turned out to be very useful in the study of social communication and significance or even of knowledge. There is no "wit" as a unit of knowledge to correspond to the "bit" as a unit of infor-

[4] Nicholas Georgescu-Roegen, *The Entropy Law and the Economic Process* (Cambridge, Mass.: Harvard University Press, 1971).

[5] Claude Shannon and Warren Weaver, *The Mathematical Theory of Communication* (Urbana: University of Illinois Press, 1949).

mation, simply because knowledge is a far more complex kind of order than information. While, therefore, we may have a fair amount of confidence that time's arrow in social as well as in biological evolution leads towards order, it is not at all clear what kind of order it leads towards, and the taxonomy of different kinds of order is a task which still remains for the future. The GNP, for instance, is a certain measure of the order of power and complexity of the society, yet this too, as we are extremely well aware these days, is highly imperfect, particularly inefficient as a measure of human welfare, and yet welfare itself involves orders of a complexity which we find extremely difficult even to describe, and still more difficult to measure.

Regretfully, therefore, I think we have to leave the entropy concept behind, as suggestive but not ultimately very informative, simply because it cannot handle the crucial problem of cultural and economic evolution, which is that of the description and measurement of different kinds of order. To rely on the entropy concept would be rather like trying to find out about the Catholic Church by studying the people who were not Catholics. The absence of order does not really tell us very much about the order that is absent.

Perhaps the greatest achievement of mechanistic economics is the macroeconomic models which come most immediately from the inspiration of Lord Keynes. Economics, however, has had a long history of what might be called a "total systems approach," that is, looking at the economy as a totality of interrelated parts and perceiving that propositions which might be true of parts might not be true of the whole. This is implied, indeed, in Adam Smith, who was the first to develop a concept of a set of "normal," "equilibrium," or in his own term "natural" prices, a concept which was later elaborated by Alfred Marshall and Leon Walras. In the early years of the twentieth century, Irving Fisher in the United States and Knut Wicksell in Sweden each developed systems which had implied macroeconomic models in them. As often happens in the history of science, however, the great breakthrough came as a result of a double thrust—an improvement in "economic instrumentation" pioneered at the National Bureau of Economic Research in New York by Simon Kuznets (who has just received an extremely well-deserved Nobel Prize), and the theoretical insights of John Maynard Keynes, who perceived with an almost poetic insight, first that profits were a "widow's cruse," which would never run dry as long as they were distributed in dividends,[6] and then the further insight in the General Theory,[7] that there could be an equilibrium level of unemployment, at the point at which the total product of the society would just be absorbed or disposed of to households and household purchases, to government and government purchases, or to business investment—that is,

---

[6] John Maynard Keynes, *Treatise on Money* (New York: Harcourt Brace & Co., 1930; London: MacMillan & Co. Ltd., 1950).

[7] John Maynard Keynes, *General Theory of Employment, Interest and Money* (New York: Harcourt, Brace & Co., 1936).

a willing increase in the total capital stock of goods held by businesses. The perception that the actual quantities of product produced, consumed, invested, and so on were not the result of the decisions of individual households, businesses, or even governments, but were the result of the interaction of the decisions of all the parties to the system, is perhaps one of the most profound insights to come out of economics.

I have sometimes called these principles the "macro-economic paradoxes." They include, for instance, the proposition that a decision on the part of individuals of a closed economy to increase their money stocks does not result itself in an increase in the stock of money, but results only in a decline in the total volume of receipts and expenditures. This follows from the principle that whereas for an individual, receipts and expenditures are something quite different, which do not have to be equal to one another, for a closed society, receipts and expenditures are exactly the same thing as each transfer of money is a receipt at one end and an expenditure at the other. Consequently, while an individual can easily increase his money stock by spending less than he receives or decrease it by spending more than he receives, all individuals taken together cannot do this. The money stock can only be increased by increasing it, or decreased by decreasing it. It is unchanged by circulating it. These are very simple and obvious propositions, yet it is surprising how long it took for even economists to perceive them clearly.

Another of the paradoxes is the paradox of saving, that decisions to save on the part of individuals may not result in the net accumulation of capital, but may merely lead to increased unemployment and a decline in output. It is much more true to say that the aggregate decision to invest determines the volume of saving, than to say that decision to save is determined by what is available for investment, for there can be forced saving through inflation, for instance, as well as voluntary saving.

Another set of propositions which, however, are less generally accepted, relate to the distribution of national income or some similar measure, as between wages or aggregate labor income and the various components of non-labor income—profits, interest, and rents. The labor market for money wages plays a surprisingly small role in this distribution. A rise in money wages can easily result in a fall in real wages and redistribution towards profits if there is an inflationary trend and prices rise faster than the money wages. This principle very severely limits the power of labor unions to redistribute income. Over the long pull, indeed, this power seems almost non-existent, and it may well be that the main impact of labor unions is to redistribute income within the working class, perhaps a little away from unorganized towards organized labor, but seems to have very little effect on the distribution of income between labor income and non-labor income. In the United States, for instance, between 1932 and 1942 there was a great rise in the power of labor unions, membership increasing four or five times, and a large part of American industry came under collective bargaining. Nevertheless, in this period the proportion of national income going to labor actually fell from about 72 percent to about 62 percent, a result of the economic recovery and the rise in investment and profits. In this area, indeed, "things are seldom what they seem." Skim milk not only masquerades as cream, but cream turns out quite unexpectedly to be nothing but skim milk.

A critical question which is not easily answered, is whether there is anything in the larger framework of cultural economics, or the still larger framework of cultural science as a whole, which corresponds to these macro-economic paradoxes. Are there things which can be said about the system as a whole, for instance, which are fundamentally different from what can be said about an individual or else part of it? Are there general cultural systems in which the sum of individual decisions produces results which are quite contrary to the intentions and expectations of any of the individual decision-makers? It is certainly tempting to look for propositions like this in the larger cultural framework. We can find them certainly in the field of the international system, especially in regard to national defense, where decisions to increase national security by increasing armaments frequently lead to the opposite result. Jay Forrester at M.I.T. has called attention to what he calls "counterintuitive results" in elaborate computer-operated dynamic models of urban development and also of the total world economy.[8] The detailed assumptions of these models are very much open to question. One is tempted, indeed, to call them "under-the-counter intuitive assumptions," which are hidden in the mathematics and the procedures of the model, but which determine its results. Nevertheless, the principle is a sound one, that when we make models of total systems the results are very frequently counterintuitive.

A very early example of this in economics which had a wide cultural framework is the economist's attack on the old English Poor Law, beginning particularly with Malthus, on the grounds that if the poor were supported in a way that encouraged their propagation, the result would not be ultimately to relieve poverty, but rather to increase it enormously, and to bring the whole society down into ruin. The counterintuitive model of 1834, then, which bore some resemblances to the rather grim models of Professor Forrester, is that if poverty is to be relieved in the long run, it must be relieved very little in the short run, and under conditions which make it both disagreeable to be on relief and also which discourage procreation. Here, again, however, one wonders if the counterintuitive model also did not contain certain errors. If the lot of the destitute could have been made a little more comfortable in nineteenth century England, it is doubtful there would have been much more propagation, and the system might have reached a bearable equilibrium without driving the destitute into horrible workhouses.

Similar problems emerge in the situation of foreign aid to poor countries.

[8] Jay Forrester, *Urban Dynamics* (Cambridge, Mass. and London: M.I.T. Press, 1969).

There are circumstances, certainly, under which this could simply lead to a vast proliferation of ultimately catastrophic poverty. The medical advances of the late 1940's, which resulted in the virtual elimination of malaria in a large part of the tropics, had a totally unforseen effect in population explosions which have made the ultimate development of these countries much more difficult. On the other hand, we have to be careful even here against under-the-counter intuitive systems. It is all too easy to make models which leave out some essential cultural variables. There have been occasions in history when a rapid rise in population has gone along with an even more rapid rise in productivity. There are other occasions, however, such as Ireland in the nineteenth century, where a rise in population has been totally disastrous, in this case, perhaps, because of foreign domination and absentee landlordism. Here I think great vigilance is needed on the part of social scientists to insure that in the building of these models, the essential variables are not left out. Here, indeed, is perhaps the greatest task of the cultural economics that we hope is somewhere on the way.

I must confess I am not overly optimistic about a quick breakthrough into the sort of cultural economics one would like to see. Nevertheless, there is quite widespread dissatisfaction in the economics profession with the rather barren mechanistic economics and econometrics which now dominates nearly all our journals. It may be that the time is ripe for another of Mr. Kuhn's scientific revolutions.[9] On the other hand, a good many revolutions have never come off; and a good many others have come off, only to be regretted later. While, therefore, I am prepared to exhibit a certain optimism, I find it hard to avoid restraining the optimism with a modicum of caution.

[9] S. Thomas Kuhn, *Structure of Scientific Revolutions* (Chicago: University of Chicago Press, 1962).

CULTURE AND POLITICAL SCIENCE: PROBLEMS IN THE EVALUATION OF THE CONCEPT OF POLITICAL CULTURE

LUCIAN W. PYE
Massachusetts Institute of Technology

F OR A DISCIPLINE THAT REJOICES IN IMPORTING IDEAS, POLITICAL SCIENCE was strangely slow to incorporate the concept of culture. In part the reason no doubt was that political science had long employed cognate concepts which, like culture, promised much for general explanations but proved elusive for pinning down causation in any specific case.

For example, first Montesquieu and then the German theorists conceived of law as a web of habits, customs and folk-themes common to a people. The concept of nation provided a further analogy to that of culture. The notion that a constitution reflects the basic values, predispositions and ideals of a community, which came to dominate constitutional theory by the 1930's, was hardly distinguishable from the early and more diffuse definitions of culture common in other social sciences at the time.

These classical and neo-classical concepts of political science all contained two of the basic ingredients of the modern concept of culture: human communities tend to have distinctive characteristics which last over time, and collectivities have dynamic laws with respect to development and change. By the early 1940's new concepts based upon new research techniques were welcomed into the discipline. The art of sample surveying and with it a new definition of public opinion was demanding academic recognition. At the same time it was becoming increasingly urgent for political science to come to terms with the new revolutionary concept of man which Freud's discoveries were diffusing to all aspects of Western thought.

The time was thus ripe for a new infusion and synthesis of ideas, and World War II made it urgent to get on with the task. The compelling need to train large numbers of people to understand foreign cultures so as to plan for military governments, conduct psychological warfare, and simply to interpret what made the enemy act as he did overnight legitimized area studies and interdisciplinary approaches. The wartime concerns with man and society opened the doors of political science to numerous emerging and powerful concepts from neighboring disciplines.

Quite understandably culture was one of these, particularly since for a brief period anthropology appeared as the reigning social science. The notions of area studies and of interdisciplinary research seemed less novel to the anthropologists, who at the time were being led by an extraordinary generation of imaginative literary men and women. Even if Margaret Mead, Ruth Benedict, Geoffrey Gorer, Clyde Kluckhohn, Abram Kardiner, George Murdock and others had not been at the forefront of relevant research and effective policy advising during the war, their collective brilliance and exciting expositions of the relations of culture and personality would have certainly penetrated political science. It is true that these anthropologists, fortified primarily with the concept of culture, greatly overstated their potential contribution to the making of a brave new world of social science in the public service; and to re-read today Clyde Kluckhohn's assertions in *Mirror for Man*[1] that once anthropologists "returned home" it would soon be possible to solve the problems of advanced societies and world politics is to capture a sense of nostalgia and also to blush that such hubris was once routinely accepted. Inflated claims aside, Clyde Kluckhohn did lead in the establishment of the model postwar area study program at the Harvard Russian Research Center.

In retrospect it seems strange that in a postwar environment in which the concept of culture was so pervasive in the social sciences it still took nearly a decade for the concept of political culture to be formulated. Gabriel A. Almond's initiation of the term and the concept came in his classic article in 1956,[2] and two years later Samuel H. Beer and Adam B. Ulam made the concept of political culture central in their jointly edited comparative politics text.[3] While these were the first explicit uses of the term political culture, other writers during the decade after World War II were contributing to a substantially rising interest in the implicit use of the concept of culture in political analysis. Studies of national character were increasingly based on more sophisticated views about socialization and cultural transmission. In the strictly political field, Nathan Leites made a completely original innovation in elite analysis with his concept that leadership elements tend to share a common "operational code."[4] In his monumental *Study of Bolshevism*[5] Leites demonstrated that the insights of depth psychology could be applied to study the collective "style" and "spirit" of a political class that shared important common experiences.[6] In positing a basically characterological concept of the dynamic bases of political behavior Leites operated with the basic anthropological concept that personality and culture are the opposite sides of the same coin. He thus succeeded in advancing the application of psychological, and particularly psychoanalytical, insights from the study of individual political figures (as for example in the Georges' analysis of Woodrow Wilson[7]) to the study of groups of men, that is a sub-culture.

[1] Clyde Kluckhohn, *Mirror for Man* (New York: Whittlesey House, 1949).

[2] Gabriel A. Almond, "Comparative Political Systems," *Journal of Politics*, 18 (Aug., 1956), pp. 391–409.

[3] Samuel H. Beer and Adam B. Ulam, *Pattern of Government* (New York: Random House, 1958).

[4] Nathan Leites, *The Operational Code of the Politburo* (New York: McGraw-Hill, 1951).

[5] Nathan Leites, *A Study of Bolshevism* (Glencoe, Ill.: Free Press, 1953).

[6] Two important reviews that displayed deep understanding of Leites' objectives and methods are: Daniel Bell, "Ten Theories in Search of Reality," *World Politics*, 10 (April, 1958), pp. 327–365, and Clyde Kluckhohn, "Politics, History, and Psychology," *World Politics*, 3 (Oct., 1955), pp. 112–123.

[7] Alexander and Juliette George, *Woodrow Wilson and Colonel House* (New York: John Day, 1956).

The stage was set for the explicit adoption of the concept of culture in political science. The behavioral revolution, which was bringing to the discipline a flood of concepts from psychology and its related fields, made it inevitable that political scientists would soon be employing the concept of "political culture" where they had once used such concepts as public opinion, political ideology, national ethos and the basic consensus, values and constitutional integrating sentiments of a people.

Gabriel A. Almond in recently summarizing the intellectual history of the political culture concept noted that his views were influenced by three particular intellectual currents that seemed to him to converge to produce the concept.[8] First, there was the tradition of sociological theory developed by Max Weber and Talcott Parsons which stressed the underlying subjective norms and idealized patterns in providing cohesion and structure to social systems. The second current was that of the psychoanalytically oriented anthropologists, which we have just stressed. The third current sprang from the theories, assumptions and even techniques basic to the development of sample surveys.

The concept of culture seemed to be the one that best brought together all these strands and suggested moreover that there might be a unifying basis for both society and polity.

THE SHORT STEP FROM ACCEPTANCE TO VULGARIZATION

Although the term political culture is fast becoming a common term among political sicentists and, indeed, intellectuals in general, it remains an elusive concept. Like so many concepts in the social sciences which initially represented powerful and vivid insights but which soon become vague and empty through indiscriminate use, there is a danger that the notion of political culture will become, as Sidney Verba has warned, a residual category casually used to explain anything that cannot be explained by more precise and concrete factors.[9] Because of this almost lawlike tendency towards fuzziness of all usable concepts in the social sciences—note what has happened to such concepts as "identity" and "alienation" as they have become commonplace—it is essential from time to time to re-examine concepts and see if and how they can continue to contribute to theoretical advances in the social sciences.

As used by most political scientists the concept of political culture comes from Gabriel A. Almond's observation that "every political system is embedded in a particular pattern of orientation to political actions."[10] This definition leaves open as to whether the political culture is functional to

[8] Communication to the Conference on Political Culture and Communist Studies, Arden House, November 19–21, 1971. A digest of the conference has been published in the *Newsletter on Comparative Studies of Communism*, 3 (May, 1972).

[9] Sidney Verba, "Comparative Political Culture," in Lucian W. Pye and Sidney Verba, eds., *Political Culture and Political Development* (Princeton: Princeton University Press, 1965), pp. 513–517.

[10] Almond, "Comparative Political Systems," and reprinted in *Political Behavior: A Reader in Theory and Research*, Heinz Eulau, Samuel J. Eldersveld, and Morris Janowitz, eds., (Glencoe, Ill.: Free Press, 1956), pp. 34–42.

the performance of the political system or whether it is described by the distribution of political attitudes common to the society; that is whether the political culture is related primarily to the operations of the political system or to the separate views of the population. Sidney Verba's definition that "The political culture of a society consists of the system of empirical beliefs, expressive symbols, and values which defines the situation in which political action takes place"[11] is also open to several interpretations. So is the statement with which I began the article on the subject in the *International Encyclopedia of the Social Sciences*:

> Political culture is the set of attitudes, beliefs, and sentiments which give order and meaning to a political process and which provide the underlying assumptions and rules that govern behavior in the political system. It encompasses both the political ideals and the operating norms of a polity. Political culture is thus the manifestation in aggregate form of the psychological and subjective dimension of politics.[12]

All of these definitions stress the psychological or subjective aspect of behavior. In doing so they also, however, imply that the political realm is to some degree distinct and separate from the general culture. In contrast early national character studies tended to treat all behavior as essentially interrelated so that analysis might leap from toilet training to high level policy making and back again with little sense that the political life of a society might have its own rules and the capacity to filter out some attitudes while accentuating others.

What the concept of political culture has achieved in the first instance has been to make more vivid the distinction between political attitudes and values on the one hand and general cultural values on the other. This in itself represents a substantial advance in conceptualization. What has generally remained unclear, however, is whether the concept of political culture involves only the psychological aspects of political life. Should the concept apply only to subjective considerations or does it also involve actual behavior patterns? If the term is meant to include both psychological and behavioral patterns then it would seem to come perilously close to being no more than a pretentious way of referring to political behavior.

If the value of the concept of political culture is to be maintained, and its potential fully realized, then it is important to examine its advantages and to explore the limits of what it refers to. Our purpose in these pages will therefore be to try to identify the difficulties in conceptual precision and to suggest possible solutions.

WHERE TO BEGIN? THE INDIVIDUAL OR THE POLITY?

The concept of culture when applied to political analysis has proved to be both exciting and confusing because it appears to confront an increas-

---

[11] Verba, "Comparative Political Culture," p. 513.
[12] *International Encyclopedia of the Social Sciences* (New York: Macmillan Co. and The Free Press, 1961), Vol. 12, p. 218.

ingly perplexing problem in political science—that of the gap between micro-analysis and macro-analysis—but all too often it seems to provide only a fudging answer. The basic problem of behavioral political science is that of trying to go from an understanding of individual psychology to the performance of collective entities. How is it possible to incorporate into a discipline that is ultimately concerned with macro-systems the rich insights of modern psychology and the discoveries about individual behavior?

In more traditional political theory this problem did not exist because generalizations about collectivities were readily accepted and action was seen in terms of the dynamics of such entities as organizations, parties, nations and other institutions. The general principle of political theory was that institutions were assumed to have inherent properties separate from the properties of any particular individual. Above all the concept of legitimacy meant that offices and organs of government were seen as being governed by more than just the individual who might occupy them at any time.

The behavioral revolution reversed this tendency by emphasizing that the act should be the unit of analysis, that only individuals can act, and that the actions of institutions thus always depend upon decisions which can only occur in the minds of particular individuals. This emphasis upon the central role of action by individuals provided an easy opening to bring into political science the advances of psychology and particularly the consequences of the Freudian revolution. Since all action of any political significance ultimately springs from the actions of particular individuals, the way seemed to be opened for political scientists to benefit from all the advances in psychology.

The opportunities soon proved to create new problems for the discipline because the linkages between individual action and collective action remain obscure and have not been centrally dealt with by psychology. Heinz Eulau has identified several fallacies that have crept into political science as it has grappled with the micro/macro problem:

> . . . there is the fallacy of extrapolation from micro to macro phenomena. Small units are treated as analogues of large ones, and the finds on the micro level are extended to the macro level. There is a fallacy of personification: large-scale phenomena are reduced to the individual level through the use of anthropomorphic categories of analysis, as in the more grotesque descriptions of "national character." Or there is the fallacy of misplaced concreteness: interactional and relational phenomena are reified and treated as if they were physical entities.[13]

Freud himself contributed to the fallacy of extrapolating from the individual to society when in *Totem and Taboo* and *Civilization and its Discontents* he suggested that the historical development of human societies followed the laws of personality development. This is the tradition that the

---

[13] Heinz Eulau, "Political Behavior," *Encyclopedia of the Social Sciences* (New York: Free Press-Macmillan Co., 1968).

cultural anthropologists have also tended to stress with their view that the collective culture and individual personalities mirror each other.

It is of great significance that Harold Lasswell, in first bringing psychological insights to political science, proceeded in the opposite manner and in the classic tradition of political science accepted the collective system as given, composed, however, of roles which could reflect the personalities of their occupants.[14] For Lasswell the political system has a functional integrity of its own and thus the roles that make it up have to be performed, up to a point, according to criteria inherent in the system. The psychological dimension of behavior thus becomes a way of enriching and finding greater subtlety in explaining the performance of roles by particular individuals.

Thus in the application of psychology to political analysis there have been these two basic approaches, the one which begins with the system and macro-analysis and then introduces a human and biographical-psychological dimension, and the other which begins with the formation of personality and micro-analysis and sees the larger system as essentially the manifestations of the human personality as shaped by the socialization process. Aside from national character studies the second approach has been employed in such studies as that of the relationship between personality and political opinion and prejudice[15] and in the extremely creative studies by Nathan Leites of the operational codes of various elites which suggest a characterological basis to political strategies.[16]

Against that background of intellectual history, the concept of political culture sought to reduce the gap between macro- and micro-analysis by suggesting that the linkages lie in the complex processes of political socialization by which political systems maintain their continuity and individuals learn how to perform appropriate political roles. Political socialization includes both early personality development and later cognitive learning about politics, particularly as this later involves the process of recruitment to political roles. To the extent that the emphasis is placed upon the early stages of socialization the political culture approach leans in the direction of the earlier work in psycho-cultural analysis; when the emphasis shifts more to cognitions and explicitly learned patterns of behavior the stress is more on the basic features of the political system and on the need for the individual to accommodate to the imperatives of the political process. In practice, the ease with which it becomes possible, with the political culture approach, to shift the focus back and forth between personality and political system means that the micro/macro problem becomes blurred, either by still fudging the issue, or, quite legitimately, by a systematic progres-

[14] Harold D. Lasswell, *Psychopathology and Politics* (Chicago: University of Chicago Press, 1930), and *World Politics and Personal Insecurity* (New York: Whittlesey House, 1930).

[15] T. W. Adorno, et al., *The Authoritarian Personality* (New York: Harper & Brothers, 1950).

[16] Leites, *Study of Bolshevism.*

sion of approximations in which every effort is made to work explicitly from both directions toward a consistent picture of the psychological dimensions of political behavior and the political system.

MISPLACED PRECISION: WHEN THE PARTS ARE MORE THAN THE WHOLE

The hope that the concept of political culture, reinforced by the concepts of political socialization and recruitment, might effectively bridge the gap between micro- and macro-analysis encouraged a search for greater precision in measuring all forms of political attitudes and sentiments. A source of dissatisfaction among political scientists with the admittedly very insightful psychoanalytically oriented "national character" studies has been not only their tendency to move glibly between childhood and sophisticated political behavior but also the lack of scientific precision in the generalizations. In theory, generalizations about national temperament should be no different from other generalizations about macrosystems.

Twenty years ago, writing in the first issue of *World Politics*, Nathan Leites stated the essentially logical-positivist view that "hypotheses about cultural patterns should be treated by conventional canons of social science, the terms need only to be specified and made operational and vague references to matters of degree and frequency should be made more quantitatively precise."[17] The difficulty, however, is that there is an understandable suspicion of subjective bias when people describe the traits of foreigners. In order to meet this problem and quite legitimate concerns about the possibility of validating statements of national opinion and sentiment, political scientists have turned to the most sophisticated techniques they have for measuring opinion, sample surveys. National differences based on systematic surveys would seem to be more valid than generalizations based upon such apparently less quantitative approaches as, say, the methods of the participant observer and those of the anthropologists.

The use of attitudinal and opinion surveys to gain precision has created some new problems in the conceptualization of political cultures. Specifically it has suggested that political cultures are in fact defined by the distribution of attitudes, opinions and sentiments among the given population. The prevalence of views and the differences of their percentage distributions are thus taken to provide the basis for characterizing differences among political cultures. The ability to speak with scientific assurance about differences among populations, however, obscures the fact that this approach is merely a more sophisticated version of the fallacy that macrosystems are no more than extrapolations of micro-systems.

In addition two further problems have been raised by this approach: the relationship between "attitudes" and "behaviors," and the compound-

[17] Nathan Leites, "Psycho-Cultural Hypotheses about Political Acts," *World Politics*, 1 (Oct., 1948), pp. 102–119.

ing difficulty that the individual (or sub-system) is more complex and reflects more subtle sentiments and attitudes than does the political system as a whole.

The first problem is that people seem to have more opinions than politically significant actions. Through the techniques of modern psychology we can uncover a rich subjective world, but it becomes extremely difficult to determine what aspects of the individual's inner world will govern his objective behavior.

The second problem is that, since the subjective realm of the individual is more complex than the objective reality of prosaic political systems, it becomes impossible to determine by beginning with the individual which of his attitudes are the most relevant for understanding why a political system performs as it does. Therefore, the aggregating or totaling up of the attitudes of individuals produces a "sum" that far exceeds the "sum" of attitudes essential for explaining the performance of the particular system. It is this bountifulness of subjective political attitudes which makes it so difficult to construct even the key features of a political system out of the "orientations" of its members.

AN ANALOGY FROM ECONOMICS

This macro/micro problem in political culture analysis can be illustrated by trying to imagine what might have happened if a behaviorally oriented revolution had hit economics before Keynes made his great breakthrough in depicting the basic model of national income flows. Under such conditions it is conceivable that researchers would have engaged in attitude studies and even depth interviews of entrepreneurs, investors, customers and business men in the hopes of discovering how all of their motivations, expectations and values related to each other and produced a functioning economic system. One thing we could be confident of is that no matter how skillful or precise they were in their measuring of attitudes, they never would have been able to total up the subjective worlds and arrive at the Keynesian model for macro-economic theory.

What has happened, of course, is that once basic macro-theory was accepted in economics, an appropriate context was established for micro-analysis. The fact that businessmen and customers have a wide range of emotions and motivations which influence their behavior can be introduced to modify and enrich the basic theory, but such facts do not in any way confuse the objectives of macro-analysis. It is true that the economists have reduced their problems greatly by simply keeping macro- and micro-theory completely separate and not attempting to arrive at a general theory; but to the extent that they have been interested in enriching economics with behavioral and psychological considerations it has been within the context of accepting the primacy of the macro-model as the proper starting point.

THE "AS IF" HYPOTHESIS; AND A FORM OF PREDICTION

What we have been arguing is that political culture must be studied on the basis of an understanding of how the particular political system performs. The initial hypotheses about a political culture must thus take the form of statements which hold that the system behaves "as if" certain values, sentiments, and orientations were the most critical in giving the collectivity its distinctive character. The political culture thus consists of those "orientations" that make the system distinctive, not necessarily the ones that may be most distinctive among all the attitudes a population may hold. In introducing a study of the Chinese political culture I noted that my concern was

> to describe the constellation of sentiment and attitudes that we feel must have existed for the Chinese political system to have developed as it has. We are not concerned with questions about the actual distribution of attitudes and feelings throughout the Chinese population. Even if we could obtain accurate sample survey results on the political attitudes of all Chinese, it would not serve our purposes greatly; and for the same reason that accurate attitudinal studies of investors and consumers, for example, would not have been relevant in developing the Keynesian model of national income accounting.[18]

It should be noted that these initial system-oriented hypotheses may be of the character that seek to explain either particular systems or certain more general categories of systems. The classic example of the latter type of political culture study is Almond and Verba's *Civic Culture*[19] in which their prime theoretic concern was the explanation of democratic stability for which they posited the necessity of a generalized "civic culture," and then tested samples in five different countries to determine the relative prevalence of that "culture."

It is thus the culture which imparts meaning and even gives substantial structure to the political system. Observations about the performance of a system thus suggest what attitudes are probably important in making the system operate as it does. At this point the analysis must shift to the individual for two reasons. First for the obvious need to test whether the subjective factors posited as being critical for system performance do in fact exist at all among the relevant population. Secondly, it is necessary to test system-oriented hypotheses in terms of individual psychology because of the potency of psychological theories in suggesting relationships and patterns of basic orientations. We shall in a moment return to this problem of how coherence in personality may provide guides to coherence among larger cultural themes, but first we must comment further about the use of

[18] Lucian W. Pye, *The Spirit of Chinese Politics: A Psychocultural Study of the Authority Crisis in Political Development* (Cambridge: M.I.T. Press, 1968), p. viii.

[19] Gabriel A. Almond and Sidney Verba, *The Civic Culture* (Princeton: Princeton University Press, 1963; paperback ed., Boston: Little Brown & Co., 1965).

individual psychological findings to "test" general hypotheses about a political culture.

It is far from clear what canons of science are called for to "test" hypotheses about the political culture that underlies a political system. There is first of all a question of the significance of quantitative degrees in testing such hypotheses. To what extent does a population have to demonstrate the presence of certain values and attitudes in order for us to be confident that our initial hypothesis was correct in posing the necessity of such values for the system to operate as it does? For example, in the case of democracy, to what extent do people have to have the various qualities associated with the "civic culture" for there to be a stable democracy?

Our problem here, as with so much of political science theory building, is that we are able to fairly effectively identify "necessary" conditions, but we are very weak with respect to identifying "sufficient" conditions. We can say with greater confidence what is necessary for something to happen than whether what in fact exists is sufficient to produce the expected outcome.

A second problem of "testing" in individual attitudes hypotheses about collective behaviors is that of determining what are the appropriate "indicators" or empirical referents for essentially subjective factors. For example, if we hypothesize that "nationalism" has been a decisive force shaping the political culture of twentieth century China—a statement historians, accustomed as they are to broad generalizations, would have no doubts about—we might still have found it hard to identify this sentiment in its inchoate form in sample surveys if we had been able to administer them in the first decades of this century. What are the deeply held feelings of an unpoliticized population which can give expression to nationalism once that population became politically conscious?

The problem is more than just one of interpreting the content of values, for often the test of a political culture is the combinations of values, regardless of content, that is critical. The strength of democracy in India, for example, may rest less upon how widespread are liberal democratic values among the Indian masses than upon the tolerance of Indians for the differences they have in their basic values.

In summary, these and other problems of "testing" political culture hypotheses all involve the arrival at types of approximations which can make possible the particular form of "prediction" that is the ultimate test of political culture statements. These are "predictions" which are not forecasts or even statements of probabilities of future events, but are rather statements as to what would be consistent with the assumed underlying characeristics of the political culture.

This form of "predicting" which is more a judgment of plausibility than a strict statement of customary contingency prediction is what Clifford Geertz had in mind when he said that there was a relationship between the important place that cockfighting occupies in Balinese culture and the violent intra-village slaughtering of Balinese of each other after the unsuccessful Communist coup of 1965.

This is not to say, of course, that the killings were caused by the cock-fight, could have been predicted on the basis of it, or were some sort of enlarged version of it with real people in the place of the cocks—all of which is nonsense. It is merely to say that if one looks at Bali not just through the medium of its dances, it shadowplays, its sculputure, and its girls, but—as the Balinese themselves do—also through the medium of its cockfight, the fact that the massacre occurred seems, if no less appalling, less like a contradiction to the laws of nature.[20]

CAN PLAUSIBILITY BECOME A RIGOROUS CONCEPT?

We now confront a cruel paradox: political scientists are able to be increasingly rigorous and precise with respect to measurement at the micro-analysis level, but our theories are not sensitive to the importance of quantitative differences in attitudes and sentiments, only to the necessity of "appropriate" attitudes existing among the critical elements; on the other hand, it is at the macro level that the critical hypotheses must be advanced and "tested," but it is at this level we lack capacity for rigor and precision. In part this is because in political science we do not have a tradition for systematically evaluating plausibility statements. In journalism and government service there is greater awareness of skill in applying knowledge and judgment to understanding why events occur as they do.

There is a need at this stage in the evolution of the concept of political culture to try to design better ways of judging whether hypotheses about particular political cultures have provided the kind of highly qualified predictive powers necessary to suggest their validity. The danger, of course, is that any analyst, if left to himself, can always see his own work as providing a completely plausible understanding for whatever may have happened in the country of his analysis.

Possibly the problem might become more manageable if there was a tendency for studies of political culture to focus on common themes. Fortunately there are several candidates that have attracted widespread interest, and they include the themes of attitudes towards power and authority, the character of hierarchical relations, the acceptance of freedom, and patterns and expectations of participation. If studies of political culture were to converge more with respect to key themes then it would be easier to judge the extent to which particular studies have successfully added to our capacity to understand particular systems.

SUMMARY AND CONCLUSIONS

The concept of political culture has been an exciting addition to political science which has enriched comparative analysis. Above all the concept has provided a promising way of incorporating psychological insights into the study of political systems. In so seeking to bridge the gap between macro- and micro-analysis, political science has sought to move ahead of economics.

[20] Clifford Geertz, *Balinese Cockfight,* "Deep Play: Notes on the Balinese Cockfight,' *Daedalus; Myth, Symbol, and Culture,* 101 (Winter, 1972), p. 37.

At the same time the concept of political culture leaves many problems unresolved and it highlights the inherent difficulties in achieving systematic analysis with respect to macro-systems in political science. The concept of political culture has made it clear that it is impossible to extrapolate from the richness of individual psychology to the less coherently structured patterns of collective behavior common to political systems. The basic problem is that while the sub-systems (that is, the individuals) condition and limit, and thus in a sense "determine" the behavior of the macro-system, it is impossible to infer the character of the larger system from a detailed examination of its component "sub-systems." The situation is analogous to our ability to say "something" about what a building will be like from knowledge about what its building elements are like, but to truly "picture" the building we need also to know the blue-prints and the total design.

Progress in the use of the political culture concept thus calls for more effective ways of describing total systems and for identifying what are likely to be the most critical factors in improving our ability to understand and in a limited sense "predict" system performance. Until we can arrive at better standards for evaluating system performance, and hence determining the "accuracy" of "predictions," the concept of political culture will still be of great value in making analysts more sensitive to the significance of underlying psychological factors in political life.

The concept of political culture does imply that there is an underlying and latent coherence in political life. Among political scientists there has been a long standing acceptance of the idea of such a basic and implicit force in human societies, as demonstrated in general acceptance of such concepts as collective will, social contract, constitutional consensus, and inherent values. At the same time political scientists tend to treat such underlying forces as being somewhat vague and only a determining factor at the extremes of behavior—it is accepted that within the limits of the constitutional consensus, that is of the political culture, there can be a fair variety of behavior that is still "consistent," and hence culturally acceptable. In this sense the concept of "culture" in political science suggests less rigorously defined and precise patterns of behavior than does the concept of culture in anthropology. In fact this may be exaggerated because political scientists tend to work on more diffusely structured and less culturally homogeneous societies.

In sum we can say that in spite of the difficulties in rigorously applying the concept, political culture will continue to attract attention among political scientists. Indeed awareness of the difficulties may serve to produce sensitive but also balanced and judicious uses of psychological insights in political science. Concern with these problems may reduce the ever present temptation to use "psychologizing" as a veiled technique for prejudicial studies of political actors. The concept of culture is much too valuable to be allowed to be discredited by being used for base purposes.

CLIO AND THE CULTURE CONCEPT: SOME IMPRESSIONS OF A CHANGING RELATIONSHIP IN AMERICAN HISTORIOGRAPHY

ROBERT F. BERKHOFER, JR.
University of Wisconsin, Madison

THE HISTORY OF THE WRITING OF HISTORY HAS ITS OWN HISTORY, AND ONE of the current fashions in this form of disciplinary narcissism is for today's American historians to berate yesterday's for exhibiting Cold War partisanship. Established historians, young professionals of New Left persuasion, and doctoral candidates in search of a thesis alike read the works produced by historians in the two decades after World War II as mirrors of the era of Joseph McCarthy and Josef Stalin. These latter-day commentators on their professional forebears see the repudiation of Frederick Jackson Turner, Charles A. Beard, Vernon L. Parrington, and others of the so-called progressive or economic interpretation school of American history by historians Daniel Boorstin, Robert E. Brown, Richard Hofstadter, and Edmund Morgan or political scientists Louis Hartz and Clinton Rossiter as a search for stability in a time of crisis for American traditions at home, as a reaction to ideology and morality in politics, and as a reaffirmation of American unity and traditions in the face of a hostile world.

Ample evidence for this view can be found in the prefaces and pronouncements of the period, but these critics point also in support of their contentions to the larger assumptions and frameworks of these and other interpreters of the American past who wrote after World War II. Whereas the earlier school saw an American past dominated by class and sectional conflict and United States history therefore determined by the continuing struggle between the "haves" and the "have nots" in the economic and political realms of life, the newer interpreters emphasized the ideas and values common to all Americans throughout the course of their history. Rather than focusing on the rich and the poor, their representatives, and the clash of ideologies and interests, many historians writing in the post-war decades stressed the adherence of almost all shades of past political opinion to the liberal, capitalistic tradition defined generally as the American way of life. Worst of all, perhaps, from the point of view of the recent critics was the tendency of the post-war historians to play down or avoid conspicuous moral partisanship in recounting the ideas and actions of past Americans and therefore seemingly to accept the outcomes of past struggles, regardless of who won, as all for the best. For these reasons, the critics dubbed this interpretation of the American past "the cult of consensus," because it excluded the conflicts of groups in order to exaggerate the adherence of all the population to a basic consensus. Therefore, the progressives' tale of the American past as a succession of struggles dissolved in the writings of the consensus school into a bland story of the essential continuity of American traditions pervading the entire course of United States history.[1]

Such a view of post-war American historiography is not wrong but partial in my opinion, because the criticism accents the social determinants of historians' ideas at the expense of their relationship to the scholarship of the period and the internal development of history-writing. I believe that much of the so-called consensus history, regardless of the political circumstances that gave rise to it, can be seen equally well as an application of the culture concept, popular in the social sciences and scholarly discourse at the time, to the history of the United States. In brief, I shall argue that the intellectual foundations of consensus history rest upon the premises about human nature and behavior represented in the changed meaning of culture adopted by social scientists and the educated public after World War II.

If this hypothesis—or, more accurately, impression—is correct, then the newest trends in history-writing in the past decade are not due merely to the changing mood in domestic politics and foreign policy. Rather, the exploration and application of the culture concept to historical analysis revealed its limitations in use just as it did in the social sciences. In other words, just as the concept of culture came to dominate so many phases of the social sciences after World War II and now is being refined or discarded in the social scientists' quest for greater analytical precision, so too a parallel trend is appearing in the American historical profession. Thus I see the rise of the culture concept to explanatory prominence in the social sciences and history and its subsequent decline occurring at the same time and for the same scholarly—and extra-scholarly—reasons.[2]

Proof of my contentions, or impressions, does not lie in the explicit discussion of the modern technical concept of culture by historians, because such examination only happened after consensus was already being challenged and new trends in techniques and analysis were becoming apparent

---

[1] The term derives from John Higham, "The Cult of the 'American Consensus'; Homogenizing Our History," *Commentary*, 27 (Feb., 1959), pp. 93–100; and "Beyond Consensus: The Historian as a Moral Critic," *American Historical Review*, 67 (April, 1962), pp. 609–625. Compare J. Rogers Hollingsworth, "Consensus and Continuity in Recent American Historical Writing," *South Atlantic Quarterly*, 61 (Winter, 1962), pp. 40–50; and Dwight W. Hoover, "Some Comments on Recent United States Historiography," *American Quarterly*, 17 (Summer, 1965), pp. 299–318. For a New Left interpretation, see the introduction to Barton Bernstein, ed., *Towards a New Past: Dissenting Essays in American History* (New York: Random House, 1968), pp. v–xiii. A more vitriolic attack in this vein was delivered by Jesse Lemisch at the American Historical Association's annual meeting in Washington, D.C., Dec. 30, 1969, in a speech entitled "Present-Mindedness Revisited: Anti-Radicalism as a Goal of American Historical Writing Since World War II." One example of a dissertation on the topic is Marian Morton, "The Terrors of Ideological Politics: Intellectuals, Liberals, and Intellectual History," (Unpubl. Ph.D. diss., Case Western Reserve University, 1970).

[2] Given the effect of nationalism on the outlook and the tasks of the historical profession, I shall, on the whole, confine my speculations to historians in the United States and more particularly those who deal with the past of their own country.

in the profession. Given its timing, as we shall see, explicit discussion of the culture concept signified what had happened in the profession rather than what was to happen. What had happened was the conjunction of three parallel but related intellectual trends in the period after World War II, and their combination produced consensus history. The first trend was the changed definition of culture in the social sciences and the new conception of man embodied in it. The coming into popular use by the educated public of this new technical meaning of the word culture comprises the second trend. The rise of intellectual history to a place where it dominated the historical profession after World War II constitutes the third trend. Thus I shall sketch a rather selective and speculative genealogy of ideas to show the use of the culture concept in history-writing.

The conception of culture prevalent in the American social sciences after World War II possessed a definition quite different than the first technical one given the term in English by Edward Tylor in 1871. Although Tylor's oft-quoted definition contained the idea of totality or comprehensiveness ("complex whole") present in the current usage of the word, its enumeration of the components of culture, unlike modern usage, implied the equal importance of mental, behavioral, and artifactual aspects. Not until the 1920's did even Tylor's definition attain frequency in American social science, and not until well into the 1930's did the two additional elements of normativeness and patterning long traditional in the German meaning of the word enter into the common definition given the term by social scientists in the United States. Surely, part of the reason behind the extensive survey of definitions of culture by Alfred Kroeber and Clyde Kluckhohn published in 1952 was to establish finally and completely the legitimacy and necessity of these latter aspects of the term in scientific use. Accordingly, they summarize the common definition of the term as they say it was and as they wish it to be:

> Culture consists of patterns, explicit and implicit, of and for behavior acquired and transmitted by symbols, constituting the distinctive achievement of human groups, including their embodiments in artifacts; the essential core of culture consists of traditional (i.e., historically derived and selected) ideas and especially their attached values; culture systems may, on the one hand, be considered as products of action, on the other as conditioning elements of further action.[3]

As this statement shows clearly, social scientists had moved from a meaning based upon the equality of physical artifacts, outer behavior, and ideation to a definition purely in terms of the latter, and causality and integration as well as the manifestations of behavior were sought in terms of patterns of ideas and values. From the enumeration of traits and char-

[3] Alfred Kroeber and Clyde Kluckhohn, *Culture: A Critical Review of Concepts and Definitions*, Papers of the Peabody Museum of American Archaeology and Ethnology, Vol. 47, No. 1 (Cambridge, Mass.; Harvard University, 1952). I used the Vintage edition (New York: Alfred A. Knopf, 1963), p. 357.

acteristics, social scientists had progressed to seeking the organized inter-relation of the ideational components behind them. From an interest in observable customs and physical artifacts and behavior, anthropologists turned to exploring the subjectivity said to cause them. Culture was given causal efficacy as well as being caused. As a result, ethnography changed from eclectic descriptions to searches for "themes," "patterns," "foci," "configurations," "tacit premises," "value-orientations," or "ethos" that gave meaning to the observed multiplicity of men's activities in various societies.[4]

The changed definition of culture entailed a changing conception of man as well. Just as the word "attitude" had been transformed in meaning during the same period of time from a physical stance to inner mental state behind the behavioral manifestation,[5] so too "culture" had come to emphasize the ideational over the other aspects of the Tylor definition and even was used, in a sense, to explain them. The increasing frequency of the terms "norms" and "values" in social science books and articles indicated in yet another way the newer emphasis on the ideational and norma-tive realm of human existence. The trend to normative and evaluative understanding of human behavior, although begun in the late 1920's and early 1930's in the United States, reached full-blown proportions only after World War II and radiated chiefly from the Harvard Department of Social Relations under the leadership of Talcott Parsons in sociology and Clyde Kluckhohn in anthropology.[6] What these men and others accomplished in their fields was to reorient the social sciences in this country along lines familiar to continental philosophers and social scientists in understanding social order as the product of normative rules and orientations.[7]

Although social scientists did not agree on any standard definition of norm or value in the post-war period, the interpretation of man rep-resented in these terms can be seen clearly in Kluckhohn's influential defi-nition of a "value-orientation" as a "generalized and organized conception influencing behavior, of nature, of man's place in it, of man's relation to

[4] I omit the social structure approach to culture in American anthropology in favor of the pattern theory of culture. Compare the brief histories of the concept by Fred W. Voget, "Man and Culture: An Essay in Changing Anthropological Interpretation," *American Anthropologist*, 62 (Dec., 1960), pp. 943–965; Eric R. Wolf, *Anthropology* (Englewood Cliffs, N.J.: Prentice-Hall, 1964); and Milton Singer, "The Concept of Culture," in David L. Sills, ed., *International Encyclopedia of the Social Sciences* (New York: Macmillan, 1968) Vol. 3, pp. 527–543.

[5] Donald Fleming, "Attitude: The History of a Concept," *Perspectives in American History*, 1 (1967), pp. 287–365.

[6] For a brief history of the concept, see William L. Kolb, "The Changing Prominence of Values in Modern Sociological Theory," in Howard Becker and Alvin Boskoff, eds., *Modern Sociological Theory: In Continuity and Change* (New York: Dryden Press, 1957), pp. 93–132.

[7] This, for example, would seem the main effect, if not purpose, of Talcott Parsons' early book, *The Structure of Social Action* (New York: McGraw-Hill, 1937). To what extent the migration of European scholars to the United States in the 1930's subse-quently fostered this development must be left to conjecture at this point.

man, and of the desirable and non-desirable as they may relate to man-environment and interhuman relations."[8] In short, this new phrasing of the good, the true, and the beautiful provided the explanation of people's actions. The emphasis on the normative and evaluative patterning at the base of human behavior quickly found its way into the studies of national character and basic personality so popular at the time.[9]

Although the culture concept was therefore only one indication of the changed conception of man so prominent in the social sciences after World War II, it was, in the eyes of Kroeber and Kluckhohn, "one of the key notions of contemporary thought." They argued, "in explanatory importance and in generality of application it is comparable to such categories as gravity in physics, disease in medicine, evolution in biology."[10] With two such prominent anthropologists claiming such a crucial place for culture in understanding human behavior, small wonder popular writer Stuart Chase in his exposition of the social sciences after the war thought the concept was "coming to be regarded as the foundation stone of the social sciences."[11] His popularization of the scientific notion of the term indicated the growing awareness by the educated public of its technical use. Perhaps no better sign exists of the increasing tendency of scholars outside of the social sciences to employ the term than the stated goal of the American Studies movement to study the culture of the United States. Suddenly professors of American literature, art, music, as well as history realized that all their narrow specialties really were engaged in the same basic endeavor encompassed in the new meaning of culture.[12] In short, the new emphasis on the symbolic basis of action, man as a valuing animal, and the patterning of ideas and norms enabled many humanists to climb aboard the cul-

[8] Clyde Kluckhohn, "Values and Value-Orientations in the Theory of Action: An Exploration in Definition and Classification," in Talcott Parsons and Edward A. Shils, eds., *Toward a General Theory of Action* (Cambridge, Mass.: Harvard University Press, 1951), p. 411.

[9] Summaries of the concept at that time are Margaret Mead, "National Character," in Alfred Kroeber, ed., *Anthropology Today: An Encyclopedic Inventory* (Chicago: University of Chicago Press, 1953), pp. 642–667; and Alex Inkeles and Daniel J. Levinson, "National Character: The Study of Modal Personality and Sociocultural Systems," in Gardner Lindzey, ed., *Handbook of Social Psychology* (Cambridge, Mass.: Addison-Wesley, 1954), pp. 977–1020.

[10] Kroeber and Kluckhohn, *Culture*, p. 3.

[11] Stuart Chase, *The Proper Study of Mankind: An Inquiry into the Science of Human Relations* (New York: Harper and Brothers, 1948), p. 59.

[12] If we judge their aim by the statement of purpose in the first issue of their journal to assist "in giving a sense of direction to studies in the culture of America, past and present," *American Quarterly*, 1 (Spring, 1949), p. 2. That many of these scholars mixed the old and new meanings of the word can be seen in "A Statement by the Committee of American Civilization of the American Council of Learned Societies," in *ibid.*, 2 (Fall, 1950), pp. 286–288, and in the nature of the articles in the journal. An explicit and extended discussion of the concept of culture did not obtain a place in the *Quarterly* until the article by Richard E. Sykes, "American Studies and the Concept of Culture: A Theory and Method." *ibid.*, 15 (Summer, 1963), pp. 253–270; unless we count the earlier one by Bernard Bowron, Leo Marx, and Arnold Rose, "Literature and Covert Culture," *ibid.*, 9 (Winter, 1957), pp. 377–386.

ture wagon—not the least of whom was T. S. Eliot—and afforded a tempo-
rary rapprochement between the humanities and the social sciences.[13]

What had happened in scholarly discourse was the addition of the long
time German meaning of the word to the more customary literary and
humanistic definition it possessed in English. The sweetness and light of
Matthew Arnold's definition of culture as the individual's "pursuit of total
perfection by means of getting to know . . . the best which has been
thought and said in the world," was replaced in the minds of social scientists and many other scholars by the teutonic interest in the totality of ideas
in a society, popular as well as scholarly—in other words, low as well as
high culture.[14] Although dictionaries lagged in attributing a modern anthropological definition to the word, let alone the latest usage of it, scholars
and even the general public—if the use of "Eskimo culture" in a comic strip
shows their thinking—were becoming quite aware of the social scientific
meaning of the term.

The impact of the new definition on the historical profession can be
traced most directly in the pleas by a few historians that their colleagues
employ the conception as an interpretative insight and as a principle of
synthesis in their writing. As early as 1939, the annual meeting of the
American Historical Association considered "The Cultural Approach to
History," as the published proceedings were titled. Anthropologist Geoffrey Gorer, later to be famous for his swaddling hypothesis of Russian
national character, provided the historians with a definition of culture
stressing ethos and rules, and the editor, Caroline Ware, spoke of integration and the pattern of culture in a manner reminiscent of Ruth Benedict.[15]
None of the historians in the volume applied or exemplified these definitions, and lack of explicit and extended discussion of the culture concept
in historical analysis typified the profession until the 1950's.[16]

Then, in 1954 appeared two books asserting the utility of the concept
for historical understanding. In the second report of the Social Science
Research Council's Committee on Historiography, culture, norms, and
values received an important place in Thomas Cochran's "Survey of the
Concepts and Viewpoints in the Social Sciences" of worth to historians—
perhaps at the behest of the consulting anthropologists to the report, Kroeber and Kluckhohn—and a lengthy discussion of culture change appeared

[13] The basis for such a rapprochement was examined by social scientists Gertrude
Jaeger and Philip Selznick, "A Normative Theory of Culture," *American Sociological
Review*, 29 (Oct., 1964), pp. 653–669.
[14] Kroeber and Kluckhohn, *Culture*, pp. 54–62; For a history of ideological conflict
over use of the word in English, see Raymond Williams, *Culture and Society, 1780–
1950* (London: Chatto and Windus, 1958).
[15] Caroline Ware, ed., *The Cultural Approach to History* (New York: Columbia University Press, 1940), pp. 10, 22, 25–26.
[16] For an example of the lag in usage, see the definitions of "Civilization and Culture" presented by Sidney Hook for historians in *Theory and Practice in Historical
Study: A Report of the Committee on Historiography*, Social Science Research Council
Bulletin 54 (New York, 1946), pp. 118–119. Admittedly, Hook was a philosopher, not
an historian, professionally.

in two other essays.[17] In the same year, David Potter argued the central importance of culture for understanding national character and basic personality in his *People of Plenty: Economic Abundance and American Character*.[18] In fact, he spent the first half of his book castigating his fellow historians for their superficial understanding of national character and praising through explication the contributions of the social scientists. That not all historians thought the concept so useful can be seen in Jacques Barzun's repudiation in the same year of the broader meaning of the term as of any value in the work of the cultural historian.[19] Four years later, the English scholar Philip Bagby offered in his book, *Culture and History*, a sophisticated analysis of the nature of history (influenced by Frederick Teggart) and an equally sophisticated definition of culture (influenced by Kroeber) as a basis for the comparative study of the history of civilizations in opposition to the superficial treatment of the same subject by Toynbee.[20]

By 1960, the intellectual historian H. Stuart Hughes thought anthropology the most congenial of the social sciences for historians. Following Benedict's emphasis on pattern and configuration, Hughes said the historian's main task was the search for the "central grouping symbols" of a society.[21] Four years later, in his enthusiasm for his discovery of culture, he proclaimed: "By the late 1950's a number of historians were at last ready to endorse the view that the widest and most fruitful definition of their trade was as 'retrospective cultural anthropology'."[22] And for his own specialty of intellectual history, he observed correctly.

[17] *The Social Sciences in Historical Study: A Report of the Committee on Historiography*, Social Science Research Council Bulletin 64 (New York, 1954), pp. 35–41, 43–44, 46–47, 65–66, 98–104, 120–125.

[18] David Potter, *People of Plenty: Economic Abundance and American Character* (Chicago: University of Chicago Press, 1954). Aside from Potter, few historians devoted professional attention to the most influential book of the time on national character, David Riesman, Nathan Glazer, and Reuel Denny, *The Lonely Crowd: A Study of the Changing American Character* (New Haven: Yale University Press, 1950). No historian, for example, appears in the volume of essays *Culture and Social Character: The Work of David Riesman Reviewed*, ed. by Seymour M. Lipset and Leo Lowenthal (New York: The Free Press, 1961). A later exception is Carl Degler, "The Sociologist as Historian: Riesman's *The Lonely Crowd*," *American Quarterly*, 15 (Winter, 1963), pp. 483–497. The third bulletin of the Social Science Research Council Committee on Historiography was to be devoted entirely at one point to the concept of national character, but in the end only one chapter discussed the notion: Louis Gottschalk, ed., *Generalization in the Writing of History* (Chicago: University of Chicago Press, 1963), pp. viii, 77–102. The concept as applied to the United States has found its own historian, however, Thomas L. Hartshorne, *The Distorted Image: Changing Conceptions of the American Character Since Turner* (Cleveland: Press of the Case Western Reserve University, 1968).

[19] Jacques Barzun, "Cultural History as a Synthesis" in Fritz Stern, ed., *The Varieties of History From Voltaire to the Present* (New York: Meridian Books, 1956), pp. 392–393.

[20] Philip Bagby, *Culture and History: Prolegomena to the Comparative Study of Civilizations* (London: Longmans, Green and Co., 1958).

[21] H. Stuart Hughes, "The Historian and the Social Scientist," *American Historical Review*, 66 (Oct., 1960), pp. 20–46, but esp. pp. 42–43.

[22] H. Stuart Hughes, *History as Art and as Science: Twin Vistas on the Past* (New York: Harper and Row, 1964), p. 24.

Intellectual history as cultural analysis is both very old and quite new in the profession. If we include the search for the spirit of an age, for the genius of a civilization, or for the *Zeitgeist* as an effort by historians and other writers to understand a culture as a patterned whole in terms of its leading ideas or ethos, then such analysis can be traced through the *Kulturgeschichte* of the nineteenth century back to Voltaire.[23] Full development of this school occurred no later than Jacob Burckhardt's *Civilization of the Renaissance in Italy* (1867), and in fact this approach influenced the development of the concept of culture.[24] But American historians were little influenced by this development because of their fear of the speculativeness of the search in the hands of the philosophers of history and by the political overtones of the German practice.[25] Intellectual history as a specific course in American colleges began no earlier than the twentieth century,[26] and as a recognized specialty in the historical profession in the United States can be said to date from the 1930's.[27] If the founding of a journal marks the institutionalization of a professional specialty, then the date becomes 1940.[28] The leading spirit behind this modern phase of intellectual history must be ascribed to the Johns Hopkins philosopher Arthur O. Lovejoy, who, in opposition to the sociology of knowledge and hazy attribution of socioeconomic determination prevailing in historical writing at the time, turned to the interior analysis of ideas through their internal logic and immanent development. Such analysis in his opinion involved tracing what he called "unit-ideas," but what we might call core values or orientations, through their histories of combination with other ideas to form the great belief systems of mankind.[29] Lovejoy's approach to the subject became known as the history of ideas, or intrinsic approach, as opposed to the extrinsic approach to intellectual history, which explored the social context giving rise to the ideas.[30]

[23] Both Hajo Holborn, "The History of Ideas," *American Historical Review*, 73 (Feb., 1968), 683–695; and Karl J. Weintraub, *Visions of Culture* (Chicago: University of Chicago Press, 1966), commence with Voltaire and proceed through *Kulturgeschichte* in tracing the history of ideas and the conception of culture in historical writing respectively.

[24] In addition to Weintraub, see Kroeber and Kluckhohn, *Culture*, pp. 11–70.

[25] Alfred G. Meyer, "Historical Notes on Ideological Aspects of the Concept of Culture in Germany and Russia," *ibid.*, pp. 403–413. See, for example, the explicit disavowal of the ideological and mystical overtones of the word culture by George Mosse in the preface to his *The Culture of Western Europe: The Nineteenth and Twentieth Centuries* (Chicago: Rand McNally, 1961), pp. 1–2.

[26] James Harvey Robinson began teaching a course entitled "Intellectual History of Western Europe" at Columbia in 1904.

[27] Although the History of Ideas Club formed at Johns Hopkins University as early as 1923.

[28] *Journal of the History of Ideas* (1940–   ).

[29] The best statement of Lovejoy's approach is the introduction to his *The Great Chain of Being: A Study of the History of an Idea* (Cambridge, Mass.: Harvard University Press, 1936), pp. 3–23.

[30] Histories of intellectual history to which I owe much in this and the succeeding paragraphs are Robert A. Skotheim, *American Intellectual Histories and Historians*

The dialectical swing of these two approaches can be traced in the histories of the role of ideas in the American past, and the synthesis of them in the form of American Studies and post-war intellectual history illustrates the impact of the culture concept on the historical writing of the time. Progressive preoccupation with the economic and environmental determination of ideas found its boldest expression in the sweeping panorama of Vernon Parrington's *Main Currents in American Thought*, published in the late 1920's.[31] His three volumes portrayed the struggle between agrarian, democratic tendencies and the anti-democratic thrust in American thinking in terms of the class and sectional interests of the heroic multitudes versus the selfish few. Some young scholars of the next decade, in deliberate reaction to such an interpretation, turned to understanding past thoughts for their own sake. One of the first and most impressive of the new histories of ideas in this vein was Perry Miller's *New England Mind* (1939). He appreciated Puritan thinking as a coherent intellectual system with its own logic and ordering. In his preface, he explicitly cast aside consideration of the social and economic influences on the Puritan mind in order to present an "organized synthesis of concepts which are fundamental to our culture," but in their language and conceptualization.[32] As the debate was joined, the author of the first modern synthesis of American intellectual history in 1943 said he would concentrate more on the "social history of American thought" than "provide an exhaustive analysis of the 'interiors' of ideas and systems of thought."[33] After the war, historians of the ideational realm, aware of the overdrawn contrast between the two approaches, sought a middle way fusing the precise description of ideas with attention to the environmental relationships.[34]

Such a synthesis seemed achieved in the American Studies approach, but in reality the new movement mainly followed the intrinsic analysis of ideas though frequently claiming otherwise. The pioneer book in the field by Henry Nash Smith, *Virgin Land: The American West as Symbol and*

(Princeton: Princeton University Press, 1966); and the important articles of John Higham gathered conveniently in his *Writing American History: Essays on Modern Scholarship* (Bloomington, Ind.: Indiana University Press, 1970).

[31] Vernon Parrington, *Main Currents in American Thought: An Interpretation of American Literature from the Beginnings to 1920* (New York: Harcourt, Brace, 1927–1930), 3 vols.

[32] Perry Miller, *The New England Mind: The Seventeenth Century* (New York: Macmillan, 1939), pp. vii, viii. See his own statement of motivation in the paperback edition (Boston: Beacon Press, 1961), pp. xi–xii.

[33] Merle Curti, *The Growth of American Thought* (New York: Harper and Bros., 1943), p. x, but see the whole introduction, pp. ix–xvii, for his understanding of the nature of the field.

[34] Particularly John Higham, "The Rise of American Intellectual History," *American Historical Review*, 56 (April, 1951), pp. 453–471; "Intellectual History and Its Neighbors," *Journal of the History of Ideas*, 15 (June, 1954), pp. 339–347. But see also, Skotheim, *American Intellectual Histories*, pp. viii–x, 256–288; and Rush Welter, "The History of Ideas in America: An Essay in Redefinition," *Journal of American History*, 51 (March, 1965), pp. 599–614.

Myth (1950), altered the view of the frontier heretofore held in the profession by transmuting the American West from reality into a series of images held by Americans in the nineteenth century and subsequently by historians. He used the terms "myth" and "symbol" of his title to "designate larger or smaller units of the same kind of thing, namely an intellectual construction that fuses concept and emotion into an image. The myths and symbols with which I deal have the further characteristic of being collective representations rather than the work of a single mind."[35] Quickly in succession followed books in the same school. Chief among these were: *Andrew Jackson: Symbol for an Age*[36]; *The American Adam: Innocence, Tragedy, and Tradition in the Nineteenth Century*[37]; *Cavalier and Yankee: The Old South and American National Character*[38]; and *The Machine in the Garden: Technology and the Pastoral Ideal in America.*[39]

All these works claimed to illuminate American culture through their concentration on the major myths prevalent in the nineteenth-century United States. Thus an intellectual historian of prominence in the late 1960's cited these classics of the genre as examples of ""Some Recent Directions in American Cultural History" during the preceding two decades.[40] Summarizing and extending the insights of the earlier works in American studies and the history of ideas was Stow Person's aptly titled *American Minds: A History of Ideas* (1958). He defined his main task as the description of "the principal focal concentrations of ideas, or 'minds,' that determined the profile of American intellectual life during its historical development." In elaboration of his aim, he stated: "A social mind is the cluster of ideas and attitudes that gives to a society whatever uniqueness or individuality it may have as an epoch in the history of thought."[41] In this exposition of goal we have essentially the concept of culture applied to past peoples' ideation.

Whether intellectual historians stressed the context of ideas or the ideas themselves, whether they studied ideation as myths, symbols, images, ideals, or ideology, they reflected the new conception of culture and the

[35] Henry Nash Smith, *Virgin Land: The American West as Symbol and Myth* (Cambridge, Mass.: Harvard University Press, 1950), p. v. He goes on to say in a confused and confusing fashion: "I do not mean to raise the question whether such products of the imagination accurately reflect empirical fact. They exist on a different plane. But as I have tried to show, they sometimes exert a decided influence on practical affairs."

[36] John W. Ward, *Andrew Jackson: Symbol for an Age* (New York: Oxford University Press, 1955).

[37] Richard W. B. Lewis, *The American Adam: Innocence, Tragedy, and Tradition in the Nineteenth Century* (Chicago: University of Chicago Press, 1955).

[38] William R. Taylor, *Cavalier and Yankee: The Old South and American National Character* (New York: George Braziller, 1961).

[39] Leo Marx, *The Machine in the Garden: Technology and the Pastoral Ideal in America* (New York: Oxford University Press, 1964).

[40] David B. Davis, "Some Recent Directions in American Cultural History," *American Historical Review*, 73 (Feb., 1968), pp. 696–707.

[41] Stow Persons, *American Minds: A History of Ideas* (New York: Henry Holt and Co., 1958), p. vii.

conception of man embodied in it. As a result, scarcely any phase of American history escaped some revision through reassessing the role of ideation in the past. Aside from the reappreciation of the complexity and subtlety of Puritan thought and the reinterpretation of the frontier as images, historians explored the myth of the self-made man,[42] the ideology of businessmen,[43] the Populist and Progressive mentalities,[44] the ambiguous ideals of Jacksonian Democracy,[45] the anti-institutional biases of many ante-bellum reformers,[46] and the efforts of the founding fathers to apply in practice the enlightened ideals of their time to foreign policy and separation of church and state as well as in framing new governments.[47] Religious history experienced its own revival as a consequence of the new interest in past ideals and values that shaped American lives in the past.[48] With so many historians reconstructing the ideation of past actors as they understood their times, no wonder Hughes proclaimed that the day of the historian as retrospective cultural anthropologist had arrived.[49] The popularity of intellectual history in the historical profession after World War II should be viewed as the counterpart of the prevalence of cultural analysis in the social sciences at the same time.[50]

[42] Irvin G. Wyllie, *The Self-Made Man in America* (New Brunswick: Rutgers University Press, 1954); Sigmund Diamond, *The Reputation of the American Businessman* (Cambridge, Mass.: Harvard University Press, 1955); John G. Cawelti, *Apostles of the Self-Made Man: Changing Concept of Success in America* (Chicago: University of Chicago Press, 1965).

[43] Edward C. Kirkland, *Dream and Thought in the Business Community, 1860–1900* (Ithaca: Cornell University Press, 1956); Thomas C. Cochran, *Railroad Leaders, 1845–1890* (Cambridge, Mass.: Harvard University Press, 1953).

[44] Richard Hofstadter, *The Age of Reform: From Bryan to F.D.R.* (New York: Alfred A. Knopf, 1955); David Noble, *The Paradox of Progressive Thought* (Minneapolis: University of Minnesota Press, 1958).

[45] In addition to Ward, *Andrew Jackson*; Marvin Meyers, *The Jacksonian Persuasion: Politics and Belief* (Stanford: Stanford University Press, 1957).

[46] Stanley Elkins, *Slavery: A Problem in American Institutional and Intellectual Life* (Chicago: University of Chicago Press, 1959).

[47] Felix Gilbert, *To the Farewell Address: Ideas of Early American Foreign Policy* (Princeton: Princeton University Press, 1961); Sidney E. Mead, *The Lively Experiment: The Shaping of Christianity in America* (New York: Harper and Row, 1963), pp. 16–71; Edmund Morgan, *The Birth of the Republic, 1763–89* (Chicago: University of Chicago Press, 1956). This trend perhaps reached its culmination in Bernard Bailyn, *The Ideological Origins of the American Revolution* (Cambridge, Mass.: Harvard University Press, 1967); and Gordon Wood, *The Creation of the American Republic, 1776–1787* (Chapel Hill: University of North Carolina Press, 1969).

[48] Henry F. May, "The Recovery of American Religious History," *American Historical Review,* 70 (Oct., 1964), pp. 79–92.

[49] Although the word culture was popular, it was not always used or exemplified in a technical sense in intellectual history let alone in other areas of writing history. See, for example, the eclectic volume by Howard M. Jones, *O Strange New World! American Culture: The Formative Years* (New York: Viking Press, 1964); or the miscellaneous topics discussed in John F. McDermott, ed., *Research Opportunities in American Cultural History* (Lexington: University of Kentucky Press, 1961).

[50] The rising popularity of intellectual history during the twentieth century is discussed by Skotheim, *American Intellectual Histories and Historians,* pp. 291–298.

The significance attributed to ideas in past human behavior produced a reinterpretation of American history. In effect this reinterpretation destroyed the progressives' easy correlation of social and physical environment, economic interests, and ideology by injecting the intervening variable, so to speak, of ideation between environmental stimuli and behavioral responses. As a result, people in the past no longer reacted directly to their sectional and economic interests but only indirectly through their culturally perceived and defined social and economic environment. According to the latter view, the frontier was not a physical environment alone but a collective image of the West composed of the myth of the yeoman farmer, the image of the productive capitalistic garden, and the abode of the "savage"—all based upon the fundamental value-orientations of progress, social evolution, manifest destiny, and the ideal of the virtuous, self-subsistent farmer.[51] Likewise, the leaders of the Revolution ceased being men in pursuit of their own economic independence from England and the establishment of a common market under the guise of the federal Constitution and became, instead, persons frightened of a conspiracy against their liberty as traditionally defined by Englishmen and earnestly attempting to practice the most enlightened political ideals of the time, although they might differ over the means to that end.[52]

Applying the same view to the nineteenth century, people voted for Jackson not on the basis of their sectional and economic alignment but because he symbolized their fears for traditional ideals in a time of apparent rapid change or because of their ethno-cultural and religious prejudices.[53] Populists measured their economic plight against the myth of the happy yeoman farmer and fabricated a world conspiracy directed against them to explain their low prices and help them decide what to do about their situation—rather than face up to their position as primary producers in a complicated national and international trade network.[54] In each of these cases and others, the newer interpretation substituted for an "ob-

[51] In addition to Smith, *Virgin Land*; Arthur K. Moore, *The Frontier Mind: A Cultural Analysis of the Kentucky Frontiersman* (Lexington: University of Kentucky Press, 1957); Roy H. Pearce, *The Savages of America: A Study of the Indian and the Idea of Civilization* (Baltimore: Johns Hopkins University Press, 1953); William H. Goetzmann, *Exploration and Empire: The Explorer and the Scientist in the Winning of the American West* (New York: Alfred A. Knopf, 1966); Roderick Nash, *Wilderness and the American Mind* (New Haven: Yale University Press, 1967). My own effort to point out the implications of the culture concept for understanding the history of the American West was "Space, Time, Culture and the New Frontier," *Agricultural History*, 28 (Jan., 1964), pp. 21–30.

[52] Bailyn, *Ideological Origins*; Wood, *Creation of the American Republic*.

[53] Meyers, *Jacksonian Persuasion*, presented the first thesis, and Lee Benson offered the second in his pioneering historical study of election statistics, *The Concept of Jacksonian Democracy: New York as a Test Case* (Princeton: Princeton University Press, 1961). Charles Sellers, Jr., traces changing historical interpretations of the period in "Andrew Jackson Versus the Historians," *Mississippi Valley Historical Review*, 44 (March, 1958), pp. 615–634.

[54] Hofstadter, *Age of Reform*, pp. 23–130, develops such a viewpoint. Compare the arguments over his thesis in *Agricultural History*, 49 (April, 1965), pp. 59–85.

jective reality" shared alike by past actors and historian a symbolic reality in the actors' perception and definition of the situation quite different, perhaps, than if the historian had been there to see for himself according to his own values and orientations.

In consequence of these new interpretations, the outline of American history assumed a different shape from that given it by older progressives. For the conflict of economic and class differences were substituted symbolic tensions and cultural antimonies. Actual conflict over the allocation of political power and economic wealth disappeared in either inherent cultural strains or in the multiplicity of subjectively perceived and defined social and physical environments.[55] The dramatic dialectics of struggle between haves and have-nots were subsumed in the common adherence to those basic values dominating the outlook and actions of most Americans for a century or more. Periodization became more difficult as complexes of values pervaded periods far longer than the short eras of progressive historiography and the changing configurations of ideas did not afford the same clarity of transition from one epoch to another as had the victory of the few or the many in the battle for wealth and power.[56]

In effect, if not in intent, this reinterpretation of the American past through cultural analysis produced much of what the later critics deprecated as consensus history. Not everything castigated as consensus history was due to the application of the cultural image of man to American history, but to the degree that overlap occurred then the charges against consensus history pertained also to the use of the culture concept in United States history.[57] Consensus history as cultural analysis often did accept the rhetoric of the past on its own terms and as explanatory of human behavior at the time, as the critics charged, instead of probing beneath the surface for underlying motives and interests. This form of historical interpretation did abrogate the duty of Clio's followers to judge the past as well as to describe the past by accepting previous verbal behavior at face value and thereby seeming to sanction the values of all men in history indiscriminantly. For the conflict and dynamism assumed by the progressives, the newer interpretation substituted the slow evolution of basic values and orientations subscribed to by an entire population. For the whiggish emphasis on the "American reform tradition" in progressive historiography,

[55] For example, see the intensive analysis of the interests of persons for and against the Constitution in Forrest McDonald, *We the People: The Economic Origins of the Constitution* (Chicago: University of Chicago Press, 1958).

[56] My book, *A Behavioral Approach to Historical Analysis* (New York: Free Press, 1969), pp. 98–168, treats at greater length implications of the culture concept for the reinterpretation of American history in particular and history-writing in general.

[57] The ambiguity of the relation between cultural analysis and consensus history in the works of one of the chief practitioners is ably examined by Jack Diggins, "Consciousness and Ideology in American History: The Burden of Daniel J. Boorstin," *American Historical Review*, 76 (Feb., 1971), pp. 99–118; "The Perils of Naturalism: Some Reflections on Daniel J. Boorstin's Approach to American History," *American Quarterly*, 23 (May, 1971), pp. 153–180.

cultural analysis substituted the disjunction between the roles and outlooks of past persons in history and those of present day historians.

True in one sense, these accusations miss the point in another sense. Moral relativization of men's experiences was not the purpose of cultural analysis but the result of the separation of the various levels of understanding according to who was defining the situation in keeping with what criteria or values. Cultural interpretation assumed a multi-faceted reality in opposition to the single, simple reality presumed common to the historian and his subjects in progressive understanding of the past. To the extent that cultural analysis presumed almost all Americans shared common or similar values and beliefs, then they homogenized the past as their critics charged. To the extent, however, that progressive historiography assumed one value system appropriate for all times and a single explanation of human behavior valid throughout all of American history, then it was the progressive historians who homogenized the past according to the modern conception of culture. At the heart of the different approaches lay two divergent models of social reality and of the nature of social order: Consensus and continuity versus conflict and coercion.[58]

If my impression is correct that many of the criticisms against consensus history represented objections to the model of man and society presumed in the cultural approach, then the critique came chiefly from without rather than from within the framework of analysis. Even the commentary from within the framework seemed less sophisticated than the searching debate over the concept taking place among anthropologists during the same period of time. That the notion created its own intellectual paradoxes and polemical tensions can be witnessed in a comparison of Kroeber's and Kluckhohn's summary analysis of the concept and the one given recently by Milton Singer in the new *International Encyclopedia of Social Sciences*.[59] Although the controversy is not entirely new, the latest phase depends upon the criteria of explanation posed to all social science disciplines by the philosophers of science and the newest developments in linguistics, always a potent influence in the anthropological idea of culture. To what degree the debate also involves an alteration in the anthropological model of man is uncertain.

Inherent in the conception of culture is the contradiction between the universal and partitive meanings of the term, or the conflict between the notion of culture as common to all mankind versus the idea of specific, individual cultures into which all men are divided. If culture is common to all men as men, then what is shared universally as opposed to relatively? Can the assumption of the psychic unity of mankind be demonstrated empirically in the modes of cognition, in logic, or in some other way? If different cultures are as various as some anthropologists claim, must they

---

[58] Gene Wise, "Political 'Reality' in Recent American Scholarship: Progressives Versus Symbolists," *American Quarterly*, 19 (Summer, 1967), pp. 303–328, arrives at many of the same conclusions but phrases them differently for his purposes.

[59] Singer, "The Concept of Culture," pp. 527–543.

be understood in totally different ways, or can they be analyzed according to the same basic categories? Furthermore, if a culture is to be understood as the people said to hold the culture understand it, then can the results be translated for people outside the culture? Thus does the dilemma of relativism bedevil the modern anthropologist.

The post-war conception of culture generally slighted these questions or, worse, presumed the answers to them. In short, the modern definition of the concept incorporated a complete theory of culture without a valid foundation in research. By assuming the components of culture in the definition, anthropologists presumed the results of their analyses of various cultures. In other words, their conception contained by definition the components they were supposed to derive from empirical, comparative research. Moreover, they hypothesized the articulation of those components according to the definition, so their research more frequently proved how things related according to the mind of the anthropologist than according to the minds of the people said to bear the culture. Anthropologists during the past decade came to realize increasingly that their version of culture was a pseudo-theory, because it was at best an eclectic description of what they were supposed to look for among various peoples according to their ethnocentric ordering of the categories. The definition did not foster comparison, because the parts had not been isolated through research but merely by assumption. Culture as it had come to be defined, in the end, did not and could not serve an explanatory function. As a result of this awareness, anthropologists focused their attention more strictly on just what was culture and how does an investigator discover it.

Whether praised for its aims or condemned for its pretensions and few accomplishments, the "new ethnography," "ethnosemantics," "cognitive anthropology," the "etics" versus "emics" debate, or even some of the controversy over Lévi-Strauss and his brand of "structuralism," all seem to be the latest anthropological equivalent of the perennial problem of understanding other men's minds. The debate revolves about two issues at the least: the method of validating the knowledge of informants' understandings of their own lives, and, second, how the anthropologist synthesizes the validated descriptions he obtains into an overall model of those understandings. Since the new breed of anthropologist assumes that what is shared by a population said to possess a culture is problematical, new approaches were devised to elicit more exactly how informants see their activities in order to compare how many informants have how many cognitions (and, presumably as this science develops, values) how alike. Next arises the problem of whose terms should describe their own ways of looking at things, or the problem of translation. Should the anthropologist's model of an informant's world appear psychologically real to the latter as well as accurate to the former? From these psychologically-validated cognitive models of each informant's culture, the anthropologist proceeds to construct his own inclusive model of these partial models, or his version of the people's culture. The validity of the inclusive model is to be tested by how well it predicts the actions of the people said to possess the culture in the way they understand it, or how well it will generate the partial models from which it was derived.

In the new anthropology, great stress is placed first upon discovering the cognitive ordering by the culture-bearers of their lives, and then on the formal analysis by logic or mathematics of those models to produce a theory of that culture. Each person is presumed to hold what is in effect his own model of his culture, which in fact is his culture, and the anthropologist constructs still another model of those models, which is his version of the culture of those people. Ideally under this system, the universal definition of culture would apply to the model synthesizing or generating the many partial, or anthropological, models of various cultures. The word culture thus pertains to three levels of cognitive analysis: the informant's model, the anthropologist's model, and the ultimate, or universal, model of sundry anthropologists' models. Only the latter model would be a true theory of culture in the eyes of the proponents of the new ethnography, because it would be a theory based on the different theories of the various cultures constructed by the anthropologists, which were derived originally from the culture-bearers' own theories of their ways of living. Such an overall theory would also be a true meta-language, as opposed to the pseudo-one of the present conception, for its language of description would be developed ·from the languages of description of the partitive cultures. In summary, recent conceptualization of the culture concept refines the previous levels of meaning in the word and increases the explicit gap between the anthropologist's and informant's conceptualization of the latter's culture.[60]

Just as the problems raised by the new ethnography were not entirely new in anthropology but a refinement of traditional perplexities inherent in the culture concept, so the issues posed by this thinking for the cultural analysis of history are new ways of putting old questions that are more congenial to current images of man embodied in the social science research of the past decade. From even this brief exposition of the new anthropology, the questions revolve essentially about each step of model con-

[60] This impression of the new ethnography is based upon the article with comments by B. N. Colby, "Ethnographics: A Preliminary Survey," *Current Anthropology*, 7 (Feb., 1966), pp. 3–32; the introduction and the articles collected by Stephen A. Tyler, ed., *Cognitive Anthropology* (New York: Holt, Rinehart and Winston, 1969); Anthony F. C. Wallace, *Culture and Personality* (2nd ed.; New York: Random House, 1970); and Pertti J. Pelto, *Anthropological Research: The Structure of Inquiry* (New York: Harper and Row, 1970), pp. 67–86. For a sarcastic view of the new trend, see Marvin Harris, *The Rise of Anthropological Theory: A History of Theories of Culture* (New York: Thomas Y. Crowell Co., 1968), pp. 568–604. By fragmenting a culture into the informant cultures, the anthropologists increased the problem of relating a culture to a society. Who bears the culture-model the anthropologist constructs and how does he know, when the presumption of correlation between society and culture is eliminated? For views of this question in relation to the idea of a tribe, see June Helm, ed., *Essays on the Problem of Tribe*, Proceedings of the 1967 Annual Spring Meeting of the American Ethnological Society (Seattle, 1968).

struction and the problem of translation: How and which folk analyses should be combined into the historian's conception of the culture of a people in a given era? In whose terms and from whose viewpoint does he tell his story of the time? Phrased according to traditional problems in historical method, the questions concern the synthesis of diverse but incomplete data sources and the problem of perspective.

From whose view among the actors in the historical drama should the tale of the past be told? Older historians debated this issue in terms of popular versus intellectual thought or of cosmopolitanism versus localism in outlook, but the younger generation tends to consider the question in relation to the role of minorities in general American history or whether to view history from the top-down or the bottom-up.[61] Can and must blacks, Indians, women, lower classes and other people previously treated as passive objects in the determination of their own futures be given their own place in the larger history of their societies? (The novelist faces the same basic problem of multiple consciousness in the adoption of viewpoint in the novel.) Phrased in terms of the new ethnography, the question would seem to be: Which folk cultures are to be combined into the analyst's model of their culture? And the answer is obvious: the entire population, of course. The problem, therefore is how to aggregate the many folk cultures or views to produce the complete social system of the period, for the very partialness of the various viewpoints makes the system work as a whole. As one of the new ethnographers puts this approach, in a narrower context but applicable here:

> This is an argument for a different kind of unitary description which sees unity as emerging from the ordered relations between variants and contexts. Variants are not mere deviations from some assumed basic organization; with their rules of occurrence they are the organization. It must be emphasized, however, that such a unitary description can only be achieved by the anthropologist. It is highly unlikely that the members of the culture ever see their culture as this kind of unitary phenomenon. Each individual member may have a unique, unitary model of his culture, but it is not necessarily cognizant of all the unique, unitary models held by other members of his culture. He will be aware of and use some, but it is only the anthropologist who completely transcends those particular models and constructs a single, unitary model. The cognitive organization exists solely in the mind of the anthropologist. Yet to the extent that it will generate conceptual models used by the people of a particular culture, it is a model of their cognitive systems.[62]

In one sense, this approach eliminates the false dichotomy between the consensus and conflict models of society as well as the top-down versus

---

[61] An argument for bottom-up history is presented by Jesse Lemisch, "The American Revolution Seen From the Bottom Up," in Bernstein, ed., *Towards a New Past*, pp. 3–45.

[62] Tyler, *Cognitive Anthropology*, p. 5. Compare Wallace, *Culture and Personality*, pp. 24–36.

the bottom-up views by saying that the overall model is to be empirically derived from variant folk cultures. One can ask, however, whether the view from the top-down or the bottom-up resembles the analyst's model more, and the answer provides clues as to who has the power in the society through control of knowledge and information. Thus, the historian does not presume people understand their position and function in the social system in the same way he does. Rather, congruence or dissimilarity of the various folk models and the historian's formal model must be demonstrated, whether analyzed in terms of interests and ideology or ideals and values. In place of the preconceived view of the interests of a group of people, the historian must show the emergence of the collective consciousness of a group of people as a group. One such approach to the mobilization of group opinion in this manner is manifested in E. P. Thompson's *The Making of the English Working Class*.[63]

For the historian to aggregate folk cultures in conformity to the advice in the last paragraph presents problems peculiar to the discipline. Given the fragmentary evidence remaining today of many past persons' cognitive models, how does the historian piece together enough past folk models to construct his overall model? In short, how does he know what and how much was shared by how many? Content analysis appears one valuable technique to answer this question for what evidence does exist of past persons' ideation. Historians have little used this device, because the 1950's cultural model of man presumed the sharing of ideas, attitudes, and motives. Such an assumption made the examination of a few cases equivalent to the consideration of all if they appeared representative. Under the new version of cultural analysis, the presumption of lack of sharing makes the representativeness of a small sample quite uncertain and the quest for diversity crucial to constructing the overall model. The use of content analysis and statistical tests to overcome the problem of representativeness seems the point of Murray G. Murphy's effort to redirect historical study of national character.[64] The paucity as well as the kinds of evidence available to determine past opinion leads Lee Benson to propose the use of election statistics as the historian's best substitute for opinion polls.[65]

Interwoven with these various perplexities is the problem of language and translation in the various models. On the level of individual folk cul-

[63] E. P. Thompson, *The Making of the English Working Class* (London: V. Gollancz, 1963). I presume this is also the intellectual rationale behind Eric Foner's study of ideological currents in *Free Soil, Free Labor, Free Man: The Ideology of the Republican Party Before the Civil War* (New York: Oxford University Press, 1970).

[64] "An Approach to the Historical Study of National Character," in Melford E. Spiro, ed., *Context and Meaning in Cultural Anthropology* (New York: Free Press, 1965), pp. 144–163. His technique, in turn, is criticized on the same grounds by David E. Stannard, "American Historians and the Idea of National Character: Some Problems and Prospects," *American Quarterly*, 23 (May, 1971), pp. 213–216.

[65] Lee Benson, "An Approach to the Scientific Study of Past Opinion," *Public Opinion Quarterly*, 31 (Winter, 1967), pp. 522–567.

tures, the historian is faced with the psychological validity of the model he constructs of the actor's culture: does he repeat the words and ways of thought exactly as they were expressed by the individual, or does he organize them in a manner more logical and unified than the person ever phrased them? Perhaps the most dramatic example of the recent recovery of the meaning of a word as the people of the time used it and the implications of such usage for historical interpretation is "republican."[66] As a result, the word has come back into use as the only appropriate term for talking about certain political ideation of the eighteenth century. At that time "democracy" possessed a more restricted meaning than that given the word later in the succeeding century or today. Historians have therefore revised their usage of the two expressions when writing about the late 1700's.

On the level of the entire population, the problem of translating assumes added complexity by combining with the degree of abstraction from the documentary data at the disposal of the historian. Not how much data or its representativeness is the problem here so much as how similar can the language of the historian's model of the culture be to any of his sources and still generate all the folk models of his system? John William Ward's several analyses of American thinking during the age of Andrew Jackson provide an instructive example of this and some of the other problems. In his first book, Ward explored the symbolic Jackson as an expression of the era's three main value-orientations of nature, providence, and will. In his essay on the cultural approach to history, he found the ideal of individualism manifested in areas as diverse as Jackson's justification for the expulsion by force of the Cherokees from Georgia, Ralph Waldo Emerson's essay "Politics," general acts of incorporation, landscape gardening, and the religious doctrine of the perfect law of liberty for the righteous. Lately, he pointed out how the dilemma between the ideal of equality and presumption of men's inequality was rationalized by the people of the period through the beliefs that the majority should rule and that government should be simple so every man in a country of self-reliant individualists could understand it, but such republican government would in the end give a "natural charter of privilege" to those men with the greater talents to get ahead under such a system.[67] In all instances, Ward's essays represent the impressionistic summation of printed and pictorial sources of past ideation. In each essay, the total model of the population's folk models is presented somewhat differently, so what was shared and how is not exactly

[66] The story of the recovery, so to speak, of republican thought is the theme of Robert E. Shalhope, "Toward a Republican Synthesis: The Emergence of an Understanding of Republicanism in American Historiography," *William and Mary Quarterly,* 3d ser., 29 (Jan., 1972), pp. 49–80.

[67] In order of publication: John William Ward, *Andrew Jackson*: "History of the Concept of Culture," in his *Red, White, and Blue: Men, Books, and Ideas in American Culture* (New York: Oxford University Press, 1969), pp. 9–14; "Jacksonian Democratic Thought: 'A Natural Charter of Privilege'," in Stanley Coben and Lorman Ratner, eds., *The Development of an American Culture* (Englewood Cliffs, N.J.; Prentice-Hall, 1970), pp. 44–63.

known. Who shared these values and beliefs is not carefully delineated, so whether these models will generate all the folk models in the society of the period is also uncertain. Moreover, different levels of abstraction seem to be combined in the language of the model. When Ward quotes a person directly, we see that he and the person use the same language and maybe understand the same value-orientation in the same way, but what about the attribution of individualism in the examples of general laws of incorporation and landscape gardening? Is this the analyst's abstract attribution according to his model or the models of the people at the time? Even more crucial from this viewpoint are his categories of analysis. Why are they not the same in all the essays? Are nature, providence, and will the best summary terms for the inclusive model of the folk cultures? The conception of individualism was explicitly named at the time and came into popular use then, but did the individual actors think in terms of a basic trinity of nature, providence, and will? If the latter are only the categories of the analyst's model, are they the best summative terms at that level? Are they sufficient to generate the folk models? In this example, we feel that such categorization does less violence to the actors' outlooks than the language employed by Perry Miller to divide the contents of the puritan mind: religion and learning, cosmology, anthropology, and sociology—surely a conceptualization appropriate only to modern man's approach to understanding himself.[68]

These considerations point directly to the dilemma of cultural relativism in the understanding of the past. If the historian ought not to impose his categories of analysis on the past folk models he constructs, but yet his model of these models is codified solely by him, then to what level of "reality" do the categories refer that the historian employs in his writing? Since, for example, the assumptions composing the historians' idea of the frontier did not exist full-blown apparently until the end of the nineteenth century,[69] does the historian who writes the history of the frontier before that time imply the modern codification of the term existed in the minds of Americans as well as himself before then? Can we as historians even say that a frontier existed before the mid-eighteenth century in the English colonies if none of the basic orientations that were to give meaning to that term existed prior to that time? Must a history of the frontier, therefore, even as a model in the historian's mind begin with the mid-eighteenth century? Is the history of the frontier in the nineteenth century chiefly one of showing the lessening and then the final disappearance of the difference between the historian's formal model of the frontier and the folk models of the western United States and its history?

Applying similar logic to the idea of American history, when does it commence as a formal model as opposed to folk models? Are past history

[68] Miller, New England Mind, Table of Contents, p. xiii.

[69] Or, so the argument of John Juricek, "American Usage of the Word 'Frontier' from Colonial Times to Frederick Jackson Turner," Proceedings of the American Philosophical Society, 110 (Feb., 1966), pp. 10–34.

books to be considered formal or folk models of the United States past for their times? Is what we teach and research as American history today the historians' overall model(s) of the historians' period models of the folk models of the time? What are the implications of such considerations for the assertion of "reality" in the past as opposed to the historian's conception of the past? To what extent, then, is history the myth of the myths of images of reality, to use some of the cultural historian's favorite words? To carry cultural relativism to its extreme leads to cultural solipsism whether in anthropology or in history. On the other hand, such an image of man reminds the historian of his many-leveled removal from the "reality" of past folks incorporated into their own cultural understandings of their worlds and their behavior. Written history ought to reflect this multi-leveled removal from past ideation by the nature of time as well as the nature of cultural understanding.

The nature of time presents another problem for the cultural analysis of history. New as well as old conceptions of culture share the fault of being time-bound as a method of explanation. Stress on pattern in cultural interpretation introduces an element of the static into the concept. The research of Bernard Bailyn on the American Revolution affords an interesting example of the temporal paradox of cultural analysis in history. His publications develop at length the colonists' fear of a conspiracy by the British government and its agents in the colonies against their traditional (English) notions of the fragility of liberty in the fight against power and corruption. In his original publication of this research, he found the belief present from the 1760's to the outbreak of the Revolution, and therefore the idea seemed an important explanation for the war between the colonies and the mother country. As his research continued, he traced the essential outlook back into the early eighteenth century, and its major components even earlier,[70] and this created the dilemma. The farther back in time he traced the conspiracy outlook, the less it explained the Revolution occurring when it did. Phrased differently, the longer in time the conspiracy idea existed—and necessary as it may be to the outbreak—the less sufficient it was to explain the timing of the event itself. This dilemma may be stated as a general rule in historical interpretation: The more some conception explains, the less it explains any one event. For this reason, the more racism and imperialism are used to explain the entirety of American history the less they explain the specific course of events that supposedly manifested the two conceptions.

Does this mean that historians should seek explanation for change outside cultural analysis? Must cultural analysis be supplemented by or reduced to explanation in some other form in order to introduce dynamics into history? One student of Bailyn has argued as much in asking for the reconciliation of his mentor's approach to the causes of the American Rev-

[70] Compare his General Introduction to *Pamphlets of the American Revolution, 1750–1776* (Cambridge, Mass.: Harvard University Press, 1965), vol. 1, with the revised version in *Ideological Origins*.

olution and the older, progressive school's assumptions about human behavior and social dynamics.[71] Bailyn himself subsequently turned to the peculiar instability of the colonial political system in an effort to pinpoint the reason for the particular efficacy of the conspiratorial hypothesis in the mid-1770's.[72]

That historians more and more feel the need to move beyond the cultural analysis of history accounts, I believe, for the current trend to social history and the social interpretation of history in the profession. Attention to various institutions and the nature of social organization and how they explain the general outline of the past side-step some of the perplexities of the cultural analysis of history. By concentrating on the "actual" structure of American society throughout its history, historians avoid the other minds problems of cultural analysis by constructing an observer's model of past human behavior independent of the actors' views as much as possible. This technique has been developed best by the new economic historians, who, thanks to economic theory and statistical description, can build models and test their hypotheses apart from the ideation found in the usual documentary sources of the historian.[73] Other "new" histories—political,[74] urban,[75] and social[76]—quickly followed in hopes of achieving as much with the poorer theory and statistical data at their disposal. Such an approach, in essence, allows the historian to establish past "reality" independent of the actors' perceptions and definitions of it. The difference between the cultural approach and the "new" approach is readily observed in their respective treatments of social mobility in American history. Cultural analysts traced the idea of the self-made man, but the new social historians study through quantification the amount of mobility up and down

[71] Gordon S. Wood, "Rhetoric and Reality in the American Revolution," *William and Mary Quarterly*, 3d. ser., 23 (Jan., 1966), pp. 3–32.

[72] Bernard Bailyn, "The Origin of American Politics," *Perspectives in American History*, 1 (1967), pp. 9–120. Compare his original starting place, "Political Experience and Enlightenment Ideas in Eighteenth-Century America," *American Historical Review*, 67 (Jan., 1962), pp. 339–351.

[73] Essays on the subject of its title are anthologized by Ralph Andreano, ed., *The New Economic History: Recent Papers on Methodology* (New York: John Wiley and Sons, 1970); and a collection of findings in the field edited by two of its leaders, Robert W. Fogel and Stanley L. Engerman, *The Reinterpretation of American Economic History* (New York: Harper and Row, 1971).

[74] A convenient guide to this field is Allan G. Bogue, "United States: The 'New' Political History," *Journal of Contemporary History*, 3 (Jan., 1968), pp. 5–27.

[75] For a sample of work in the field and the invention of the term, see Stephan Thernstrom and Richard Sennett, eds., *Nineteenth-Century Cities: Essays in the New Urban History* (New Haven: Yale University Press, 1969).

[76] For one man's view of the field, see Samuel P. Hays, "A Systematic Social History," in George A. Billias and Gerald N. Grob, eds., *American History: Retrospect and Prospect* (New York: Free Press, 1971). Examples may be found in two new periodicals: *Journal of Social History* (Fall, 1967–); and *The Journal of Interdisciplinary History* (Autumn, 1970–).

in various systems.[77] The new approach supplies firm answers according to the historian's suppositions about the past reality. It facilitates cross-societal and intra-societal comparisons through quantification by eliminating the relativistic cultural context.[78] It introduces dynamics through the observable changes in the social structure and accounts for the course of history through these changes, thereby getting around other problems in the cultural approach to history.

Such benefits are achieved, however, at the expense of substituting one model of man for another under the guise of the debate over explanation. At present, the two strategies of explanation and the two images of man on which they rest seem mutually incompatible. On one hand, the multiple consciousness enigma in cultural analysis leads to perplexities in knowing and talking about other minds and the attribution of internal states as explanation. At worst that form of interpretation leads to extreme relativism and even solipsism. On the other hand, study of social structure overcomes these problems primarily by eliminating the consciousness of people as explanation—a possibility morally unacceptable to some people and analytically invalid to others. This fundamental dichotomy between approaches to the study of human behavior faces the social scientist and historian alike today, and the basic methodological battle goes under various names in the social sciences presently: behaviorist versus phenomenological, structural versus behavioral, social versus cultural.

In history-writing these divergent approaches might be termed the latest phase of the old controversy between historicism and scientific history. Neo-scientific history removes analytical elements from their context in such a way as to enable comparison across time and societies. Neo-historicist studies try to put their topics in as complete a cultural and temporal context as possible. Practitioners of the former prefer structural analysis and observers' models of analysis, while those of the latter favor cultural or phenomenological analyses and therefore seek explanation by actors' viewpoint as much as possible. To have both comparison and context, both a structural and a behavioral explanation and image of man appears impossible at this moment in man's intellectual development in the West. Compromise or fusion is desirable in practice but analytically unattainable so far in historical analysis. Thus do past intellectual trends lead

159190

[77] Compare, for example, the approach of Wyllie, *Self-Made Man*, and Cawelti, *Apostles of the Self-Made Man*, with that of Stephan Thernstrom, *Poverty and Progress: Social Mobility in a Nineteenth Century City* (Cambridge, Mass.: Harvard University Press, 1964), and the authors in Thernstrom and Sennett, eds., *Nineteenth-Century Cities*.

[78] Similarly, the effort to obtain valid cross-cultural comparisons in social anthropology led to quantification. See for a summary of the trend, J. Clyde Mitchell, "On Quantification in Social Anthropology," in A. L. Epstein, ed., *The Craft of Social Anthropology* (London: Tavistock Publications, 1967), pp. 17–45. Note the emphasis on quantification techniques in a recent book on method in anthropology: Pelto, *Anthropological Research*.

to our time and create our present at the same time as the concerns of the present direct the understanding of our past. To what extent all this represents a passing phase of the paradigm of man in scholarly discourse can only be told when the future becomes past. To what degree this interpretation of recent intellectual history of the discipline of history is accurate depends as much upon the reader's model of man and explanation as upon the accuracy of my model of other men's models.

PLACE AND LOCATION: NOTES ON THE SPATIAL PATTERNING OF CULTURE

DAVID E. SOPHER
Syracuse University

How man, considered as sharer in a culture, relates to the land, changing it and being changed, is the central theme of classical cultural geography. Its focus is on the systemic links between land and culture expressed in the appearance of the cultural landscape—the land remolded by culture. While the theme of man-land relationships would appear to lead one necessarily to concentrate on place and local ecological relationships, the corrective view, always present in Carl Sauer's thought,[1] pays close attention to the significance of cultural location. One may even suggest that for Sauer, cultural ecology is always seen in its global context.[2]

Adherents of the prevailing paradigm within geography, who in their diversity comprise what Peter Haggett has called "the locational school,"[3] have had only distant relations with Sauer and his Berkeley school, a situation that itself invites analysis as a problem in cultural perception and cultural location. These separate intellectual streams, despite their clear differences of purpose, may in fact be coming closer together now.[4] However useful it might be to engineer a convergence, the intent of this essay is more modest: it is to consider some ideas about the location and spatial ordering of culture that appear, if only implicitly, in the work of cultural

[1] See especially John Leighly, ed., *Land and Life: a Selection from the Writings of Carl Ortwin Sauer* (Berkeley and Los Angeles: University of California Press, 1963) and Carl O. Sauer, "The Agency of Man on the Earth," in William L. Thomas, Jr., ed., *Man's Role in Changing the Face of the Earth* (Chicago: University of Chicago Press, 1956). Sauer, who was chairman of the Department of Geography at Berkeley from 1923 to 1957, is generally recognized as the founder and most eloquent protagonist of a cultural geography in America, a field that remains closely associated with the "Berkeley school."

[2] E.g., Carl O. Sauer, *Agricultural Origins and Dispersals* (New York: American Geographical Society, 1952). The partly overlapping substantive and theoretical contributions of geographers and anthropologists to the theme of cultural ecology are discussed in Marvin W. Mikesell, "Geographic Perspectives in Anthropology," *Annals of the Association of American Geographers*, 57 (Sept., 1967), pp. 617–634.

[3] Peter Haggett, *Locational Analysis in Human Geography* (London: Edward Arnold, 1965), pp. 12–13. A spacious treatment of the philosophy and methodology of geography with particular attention to the spatial science paradigm is given in David Harvey, *Explanation in Geography* (London: Edward Arnold, 1969). Exposition of technique is provided in Brian J. L. Berry and Duane F. Marble, *Spatial Analysis: a Reader in Statistical Geography* (Englewood Cliffs: Prentice-Hall, 1968), and Leslie J. King, *Statistical Analysis in Geography* (Englewood Cliffs: Prentice-Hall, 1969).

[4] The hope for such a convergence has been expressed by several European geographers, notably Paul Claval, *Essai sur l'évolution de la géographie humaine*, Cahiers de Géographie de Besançon (No. 12, 1964).

geographers, and to consider research directions by which these ideas can be refined and extended.[5]

THE AREAL DIFFERENTIATION OF CULTURE

For an exposition of what cultural geography is and aspires to do, we must still go to the introduction by Philip Wagner and Marvin Mikesell to their reader, now almost a decade old.[6] For these authors, "cultural geography is the application of the idea of culture to geographic problems," culture providing a means of classifying human beings into "well-defined groups," according to verifiable common characteristics, that is, numerous features of belief and behavior. It is also "a means of classifying areas according to the character of the human groups that occupy them."[7]

The impression created, though perhaps not intended, is of an expectation of high stability in place and time in the schematic relationship connecting culture–culture group–culture area. The expectation of stability, though understood to be relative, may be misleading; the processes that tend to generate culture change are continuous, and from a more distant temporal-spatial perspective than Wagner's and Mikesell's, culture is seen to be essentially plastic in form and fluid in its spatial extent. Culture group occupance of an area is, moreover, transitory and usually plural, and the identification of culture areas by matching cultural distributions is therefore difficult.[8] Perhaps geographers should turn their questions about culture around to ask under what conditions cultures and culture areas will appear to be stable, although to do away with the assumption of cultural stability would be to invite methodological difficulties.[9]

Consideration of processes that appear to lead to areal differentiation of culture calls into question the appropriateness of the stability assumption. This is to set aside the question as to how "well defined" culture groups really are, together with the related problems of scale[10] and of measure-

[5] A proposal for a systematic cultural geography that is largely concerned with spatial ordering is presented in Eugen Wirth, "Zum Problem einer allgemeinen Kulturgeographie," *Die Erde*, 100:2–4 (1969), pp. 155–193.

[6] Philip L. Wagner and Marvin W. Mikesell, eds., *Readings in Cultural Geography* (Chicago: University of Chicago Press, 1962). A new, expanded view of the field is promised in Philip L. Wagner, *Environments and Peoples* (Englewood Cliffs: Prentice-Hall, 1972); the book had not been published at the time of writing.

[7] Wagner and Mikesell, *Cultural Geography*, pp. 1–2.

[8] James L. Newman, "The Culture Area Concept in Anthropology," *Journal of Geography*, 70 (Jan., 1971), pp. 8–15, discusses the concept from the viewpoint of the geographer.

[9] That the ethnologist as well as the cultural geographer is led to identify periods of cultural standstill for the mapping of cultural distributions is conceded by Wiegelmann in a paper on the problem of defining culture areas; Günter Wiegelmann, "Probleme einer kulturraeumlichen Gliederung in volkskundlichen Bereich," *Rheinische Vierteljahresblaetter*, 30 (1965), pp. 95–117, reference on pp. 100–101. None of this is to deny the occurrence of remarkable cultural continuities in place (such as the often-cited stability since Roman days of the Romance-Gemanic language boundary in Belgium), and even more striking genetic continuities can be cited.

[10] Raoul Naroll, "On Ethnic Unit Classification," *Current Anthropology*, 5 (Oct., 1964), pp. 283–312.

ment of degree of cultural difference (distance). How difficult it can be to assess distance for a single aspect of culture is suggested by two imaginative though clearly improvisatory attempts to do so: lexicostatistical measures of linguistic difference,[11] and the technique of "cantometrics," devised to regionalize folksong styles drawn from a wide range of cultures.[12]

We may first postulate an earth surface and its biotic population that are areally differentiated as a result both of apparently chance events (e.g., gene mutations) and of spatial ordering (e.g., atmospheric insolation; adiabatic lapse rate; distance decay in the biotic colonization of islands). Perceived environmental differences, or simply "drift," the latter perhaps ultimately related to defects in intergenerational communication, lead to cultural "mutations" (inventions) that may be adaptively selected, but need not be. For example, adaptive pressure on language would seem to be slight. Interaction between culture groups differentiated in this manner enlarges the available information pool of cultural options in which selection can operate, while at the same time altering the environment in which cultural adaptation takes place. Isolation reduces the size of the pool and, as drift occurs, facilitates cultural "speciation."[13]

Other processes counteract the tendency of cultures to change rapidly. Two are associated with the related hypotheses of cultural consistency and functional adjustment, according to which needs, values, and institutions tend to conform to a pattern.[14] Since "the land," at least in the short run, does tend to be stable, the particular set of relations between the culture and it can act as an important cultural anchor. Even in conditions of severe environmental stress, the tendency, in a partly closed system, might well be for an oscillatory pattern of cultural adjustment to appear.[15] These processes of adjustment do not operate at the same rate on all cultural elements,

---

[11] Dell Hymes, "Lexicostatistics So Far," *Current Anthropology*, 1 (Feb., 1960), pp. 3–44; Morris Swadesh, *The Origin and Diversification of Language* (Chicago and New York: Aldine-Atherton, 1971).

[12] Alan Lomax, *Folk Song Style and Culture* (Washington, D.C.: American Association for the Advancement of Science, Publication No. 88, 1968).

[13] On the concept of culture drift, see Fred Eggan, "Cultural Drift and Social Change," *Current Anthropology*, 4 (Oct., 1963), pp. 347–359. Processes of human genetic differentiation over space are relevant for cultural geography since gene transmittal seems as a rule to follow in its spatial ordering the aggregate pattern of other face to face information exchanges and since biological adaptation to the cultural-ecological circumstances may occur. On the latter point, see Frederick J. Simoons, "Primary Adult Lactose Intolerance and the Milking Habit: a Problem in Biological and Cultural Implications," *American Journal of Digestive Diseases*, n.s. 14 (Dec., 1969), pp. 819–836; 15 (Aug., 1970), pp. 695–710; Stephen L. Wiesenfeld, "Sickle-Cell Trait in Human Biological and Cultural Evolution," *Science*, 157 (8 Sept., 1967), pp. 1134–1140.

[14] John C. Harsanyi, "Explanation and Comparative Dynamics in Social Science," in Robert A. Manners and David Kaplan, *Theory in Anthropology* (Chicago: Aldine Publishing Co., 1968), pp. 89–96.

[15] For a careful attempt to construct systems models of ecological change in societies of varying complexity, see W. Firey, *Man, Mind, and Land: A Theory of Resource Use* (New York: Free Press of Glencoe, 1960).

and, even within the apparent order imposed on aggregate behavior by the analytical device of culture, contradictions abound.

Behavior more consistent with that of living systems[16] appears in ethnic groups, that is, groups that are aware of their shared identity and that seek or are obliged to preserve themselves as such. One mechanism of maintenance is to exercise a degree of selective control over the inflow of (cultural) information, for example, by symbolizing certain behavior traits as alien. Fredrik Barth has recently helped to clarify the necessary distinction between culture and ethnic group. Although the culture of ethnic groups cannot but be changing, ethnic identity at a given time and place is signalled by the use of selected symbolic traits from the totality of culture, and by the avoidance of others.[17] Ethnic boundaries act as so many screens with respect to the temporal and spatial flow of cultural information. Their location on the map of culture is not fixed: except in their common use of symbolic markers, ethnic groups need not be culturally uniform nor need people having much common culture belong to a common ethnos.

Consideration of culture in a distributional sense is obliged to be reductionist, following the method developed to analyze the areal variations of one component of culture, that is, language. The range of shared symbols is seen to vary from a limited local occurrence to a distribution that is worldwide. The existence of levels of cultural commonality is implied—local varieties, sub-cultures, cultures, families of cultures, global culture, as indeed, the cultural taxonomists have recognized. For example, speaking of the most simply organized groups of forest gatherers in southeastern Asia, A. L. Kroeber pointed out that comparative analysis of the content of their culture would show much of it to be widely shared with other peoples of the region (making it "derivatively secondary," in his view).[18]

This sequence of levels of cultural commonality, it should be noted, has no necessary evolutionary connotation; continentwide and worldwide distributions of some cultural features have existed for a long time (global cultural elements being distinguished from cultural invariants by temporal criteria). If one were to map many elements of culture together, how-

[16] James G. Miller, "Living Systems: Cross-Level Hypotheses," *Behavioral Science*, 10 (Oct., 1965), pp. 380–411.

[17] Fredrik Barth, ed., *Ethnic Groups and Boundaries: the Social Organization of Cultural Difference* (Boston: Little, Brown and Company, 1969). Barth's introductory essay (pp. 9–38) is especially valuable. On the same theme, see also Richard Weiss, "Kulturgrenzen und ihre Bestimmung durch volkskundliche Karten," *Studium Generale*, 5 (1952), pp. 363–373, translated into English as "Cultural Boundaries and the Ethnographic Map," in Wagner and Mikesell, *Cultural Geography*, pp. 62–74; and F. K. Lehman, "Ethnic Categories in Burma and the Theory of Social Systems," in Peter Kunstadter, ed., *Southeast Asia: Tribes, Minorities, Nations* (Princeton: Princeton University Press, 1967), Vol. 1, pp. 93–124. Lehman claims that "ethnic categories are formally like roles," and only indirectly describe the empirical characteristics of groups (pp. 106–107).

[18] A. L. Kroeber, "The Ancient *Oikumene* as an Historic Culture Aggregate," *Journal of the Royal Anthropological Institute of Great Britain and Ireland*, 75 (1945), pp. 9–20, reference on p. 18.

ever, one should not find a neat areal packaging of levels of shared commonality. As in the large-scale maps of the linguistic geographer, the isolines would cross the map in different directions, with different groups of lines only occasionally bunching perceptibly.[19]

These patterns can be treated as spatial expressions of processes mentioned previously—selective adaptation, circulation, drift, etc. What follows is chiefly a consideration of circulation and communication as they are related to the complex areal differentiation of culture.

SPATIAL INTERACTION AND CULTURAL DISTRIBUTIONS

A tentative model may be constructed showing that the nature of the interaction of a culture group with the land will have probable systemic concomitants in group spatial structure, that is, the size and density of the group, the spacing of members, the pattern of interaction among them, and the group's aggregate circulatory range—actually, a series of such ranges occurring at different levels of frequency. This in turn will have consequences for the frequency of interaction with other populations, characterized by a certain distribution and size, and, thus, for the balance between the within-group and between-group flow of cultural information as well as for the range of sources of information related to ecological decisions at a place, that is, the creation of a landscape.

In Figure 1, two hypothetical cases are shown graphically. The curves represent variation in the amount of I, "information," including authority with regard to landscape decisions at a place, O, reaching O from points located at a varying distance, D, from it. The curve a is intended to represent the case of a small autonomous culture group of simple technology; the second curve, b, suggests the condition characteristic of a society of developed technology and complex spatial organization.

Some of these cultural-ecological relationships have been investigated for societies with fairly simple organization, but the implications for the areal patterning of culture need elucidation.[20] How, for example, are lan-

---

[19] See, for example, the maps abstracted from some of the provincial linguistic atlases of France in Pierre Guiraud, *Patois et dialectes français* (Paris: Presses Universitaires de France, 1968). To my knowledge there has been no application of the techniques of spatial analysis (ref. Footnote 3) to the data of the linguistic geographer, despite the availability of quantifiable data in requisite numbers. Culture trait distributions are analysed in this way in Harold E. Driver and William C. Massey, "Comparative Studies of North American Indians," *Transactions of the American Philosophical Society*, 47 (July, 1957), pp. 165–456.

[20] See Mikesell, "Geographic Perspectives in Anthropology." Some of these relationships are articulated in Hans Bobek, "Die Hauptstufen der Gesellschafts- und Wirtschaftsentfaltung in geographischer Sicht," *Die Erde*, 90:3 (1959), pp. 259–298, reprinted as "The Main Stages in Socio-Economic Evolution from a Geographical Point of View," in Wagner and Mikesell, *Cultural Geography*, pp. 218–247. James D. Clarkson, "Ecology and Spatial Analysis," *Annals of the Association of American Geographers*, 60 (Dec., 1970), pp. 700–716, urges the combination of these two important emphases in American geography.

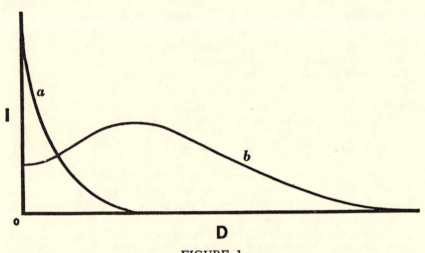

FIGURE 1

The Interaction of Two Culture
Groups with the Land

guage distributions related to circulation ranges and interaction fields, and
thus to the prevalent characteristics of particular ecologies?

One study that asks the question reports large dialect variation among
the patrilocal gathering bands in aboriginal northern Baja California,
where low density characterized the occupance of environments ranging
from coastal desert to mountain woodland.[21] The explanation of this language pattern and of within-band linguistic variability as a consequence
of band exogamy and low population density is sound. But the author fails
to take note of a change of scale when he argues that with the development
of village life as a consequence of increased population density, a lower-
ing of regional cultural and linguistic diversity would result. The interaction model used leads to a reduction of variation *within* a village, but
where, as is surmised, local endogamy is permitted, the much reduced
proportion of external transactions to internal ones could lead to greater
regional diversity, as is the case in some areas of sparse village settlement
in tropical forests.[22]

[21] Roger Owen, "Variety and Constraint in Cultural Adaptation," in Walter Buckley,
Modern Systems Research for the Behavioral Scientist: a Sourcebook (Chicago: Aldine
Publishing Co., 1968), pp. 415–419.
[22] At a different scale, the linguist Uriel Weinreich describes desert regions (in
India) as "places where we would expect communication to be impeded" in trying to
explain an apparent lack of bilingualism in a situation of apparent linguistic diversity,
both partly statistical fictions, as it happens; Uriel Weinreich, "Functional Aspects of
Indian Bilingualism," *Word*, 13 (Aug., 1957), pp. 203–233. A different assessment of
the nature and effect of communications networks in arid environments is provided
by Arnold Toynbee, *A Study of History: The Growth of Civilizations* (London: Ox-

LANDSCAPE AS SPATIAL EXPRESSION OF CULTURE: QUESTIONS OF SCALE

These considerations of areal scope have evident importance for the particular way in which geographers have apprehended culture, that is, through description of the cultural landscape. Much effort has been devoted to a puzzling out of the origins of cultural landscapes, the palimpsest, in Sauer's metaphor, on which the past record of culture is imprinted only to be effaced and inscribed over many times. Where continuity of culture is maintained in place for centuries, the landscape created may exhibit a rich, esthetically satisfying, modular integration of forms and spatial patterns, consistently replicated. But cultural landscapes may also look nondescript, disordered, blighted, and ephemeral. Deciphering the palimpsest is an elucidation of historical cultural ecology—an attempt to understand through landscape the relations between culture and land, and this task is greatly complicated by the variable scope of culture and the variable range of the authority to make decisions about the land, as illustrated in Figure 1. In many cultural landscape studies, the geographer's bias has been toward an analytical framework that corresponds to curve a, although the situation may correspond more closely to curve b, as with rural European societies in the early 1900's. A change of scale, and hence of technique, would seem to be appropriate in such circumstances.

Comparable changes of scale and perspective (perhaps the landscapes of city and highway can only be apprehended and communicated on film?) may be undertaken by those who would have the landscape tell us more, revealing the deeper nature of man and his cultures. This phenomenological approach to landscape has been advocated by Yi-fu Tuan, following a series of brilliant exploratory essays, in a recent eloquent statement of purpose.[23] One may suggest that many of the speculations and discoveries of the phenomenologist are susceptible to controlled investigation; the phenomonologist should be the indispensable critic of the geographer as scientist, and vice versa.[24]

The phenomenological view may be especially valuable for the recognition of landscape symbols that are taken as ethnic markers, if care is taken to apprehend images of very different scale; the cultural geographer may then ask how these are related to different ecological circumstances. Landmarks which may endure for long periods, as cultural markers of

---

ford University Press, 1934), vol. 3, pp. 391–394: "The 'Conductivity' of Nomadism as Illustrated in the Diffusion of Languages."

[23] Yi-fu Tuan, "Geography, Phenomenology, and the Study of Human Nature," *Canadian Geographer*, 15 (Fall, 1971), pp. 181–192. See also Edward Relph, "An Enquiry into the Relations between Phenomenology and Geography," *Canadian Geographer*, 14 (Fall, 1970), pp. 193–201.

[24] Beginning from much the same interest in the landscape of literature as did Tuan, Gerhard Hard now looks to the application of quantitative analytical and psychological techniques to aid in understanding man's symbolization of landscape; Gerhard Hard, "Noch einmal: 'Landschaft als objektivierter Geist'; zur Herkunft und zur forschungslogischen Analyse eines Gedankens," *Die Erde*, 101:3 (1970), pp. 171–197.

ethnicity go, can become, through their shared symbolic value, an especially powerful means of ethnic identification. In this way, the sense of place as home is expressed—be it for family, tribe, or nation. There is little agreement about the nature of human territorial behavior, and one may take exception to Tuan's ascription of a biological basis to human attachment to place.[25] Ethological evidence rather suggests a cultural origin, a consequence of investment of place with symbols of the group's identity. On a more complex level, groups may be maintained through symbolic attachment to a quasifictive place, as in the case of the Jewish and other diasporas. Gypsies dispense with even this degree of symbolic association with place, aspiring only to find a home, encapsulated in their separate identity, *anywhere* in the alien social world. The apparent rootlessness— let us call it *achoria*— of men in modern technologically advanced societies appears as a systemic consequence of scale changes in the relationships previously hypothesized to exist between ecology, circulation, and culture. It is the probable biological "home," that is, the familiar social field, that remains such, however widely spread. That roots in place are not natural to man is the wanderer's discovery, which Kazantsakis puts in Ulysses' mouth: "My soul, your voyages have been your native land."[26]

SPATIAL ORDER IN SOCIAL INTERACTION

Circulation and interaction entail a cost of overcoming distance—"the first hard rule of economic geography," in Sauer's phrase,[27] however variable the cost in different cultural and ecological situations; this distance-cost should be expressed in the spatial ordering of consequent cultural patterns.[28] Useful indications about such patterns are provided by recent work using a variety of spatial analytical techniques, such as the work by Torsten Hägerstrand and his followers on migration and diffusion, and Peter Gould's imaginative excursions in search of principles of spatial order.[29] Spatial order has long been recognized in cultural patterning. The vocabulary of spatial dynamics—flow, stream, front, wedge, island, backwater—is basic to the models implicit in the work of Ratzel and Sauer,[30] and in some more explicit recent expositions by cultural geographers.[31]

[25] Tuan, "Geography and Phenomenology," p. 189.
[26] Nikos Kazantsakis, *The Odyssey: a Modern Sequel*. Trans., Kimon Friar (New York: Simon and Schuster, 1958) p. 509.
[27] Leighly, *Land and Life*, p. 308.
[28] Gunnar Olsson, *Distance and Human Interaction: a Review and Bibliography*. (Philadelphia: Regional Science Research Institute Bibliography Series No. 2, 1965).
[29] L. A. Brown and E. G. Moore, "Diffusion Research in Geography: a Perspective," *Progress in Geography: International Reviews of Current Research*, 1 (1969), pp. 119–158; Ronald Abler, John S. Adams, and Peter Gould, *Spatial Organization: the Geographer's View of the World* (Englewood Cliffs: Prentice-Hall, 1971).
[30] Friedrich Ratzel, *Anthropogeographie* (2nd ed.; Stuttgart: J. Engelhorn, 1899–1912), 2 vols.
[31] E.g., D. W. Meinig, "The Mormon Culture Region: Strategies and Patterns in the Geography of the American West, 1847–1964," *Annals of the Association of American Geographers*, 55 (June, 1965), pp. 191–220; "A Macrogeography of Western Imperial-

Nevertheless, a number of recently developed approaches in quantitative geographical analysis and in other disciplines point to the existence of some little explored questions about the spatial arrangement of culture.

Work on such themes as territoriality, proxemics, and social space, in which geographers have played a small part,[32] treats in one way or another the relation of group spatial micro-structure (location, orientation, direction, and frequency of the movement of individuals) to communication, and hence with conditions affecting cultural interchange. We might reduce the scale of observation to discover whether similar relationships will still obtain. How do the positioning and spacing of structures in a settlement, and of settlements within a region, reflect spatial micro-structure and affect cultural communication?[33] Should we expect the microscopic patterns of individual spatial behavior to have relevance for the structuring of macroscopic spatial relations?[34] The enquiry proposed here may be taken as the spatial analogue of the provocative question raised by Francis L. K. Hsu as to the direction that certain key patterns of family relationship may exert on the larger social structure.[35]

In American geography, rural settlements are not commonly looked at as fields of social interaction, and analysis of internal spatial order is mostly confined to a consideration of economic inputs and outputs.[36] We may know how the labor and time expenditures associated with different agricultural uses determine their location in an Indian village,[37] but cannot find an equivalent social calculus of costs and benefits in relation to the village agglomeration itself, the compact grouping of perhaps a thousand people in one place.

Rural settlements are nodes in a social network, but social circulation patterns have been perhaps too readily equated with those of economic

---

ism: Some Morphologies of Moving Frontiers of Political Control," in Fay Gale and Graham H. Lawton, eds., *Settlement and Encounter: Geographical Studies Presented to Sir Grenfell Price* (Melbourne: Oxford University Press, 1969), pp. 213–240; and C. F. J. Whebell, "Corridors: A Theory of Urban Systems," *Annals of the Association of American Geographers*, 59 (March, 1969), pp. 1–26.

[32] David Stea, "Space, Territory, and Human Movements," *Landscape*, 15 (Autumn, 1965), pp. 13–16; Anne Buttimer, "Social Space in Interdisciplinary Perspective: Two French Pioneers," *Geographical Review*, 59 (July, 1969), pp. 417–426.

[33] Amos Rapoport, *House Form and Culture* (Englewood Cliffs: Prentice-Hall, 1969).

[34] For example, is there any validity at all to Ardrey's hunch that the "noyau" as micro-structural unit of socio-spatial organization leads to the inhibition of successful nation-building? Robert Ardrey, *The Territorial Imperative* (New York: Athenaeum, 1966).

[35] Francis L. K. Hsu, ed., *Kinship and Culture* (Chicago: Aldine Publishing Co., 1971).

[36] Michael Chisholm, *Rural Settlement and Land Use: an Essay in Location* (New York: Science Editions, 1967).

[37] P. M. Blaikie, "Spatial Organization of Agriculture in Some North Indian Villages: Part I," *Transactions*, Institute of British Geographers, 52 (March, 1971), pp. 1–40.

circulation.[38] In the Indian situation with which I am familiar, rural marriage networks extend in a lattice that links a single village with two or three hundred others without the appearance of a significant hierarchy. There are obvious implications for the historical flow of cultural information: these networks do not need market centers and regional towns to maintain them and they are capable of integrating areas and populations of remarkable size. One can estimate that through the sum of its affinal links a village today in the western Gangetic Plain can be in direct touch with a potential information field of a quarter of a million rural people.

One would like to know the cultural consequences of such spatial structures, but Indian data at the requisite scale are scanty. G. W. Skinner's remarkable model of social networks in rural China provides a basis for comparison.[39] Skinner found a regular geometric structure of social interaction corresponding closely to the pattern of market areas, and was further able to discern a coincidence of local dialect areas and market areas. Because of the spatial structure of Indian marriage networks, local dialect distributions ought to be much less definite than the Chinese ones, and distinctive speech forms ought to have a wider range. Linguistic investigations in the western Gangetic Plain show that both village to village and within-village speech variants are found within the spatial framework of a commonly used regional dialect.[40] But without comprehensive mapping or a systematic village sampling, the relationships between social circulation and cultural pattern remain uncertain.

Reversing the procedure, I have tried to detect historical paths of circulation by analyzing the distribution of castes as recorded in censuses of the British period.[41] In the middle and western Gangetic Plain, many of these groups occur widely, covering tens of thousands of square miles. Most of these caste distributions have a distinctive pattern of their own and these overlap widely, a composite pattern suggesting that pronounced circulation barriers have been absent. When place to place variation in the composition of the many-layered caste "sandwich" is measured, however, a pattern of gentle and steep gradients in the surface appears, the sharper

---

[38] E.g., Brian J. L. Berry, *Geography of Market Centers and Retail Distribution* (Englewood Cliffs: Prentice-Hall, 1967), p. 98, where the expectation is expressed that in areas of "tribal" or "underdeveloped" economies, standard market communities will be "identical with" social communities.

[39] G. William Skinner, "Marketing and Social Structure in Rural China: Part I," *Journal of Asian Studies*, 24 (Nov., 1964), pp. 3–44.

[40] John J. Gumperz, "Dialect Differences and Social Stratification in a North Indian Village," *American Anthropologist*, 60 (Aug., 1958), pp. 668–692; "Phonological Differences in Three Hindi Dialects," *Language*, 34 (April–June, 1958), pp. 212–224; "Speech Variation and the Study of Indian Civilization," *American Anthropologist*, 63 (Oct., 1961), pp. 976–988. Patterns and processes of dialect differentiation in northern India are summarized in Robbins Burling, *Man's Many Voices: Language in Its Cultural Context* (New York: Holt, Rinehart and Winston, 1970), pp. 103–116.

[41] David E. Sopher, *Essays in the Spatial Analysis of Indian Society* (in preparation). Castes designated by the census are usually clusters of related or generically similar endogamous groups.

breaks corresponding to expectable circulation impediments, such as the line of the Ganges River in the western plain. The weakly defined plural ethnic regions that are emerging from this analysis show some correspondence with major dialect regions, while the circulatory pattern implied seems unrelated to contemporary migration flows.

The pattern of movement necessary for the transmission of culture may generate a cultural surface that exhibits a gradient of receptivity to other information circulating along similar paths. With communications today rapidly and cheaply overcoming distance, the spatial ordering of innovation adoptions may be related to the existence of such a cultural response surface rather than to the pattern of information flow. A study in Sweden has found a spatial ordering of *values*—apart from the effects of such ecological characteristics as occupation and education—along an urban-rural gradient.[42] These urban-rural cultural differences may affect the rate of spread of innovations outward from the city, usually complementing distance-friction. The ambivalence of the country vis-à-vis the city and its creations and of city toward country, the variable character of these perceptions, and the nature and consequences of the filters they impose on the flow of information are important cultural geographic themes, though neglected in this country.[43] The diffusion of city ways to the country, however haltingly, is traceable in the past, prior to modern developments in transportation and communication. In Europe, the prestige of urban ways of living is recognized to have contributed centuries ago to the modification of peasant houses,[44] and the eighteenth-century life of court and city centered on Paris have been seen as sources of such varied cultural innovations, appearing in accessible rural regions, as certain fashionable linguistic usages[45] and secularist ideas and indifference to the Church.[46] When cultural replacement takes place at the center and a considerable time lag must be allowed for diffusion, what is current culture at the periphery will be archaic at the center. Such a process, enormously speeded up, is seen in the pattern of adoptions of contemporary fashions, mediated through a hierarchical spatial structure.

Such processes of spatial ordering give culture regions their internal structure, such as the morphology suggested by Donald Meinig for the Mormon culture region comprising Utah and parts of Idaho, Wyoming, New Mexico, Arizona, and Nevada.[47] In Meinig's scheme, arrived at by a

[42] Harald Swedner, *Ecological Differentiation of Habits and Attitudes* (Lund: C. W. K. Gleerup, 1960).

[43] This neglect may itself be an indication of cultural bias. Conflicting images of the city are evident in the positions expressed by participants in a symposium discussion of the topic some years ago, as recorded in Thomas, *Man's Role*, pp. 434–448.

[44] Wirth, "Allgemeine Kulturgeographie," p. 172.

[45] Albert Dauzat, *La géographie linguistique* (Paris: E. Flammarion, 1922). An example is the use of *pomme de terre* to replace terms cognate with "potato."

[46] Fernand Boulard, *An Introduction to Religious Sociology: Pioneer Work in France*, trans. M. J. Jackson (London: Darton, Longman & Todd, Ltd., 1960).

[47] Meinig, "Mormon Culture Region."

careful examination of historical-geographical data, the spatial organization of the Mormon region consists of three zones: core, domain, and sphere. The core area is a centralized zone of concentration, displaying the greatest intensity of organization, strength, and homogeneity of the features characteristic of the culture. It is also the focus of circulation, but "is not the most Mormon in the sense of numerical or relative dominance."[48] The domain is where the culture is dominant but also less intensely and complexly developed than in the core; linkages are more tenuous, and regional peculiarities are evident. The sphere is an indefinite zone of outer influence and, often, peripheral acculturation.[49]

We can construct a model that combines internal and external circulation, and derive from it spatial effects in the patterning of culture and landscape that correspond to the chief features of the Mormon region's spatial organization. With a dynamic center and focus, internal circulation alone might generate a concave cone surface expressing simple distance-decay in the intensity of interaction and, hence, of cultural vigor and dominance. The partial overcoming of distance, especially near the center, by the institution of an intense circulation—such as that characterizing the broad-based Mormon ecclesiastical organization—produces a scutate surface, a gentle dome topping the truncated base of a concave cone. But the core is also as a rule the head-link between the sub-system and the larger environing cultural or ethnic system, connecting the former with a higher level in the hierarchical structuring of information circulation. It is thus the area most exposed to a concerted flow of both ideas and people from the outside and becomes the most cosmopolitan part of the region.[50]

The domain, exhibiting strong internal cohesion, is able to screen out or retard the flow of identifiably alien and incompatible cultural features, achieving a high level of cultural exclusiveness, together with some regional variation because of its extent. The effect of external circulation on the core and of the domain's negative response to exotic features is to leave a steep-sloped central indentation or crater in the shield-shaped surface of cultural dominance. In cross-section, it would appear not unlike curve *b* in Figure 1. In the sphere, the border of the shield, three different locational consequences of space-ordering processes may be combined: interaction with proximate and interpenetrating border cultures;[51] distance-decay of the core culture; less effective resistance than in the domain to

---

48 *Ibid.*, p. 215.

49 Meinig also places in a separate category the more distant Mormon communities within large cities, but these are not considered here.

50 The concept of the cultural head-link is advanced in O. H. K. Spate, "Factors in the Development of Capital Cities," *Geographical Review*, 32 (Oct., 1942), pp. 622–631. In some cases, the principal external link does not connect directly with the core area; such situations are inherently unstable, but the degree of stability appears to depend on the balance between internal and external information flow.

51 In the Mormon case, interaction with neighboring cultures is associated with a reinforcement of practices that help to maintain identity, although these may be archaic by core standards.

alien cultural information that may be diffused from the cosmopolitan core over or through the more resistant medium of the domain. Among surfaces that appear to be described in this way, one may think of the surface of French monolingualism in the province of Quebec, or, inverted, the impact of Christian missionary activity on a predominantly non-Christian country, such as Thailand.

THE CULTURAL SIGNIFICANCE OF LOCATION

These spatial models give location a cultural weighting that itself becomes an element of cultural variation from place to place. Location thus connotes a degree of connectedness to the cultural network of the society; it is also, *ceteris paribus*, a consideration in the assignment of status. The use of locational terms as a discriminant of cultural and social standing is a commonplace of our language: consider such familiar current expressions as "in," "where it's at," "the sticks," "the boonies,"[52] "Middle America," and that astounding paradox, "inner city."

As relative location changes with alterations in the circulation pattern, so may cultural and social standing. In developing nations, a wide cultural gap separates country from primate city, where cosmopolitan life styles are concentrated. A person with some education living in the country may develop a strong sense of locational inferiority that conflicts sharply with his sense of place. The meaning of location for social and cultural position is clearly recognized in the attempt to change it in China, where, as part of the "permanent" cultural revolution, a continual spatial redistribution of intellectuals, technicians, and functionaries has been undertaken. A note in passing: a formal relationship has been hypothesized between social order and spatial order at a local scale, such that in ostensibly open societies, physical spacing appears as a social ranking device (e.g., the residential areas of American cities), while societies with formal social stratification require only a symbolic distancing.[53] The usefulness of this concept at a regional or national scale is not clear. Perhaps it needs to be tied to the range of information. Might it have been, for example, because there was not the circulation of information to confer an appropriate status significance on the location of regional lords in Tokugawan Japan, that the court required them or their representatives to be present in the capital to affirm their subordinate status in the visible hierarchy?

This discussion of location as a social variable serves to make the point that in much social theory, essentially non-spatial, society may be said to extend uniformly in space. A pictorial analogy would be the text-book diagram of an undisturbed sedimentary rock formation, the strata extending

[52] I.e., "boondocks," from Tagalog *bundok*, the highlands (of Luzon, occupied by warlike pagan peoples at the turn of the century).

[53] See, for example, John B. Calhoun, "The Role of Space in Animal Sociology," *Journal of Social Issues*, 22 (Oct., 1966) pp. 46–58; Walter Firey, "Sentiment and Symbolism as Ecological Variables," *American Sociological Review*, 10 (April, 1945), pp. 141–148.

horizontally across the profile. The focus of social theory is on dynamic "vertical" relationships. What the cultural geographer sees is a more complicated "geologic" cross-section: "dipping strata" of status and power as a function of distance; discordance in the alignment of strata along "fault lines," a serviceable metaphor for the racial interface; igneous extrusives and intrusives, ancient indigenous ethnicities or recent exotic ones. He sees the race of many inter-braided histories, whose divergence and convergence is not at an end—different cultures, different perceptions of group identity, different working beliefs about men and societies. The potential cultural creativity of "theories" of society or culture is nevertheless recognized. Marxist, Parsonsian, McLuhanite—in greatly differing degree, such constructs provide frameworks for "observation" which influence the behavior observed to the degree that they are communicated, and, as part of the culture of the observed, screen what they themselves perceive.[54]

TOWARD A GEOGRAPHY OF CONTEMPORARY CULTURE

The greatly changed scale of interaction with the land, reach of information, and areal scope of culture that characterize complex, technologically sophisticated societies oblige the cultural geographer to change his own methods and scale of investigation in order to deal with them. The adding of new tools to his kit has been slow because of practical difficulties but also because a degree of cultural bias lingers. Characteristically, attention is given to subcultures that *can* be clearly defined, such as the Mormons and nineteenth-century European immigrants in American cities. What the consequences of information flow today may be in the genesis of cultures of large dimension and what may be the nature of the landscapes these cultures create and express themselves by are questions that are still approached only tentatively. A problem is to calibrate the effect of information flow of different ranges and intensities. For example, we are not at all clear about the effect of mass media on culture. Among many unknowns, or large uncertainties, are the varying selectivity and receptivity of media audiences—readers, listeners, viewers—with regard to media messages, and the cultural effect of a variety of apparently conflicting media messages. In particular, how does the media message affect the microscopic structure of society? Since this structure appears to be quite stable, how does it relate to the macroscopic social order, as the latter accommodates developments in communications and other technologies? It is becoming clear that the prevailing model of modern urban industrial society is properly that of an industrialized and urbanized western European society that became such at a particular moment in history. It appears that this society has had a different microscopic structure—or range of structures—from, let us say, Japanese or Indian or southern Italian society. What is not clear

---

[54] See Alvin W. Gouldner, *The Coming Crisis in Western Sociology* (New York: Basic Books, 1970) for a penetrating analysis of the beliefs (background assumptions) underlying contemporary social theory.

is how far and in what ways the macroscopic structure of industrialized Japanese society, etc. is therefore predictably different from that of the West.

The increase of a common cultural content among the people of the world seems to be an undeniable consequence of developments in communications, yet the strength of ethnic identity, especially national identity, not only persists but seems to be increasing, although there is some merging and refashioning of identities. Barth's explication, applied at a national scale, makes it clear that this is no contradiction: closer interaction among ethnic groups can have different consequences for culture and ethnicity. Thus, increased interaction between, say, native French speakers and native English speakers in Canada may generate at the same time both an inevitably greater cultural sharing through increased bilingualism, and a heightened awareness of separate ethnic identity as well as increased tension between the two groups. To the casual television viewer of the violence between Protestant and Catholic civilians in northern Ireland, the behavioral shibboleths that might serve to distinguish members of the two groups—apart from their reciprocal hatred—are undetectable.

There are, of course, huge impediments to a worldwide flow of information. Powerful barriers and screens channel and filter the flow, operating even in the absence of language barriers and effective distance constraints. For example, the capital of Canada is only two-thirds as far from Syracuse, where I live, as New York, yet it might be across the Atlantic to judge by the space it is given in the local information media. Increase of internal communication can have the effect of increasing the *relative* isolation of places outside, while strengthening cultural solidarity within. Thus, the present steady growth of literacy in India may weaken rather than strengthen internal cohesion (in the absence of reinforcement of common symbols and accelerated development of inter-regional circulation) because the increase in literacy is mostly in the regional languages and is likely to strengthen the ethnic identity of their speakers. How such high-intensity internal communication systems can create or strengthen the ethnic value of selected landscape symbols has been demonstrated in a century and more of modern European history. As internal cultural commonality increased in partly closed communication fields, particularly with regard to the adoption of ethnic symbols, national boundaries became deeply incised in the cultural surface of Europe. This process appears to be on the increase elsewhere in the world.

The effect of communications is more problematic in relation to regional cultures within national territories, such as have been a traditional concern of cultural geography. Given the scales at which he has customarily worked, the cultural geographer is likely to be uneasy with the gross, apparently *ad hoc* regionalizations that are used in the sampling of American public opinion. Nevertheless, he recognizes that these surveys appear to provide strong evidence of persistent cultural differentiation, despite large temporal changes in cultural content. This regional differentiation within a "mass society" can be inferred as the effect of locational difference; of ethnic selectivity however weakly developed (one example would be possible Southern attitudes to innovations from the North); and of the varying content of formal education which reinforces family and local community transmission of regionally differentiated attitudes and histories from one generation to another. Ways of adapting the methods of landscape study to cultural differences at this scale need to be refined. Another useful direction would be to analyse regional variation in the content and consumption of mass media. A preliminary study of American mass magazine circulation discloses regional variation in total volume and in magazine preference, not all of which is to be associated with such ecological variables as urbanism, age structure, occupation, education, and income. Undefined regional factors seem to be related to part of the variation.

The work of D. Elliston Allen, a market research specialist in Britain, affirms the usefulness of this approach.[55] While landscape and other symbols of regional ethnicity may have a stronger hold on people in Britain than in the United States, the internal circulation of information, e.g., of metropolitan newspapers, can transmit it to the whole population more effectively. Despite the reality of a mass taste, Allen finds that, when they are collated, regional variations in a large number of apparently trivial consumer preferences suggest the outlines of consistent regional cultures.

The relevance of other media for the formation of consistent value systems, including attitudes toward the land, must be apprehended by the cultural geographer. By visually dramatizing "the ecology issue," for instance, it seems that television has encouraged the formulation of mass decisions regarding the American landscape. Yet there are at present no firm answers to questions about the role of broadcast media in the formation of culture, and whatever commonality of culture is generated need not connote the generation of common identity, as McLuhan has noted of radio.[56] Attention has been given to the presumed homogenizing effects on national culture (and, potentially, on international culture) of developments in transportation and communications; one might also look at the reinforcement they may provide to the social micro-structure by their effects on spatial interaction patterns and the possibilities they offer for the creation of new identity groupings. The general availability in the United States of cheap domestic air travel and long-distance telephone communication may be effecting a "retribalizing" by renewing and strengthening intimate social compacts among members of families, communities, or ethnic groups otherwise widely dispersed by the complex spatial organization of the economy. (One recalls poor Portnoy, prisoner of those formidable allies, his mother and Ma Bell.) Even before World War II,

55 D. Elliston Allen, *British Tastes: An Enquiry into the Likes and Dislikes of the British Consumer* (London: Hutchinson and Co., Ltd., 1968).

56 Marshall McLuhan, *Understanding Media* (New York: McGraw-Hill Book Co., 1964), p. 267.

widely separated but related Gypsy bands in Europe were receiving long-distance telephone calls and letters through trusted contacts, thus keeping informed of each other's movements.[57] Telephone and bush-plane contacts form communities among the residents of widely scattered ranches in the Australian outback. And the whole youth "counter-culture" in the United States and abroad, with its unusually ephemeral ties to place, is largely maintained by these systems of cheap long-distance communication.[58]

The concept of culture has never been more elusive in its geographical application than in the world of today. We may recall the situation noted earlier among the aborigines of Baja California, where internal linguistic variability was seen as a consequence of proportionally high inflow of external information in the form of different mother tongues. By analogy, internal cultural variability—among communities, ethnic groups, nations —should be unusually high today. As the scope of cultures becomes extended, landscape anchors less effective, and circulation more intense, does not culture also become increasingly plastic, increasingly fluid? The challenge to cultural geography is to discover whether, with appropriate changes of scale and technique, it can still use the concept of culture successfully in elucidating man's present and future, as it has his past.

[57] Jan Yoors, *The Gypsies* (New York: Simon and Schuster, 1967), pp. 87, 88, 103.
[58] Even seemingly trivial indices of this kind need not be ignored. May we, for instance, find meaning for a map of social linkages in a recent report that tells of the annual exchange in the United States of between 15 and 20 billion greeting cards?

THE IDEA OF CULTURE IN THE SOCIAL SCIENCES: CRITICAL AND SUPPLEMENTARY OBSERVATIONS*

LOUIS SCHNEIDER

University of Texas at Austin

THE OBSERVATION, BY JAMES BOON,[1] THAT THE IDEA OR CONCEPT OF CUL-ture is "tenacious to a degree which suggests it is indispensable" will seem persuasive to many; and it may be taken to reinforce the statement in the Introduction to these papers that "the idea of culture in the social sciences is worth consideration again and again." But the papers themselves, granted their merits, occasion a certain unease. The present commentary is designed to give expression to this unease and to suggest some turns of thought that may help to make the idea of culture a bit more "useful" in the social sciences than it now is. If the idea has a potential organizing power, or even merely illuminating quality, not yet realized in the social sciences, there are still large difficulties in the way of this sort of happy possibility, and, as also seems to be the case to this commentator, there are matters that need more emphasis than they are here given.

The following observations divide into four sections. A start is made with a section on "Conceptual Looseness." Then I have commented on how "culture" is handled in the several social science areas by the contributors to this symposium. " 'Culture' in the Social Sciences" has seemed an appropriate enough heading here. I have given a third section the label, "Notions Relating to Culture in Need of Further Development." The contributors of the papers worked within strict limitations of space and were at the same time allowed their own preoccupations. These circumstances at least partly explain a near-omission of concern with a number of notions pertaining to culture that I believe it would be profitable to try to develop further. Here I comment on matters that "everybody knows" but that it appears unwise to forget. Finally, I have not hesitated to express a critical reaction against certain tendencies in social science today that strike me as being likely to create as much difficulty in cultural theory as anywhere else and that I present under the heading of "Misplaced Humanism."

CONCEPTUAL LOOSENESS

When Tylor wrote his famous definition of culture—"Culture . . . is that complex whole which includes knowledge, belief, art, morals, law, custom, and any other capabilities and habits acquired by man as a member of society"—a definition reprinted here for perhaps the ten thousandth time—

---

* I am indebted to Charles M. Bonjean for helpful comments on this statement.
[1] P. 1.

he could not possibly have foreseen what would happen to this reasonably sagacious formulation. Tylor's definition appears to have become inordinately swollen if we go by what social scientists do, at any rate in their less formal moods.

One is tempted to say that by now just about everything has been thrown into "culture" but the kitchen sink. But hold. The kitchen sink clearly has to be thrown in too. There is that wondrous and gargantuan category called "material culture," which takes in pants, textile machinery, houses, computers, salt-shakers, sledgehammers, blackboards, children's toys—and of course the kitchen sink among yet other things. "Material culture" is still fairly well established as an anthropological and sociological term and few of its users are likely to repudiate it despite its defects. To some, it will undoubtedly seem intellectually prudish to quarrel about it and strained and whimsical, in particular, to suggest that if something is material it is not cultural, and vice versa. But "material culture" may not be so terribly bad after all. It is a worse trouble that people have somehow gotten into "culture" too.

Putting people into culture is a sad maneuver into which social scientists slip time and again. Boon, who is certainly not an unusually loose writer, remarks,[2] "What the outside observer frequently confronts are responses of some well-versed *member of the culture* to some inarticulate, unversed interrogator." (My italics.) Pye refers[3] to "the study of groups of men, *that is* a sub-culture." (My italics.) Berkhofer writes of "specific, individual cultures *into which all men are divided.*" (My italics.) Any number of others, not contributors to this symposium, do the same kind of thing. In the course of his paper Berkhofer also quotes the anthropologist Stephen Tyler thus: "It is highly unlikely that the *members of the culture* ever see their cultures as. . . ."[4] (My italics.) But the earlier Edward Tylor, let us note again, listed knowledge, belief, art, morals, law, custom, capabilities and habits acquired in society. Is it tiresome or dull to ask, How can a person be a *member* of "knowledge," and so on? To say that a person is a member of a culture or a subculture is rather like saying that the Catholic ritual of the mass is a member of a street corner gang. In the worst case— and that case all too frequently confronts us—laden with an enormous freight of toys and tools and machines and practically all the people (certainly, all the persons or role-playing agents) in the world, in addition to the content of the "proper" categories Tylor originally included, the concept of culture becomes so "heavy" that it must end by depressing us all.

This may be thought to be taking undue advantage of somewhat accidental if unfortunate turns of phrase. I believe not. There is some merit in Pye's reference[5] to "an almost lawlike tendency towards fuzziness of all

[2] Pp. 28–29.
[3] P. 66.
[4] See above, P. 93 and Stephen Tyler, *Cognitive Anthropology* (New York: Holt, Rinehart & Winston, 1969), p. 5.
[5] P. 67.

usable concepts in the social sciences." Current anthropology texts tend to reinforce Pye's notion. Hammond writes in his recent text, "Wherever the term *culture* is used alone here it is intended to encompass the somewhat more restricted concept of *society*." Hammond's glossary does not define culture but it does define society as "a generally large group of people who share a common culture" (although it also makes society refer to "the system of interpersonal and intergroup relationships" among the members of such a group).[6] It is not easy to avoid the suspicion that Hammond, too, has some inclination to inflate the concept of culture by putting people into it. Harris's recent text presents a brief, sensible discussion of the terms "social" and "cultural," stating that "society" signifies a group of people who are dependent on one another for survival and well being, while culture refers to "a society's repertory of behavioral, cognitive, and emotional patterns." But later in the book there comes the almost standard lapse into referring to "members of the culture" when Harris means humans or persons, *not* items in a "repertory of patterns."[7]

The situation is not always so desperate. At least one merit of Parsons' paper and of the additional work he has done in this field is that his careful differentiations of concepts make it more difficult to corrupt cultural and social analysis on certain lines. Parsons, it should also be remarked, is surprisingly close to Tylor. His categories for what he calls the four primary subsectors of the cultural system overlap appreciably with Tylor's sheer listing of items. Parsons writes of a cognitive sector; and Tylor lists knowledge first. There is a moral-evaluative sector, for Parsons; and Tylor lists "morals, law, custom." Parsons refers to an expressive sector; and Tylor lists art. While for Parsons there is a constitutive symbolic sector, for Tylor there is belief, and he unquestionably means to include religious belief. It is enough to note the broad overlap. Tylor did not include "society" (as group) or "social system" (as scheme of interrelationships). Even when he added "capabilities and habits," he clearly indicated that he meant those that are "acquired by man as a member of society." (To include any and all "capabilities and habits" would involve still another terminological inflation moving toward the complete stultification of the concept of culture.) The concept of culture is "large" enough even when it is held within "proper" bounds.

Parsons' work in this whole conceptual area, however one may react to it in detail, is far more extensive than Tylor's, and it is certainly not necessary to hold Tylor up as an unsurpassable model. But it is necessary to insist on the point, even at this late date, when social scientists have repeatedly mulled over some of their essential terms, that there is still insufficient clarity among them about "culture" and cognate categories, which

[6] Peter B. Hammond, *An Introduction to Cultural and Social Anthropology* (New York: Macmillan, 1971), pp. 5, 419.

[7] Marvin Harris, *Culture, Man, and Nature: An Introduction to General Anthropology* (New York: Crowell, 1971, pp. 136–137, 345.

too often are messy items. It is granted that there are notable exceptions to this, and it would obviously be irrational to stand in the way of creative efforts at redefinition that reflect more than merely verbal issues, while it is useless to try to "legislate" a uniformity of definitions for all. The crucial matter is plainly whether the confusions that exist stand in the way of making the idea of culture a more potent social-science instrument. I am persuaded that they do, and this persuasion on my part should gain strength from the general burden of the present observations.

There are other things that come up in the present papers that it is convenient to comment on here. Berkhofer has a tendency (to which I shall also refer again below) to associate the idea or concept of culture with broad theories of history and society that appears to me to be questionable. He argues[8] that Tylor's definition, in its enumeration of the components of culture, "unlike modern usage, implied the equal importance of mental, behavioral and artifactual aspects." Tylor's definition does not mention artifacts. Nor is it clear that it "implied" anything like "the equal importance" referred to. It did indeed present a listing. It sought to define a concept. It indicated the range of that concept via the procedure of listing. *Qua* definition it did not propose an entire social theory or theory of history. It is possible that Tylor was misguided to be as concerned about culture as he was. But that is something quite different. (And it is not necessary to deny that ostensibly "neutral" definitions can conceal or half conceal all sorts of orientations that need the full light of day or that this often happens in social science.)

When Berkhofer contends[9] that at a certain juncture social scientists moved from "a meaning of culture based upon the equality of physical artifacts, outer behavior, and ideation to a definition purely in terms of the latter," he may have some justification. But again I would suggest that, in line with his general thesis, he confuses matters by over-reliance on his own critical stance toward the Kroeber-Kluckhohn definition. He addresses this definition apparently as a kind of central item in his effort to document the change in orientation of social scientists just referred to. He quotes Kroeber and Kluckhohn as saying that culture consists of "patterns, explicit and implicit, of and for behavior acquired and transmitted by symbols." Kroeber and Kluckhohn, then, included "behavior," at least on their terms. Precisely what did they miss or fail to stress that makes their view excessively "ideational"? Might they have included "outer behavior" with a clear indication that they thought of it as separate from meanings, values, and the like? Such "behavior" would hardly be worth considering. Might they have included "unpatterned behavior" (in order to avoid celebrating a presumed and ideologically tainted consensus)? They were certainly aware of the after all elementary point that there are such things as innovative behavior or behavior that defies "central" or "accepted" or

[8] P. 79.
[9] P. 79.

general-normative patterns, "deviant" behavior, "conflicting" behavior. Perhaps this awareness should have been incorporated into their quoted general definition? Their definition referred to cultural "embodiments in artifacts." Might they then have emphasized that artifacts, being artifacts, are "material" or have a "material" side? The point seems obvious. It is of course possible, once more, that the idea of culture has a more limited utility in social science than some have been inclined to think, but—once more—that is something else. Berkhofer's case, insofar as it rests on an appeal to the ostensible slanting of definitions like that of Kroeber and Kluckhohn, is, at the least, not sufficiently clarified.

I would urge that there has actually been more continuity and less dis‑ crepancy in views of culture, simply as culture, entertained by anthropologists than Berkhofer inclines to see, given the way in which he evidently thinks his thesis must be supported. He writes:[10] "That the notion of culture created its own intellectual paradoxes and polemical tensions can be witnessed in a comparison of Kroeber's and Kluckhohn's summary analysis of the concept and the one given recently by Milton Singer in the new *International Encyclopedia of the Social Sciences*."[11] The Kroeber-Kluckhohn "pattern" approach is opposed to the "social structure" approach. But, as Singer's article reveals, the two "approaches" are not really different approaches to culture if we mean by that that their proponents conceive culture as such in markedly different terms. Their proponents wish to do rather different things and operate with different emphases, while in effect they substantially agree on the character of culture.

Culture is involved in social relations. It "molds" them. (I avoid the word "patterns" for what small value this switch in metaphors may have in the immediate context). We accordingly get "molded" relations of "father and son, buyer and seller, ruler and subject."[12] These relations, like countless others, have a cultural content (of norms, beliefs, traditions, "theories"). The structural approach wishes to examine that content as it is involved in the relations. (One might call its proponents "sociologists.") The pattern approach is more immediately concerned to concentrate on the content as content. (One might call its proponents "anthropologists.") This is clearly not to say that there are no significant differences between the two approaches, nor that one can expect that, conceptually, "culture" must forevermore remain uncontaminated by large theoretical views. It is to say, again, that on the character of culture as such the two approaches now show little difference.

Yet more items in the present papers are somewhat disconcerting, on the lines of conceptualization. Pye makes me, for one, uncomfortable with

---

[10] P. 90.

[11] Cf. also Berkhofer's footnote 4, p. 80.

[12] See Singer in *International Encyclopedia of the Social Sciences* (New York: Macmillan and Free Press, 1968), vol. 3, p. 533, col. 1, where he quotes Radcliffe-Brown.

his reference[13] to "the basic anthropological concept that personality and culture are opposite sides of the same coin." Boulding observes at one point[14] that "even here . . . the emphasis has been on the legal rather than the cultural." Surely the law is part and parcel of culture. I hasten to add that what Boulding has in view does seem quite clear from his context. He evidently intends a contrast between certain studies that concentrate on the detail of legal prescriptions and other studies that allow a broader social and cultural framework. The matter is referred to here not to make a paltry verbal "point" but because it, too, may be allowed to suggest the question of just how the idea of culture is "integrated" or "incorporated" in the different social science areas. How is the broader "social and cultural framework" introduced? Should it indeed be "social *and* cultural"? "Culture" is so diffusely conceived at some points in these papers that one may have a number of misgivings as one turns to how our central idea or concept is to be utilized or is in fact utilized in the particular disciplines.

"CULTURE" IN THE SOCIAL SCIENCES

Anthropology and Sociology. The idea of culture is "native" to anthropology and sociology and it is not needful to say much here about how it is "integrated" or "incorporated" in them. Boon's preoccupations do not cover a concern with culture on certain terms that will be taken up later. Parsons gives a brief statement which summarizes views he has been developing over a long time. He has been much occupied with culture both on its own terms[15] and in relation to society. This is hardly the place for an effort at extensive criticism of his views. Not the least of the questions his work suggests is the ultimately always unavoidable one of how well advised sociologists and anthropologists, in particular, have been to make the idea of culture so central to their disciplines. Near the end of his main statement of his evolutionary outlook, Parsons expresses the view, now often quoted, that "within the social system, the normative elements are more important for social change than the 'material interests' of constitutive units."[16] It is regrettable that the full context of this statement cannot here be developed, but at least it may serve as another reminder that one may always ask just how "important" culture itself is. "Interests" or "material interests" are likely enough to be closely associated with, affected by, impregnated with values, beliefs, and the like, but it surely makes some sense to conceive them as suggesting one kind of background for, say, political action, while values, beliefs, traditions suggest another. But for Parsons

---

[13] P. 66.

[14] P. 49.

[15] For his concern with culture more or less on its own terms, see especially his Introduction to Part IV, "Culture and the Social System," of *Theories of Society* (New York: Free Press, 1969), vol. 2, pp. 963–993.

[16] Talcott Parsons, *Societies: Evolutionary and Comparative Perspectives* (New York: Prentice-Hall, 1966), p. 113.

himself, the idea of culture is very important indeed. Culture patterns action systems. It is wholly indispensable in his cybernetic view of social phenomena in the large.

Economics. Boulding expresses cautious hope for a "cultural economics." Yet he is plainly unhappy with what he sees as an almost complete divorce between analytical economics and cultural economics in the work of various institutionalists; and of course he would not wish to drop the core analytical apparatus of economics. In fields such as labor economics, legal economics, the relation of government to economy, there have been forays in which cultural dimensions in some sense have been explored and may be further explored with advantage. Yet Boulding cannot say a great deal for what has thus far been achieved, even when he comes to what is evidently a favorite notion with him, namely, that a cultural economics needs to be evolutionary, for evolutionary economics has much to "propose" but not very much to "say".[17]

In the end it is not quite clear how a systematic job of relating culture to economy is to be undertaken. Although Boulding admires the cultural richness of Adam Smith's work, Smith is hardly now of much help, as Boulding unquestionably knows. Smith's economics came out of a larger matrix of moral philosophy and natural law.[18] It is still drenched, as it were, in the various juices inherent in these sources. There is considerable "cultural" discussion in *The Wealth of Nations* which is apt and highly relevant to the economic sphere—as in the case of the discussion of the "habits" of merchants versus those of country gentlemen, in their bearing on the prospects of the improvement of land (*The Wealth of Nations*, Bk. III, ch. 4). But there is also much that is digressive and only tenuously related to the economic sphere. Thus, however one may appreciate Smith's extensive analyses of education and religion in the massive first chapter of Book V of *The Wealth of Nations*, there is a good deal in these analyses that is to no special economic purpose. It is simply what must now be called "sociology."

Boulding does not even mention the effort to relate "economy and society" made by Parsons and Smelser,[19] although he certainly knows of it. Rightly or wrongly, Parsons' and Smelser's efforts would be regarded with serious dissatisfaction by him, as less than adequate in theoretical terms to relate or integrate economic and sociological (including "cultural") modes of analysis. Nor would Weber or Marshall (to whose memory the Parsons-Smelser volume is dedicated) presumably provide *enough* for the kind of systematic integration one might hope for. Boulding mentions

[17] P. 59.
[18] A matrix that is classically and exhaustively discussed in Wilhelm Hasbach's *Untersuchungen über Adam Smith* (Leipzig: Duncker und Humblot, 1891).
[19] Talcott Parsons and Neil J. Smelser, *Economy and Society* (Glencoe: The Free Press, 1956).

Weber as an "European institutionalist"[20] and refers to his work on Protestantism and capitalism but can apparently exploit him for his purposes only to a limited extent. In Marshall's case, he regrets[21] that Volume II of his *Principles* ("which should have been evolutionary economics") was never written. At least we can say that by the high standards Boulding himself apparently wishes to sustain, the idea of culture in economics still awaits considerable work before anything truly imposing is done with it, if that work is indeed ever to be done.

Political Science—And Beyond. "Culture" is evidently more intimately woven into the texture of political science today than it is into that of economics. Much political science now evidently tends to be a kind of political sociology. Pye also indicates infusions of anthropology, psychoanalysis and survey research. The notion of political culture stimulates some apt descriptions and suggests some significant political problems. But although the notion is well worked into political science it would seem that it is given no special articulation or theoretical development in the discipline. It is, precisely, part of a larger baggage imported into the field as an incident of its "behavioralization."

Political science, in Pye's view, concerned as that discipline is with "macro" problems, yet is also concerned with relating "micro" to "macro" phenomena. The micro-macro matter, however, suggests some distinctions that help to bring together considerations usefully transcending the particular political science field and generally advancing the purposes of these observations. Pye is concerned with micro-macro in the sense of relating personality (at the micro level) to larger political-cultural and structural and organizational realities. Does a certain kind of upbringing predispose toward "authoritarianism," and thereby at least give support to, if it does not generate, certain over-all political biases and structures? Pye is certainly appropriately wary of naive "extrapolation from micro to macro phenomena," and the sins of that kind of "personality-culture" theorizing that swallows both history and culture or social structure in an effort to move from familial and psychological data to the "macro" level are notorious. But there is a legitimate enough field here, no matter how carefully it needs to be approached, and one aspect of micro-macro relations is hereby covered.

One may also understand micro-macro in a sense that very particularly concentrates on culture in abstraction from possibly influential factors of personality or personality "dynamics." Let us say that the poiltically relevant values of ordinary citizens are or are not congruous with those held by the personnel of government agencies or actually supported by those

---

[20] Weber did develop an "economic sociology," but he also opposed such particular institutionalist claims as the one that economic analysis rests on a dubious "psychology." See, for example, the first essays on Roscher and Knies in Max Weber, *Gesammelte Aufsätze zur Wissenschaftslehre* (Tubingen: J. C. B. Mohr, 1951).

[21] P. 48.

agencies; or that family norms for conduct are or are not in some significant way in conformity with norms that prevail in the industrial sphere. Here one can indeed inquire about specifically cultural congruities and discrepancies at different ("micro" and "macro") levels. Sopher suggests issues in this context where he writes:[22]

> It is becoming clear that the prevailing model of modern urban industrial society is properly that of an industrialized and urbanized Western European society that became such at a particular moment in history. It appears that this society has had a different microscopic structure—or range or structures—from, let us say, Japanese or Indian or southern Italian society. What is not clear is how far and in what ways the microscopic structure of industrialized Japanese society, etc., is therefore predictably different from that of the West.

Sopher does not specify the "microscopic structures" he refers to, but he does suggest questions of congruity or incongruity in which a large cultural component would be involved. One might indeed inquire whether Japanese family traditions and norms might have some relation to the norms of Western-type industrial systems. In both "personality-culture" and "culture-congruity-incongruity" considerations, however, the notion of cultural hierarchy is already strongly suggested. (Unless, indeed, congruity and incongruity have a hierarchical or "level" reference, they have no necessary connection with "micro-macro" relations.)

In regard to hierarchy, Parsons' work has been most suggestive.[23] One may ask whether certain political values, say, get translated "downward" in a political structure and increasingly specified as they are applied at lower political levels, while always retaining the component of their general, originally more abstract top-level content. One wants to be "democratic," and the terms or premises of "democracy" are maintained down to grass-roots political levels, although they have to be "spelled out" in more particular ways to cover increasingly concrete situations in the downward-going process. Insofar as a "democratic" orientation is maintained "all the way down," there is congruity, to be sure, at the different levels, but it is hierarchy that now comes to the fore. How strong and how deep, in fact, is the downward thrust of the top-level components? How pervasive is the macro orientation at micro levels? Does the hierarchy operate in reverse, so that micro pressures—pressures from below—may occasion revision at or near the political top? The illustrative detail may be varied. "Free enterprise," as Smelser indicates,[24] is as abstract in its way as "democracy" and as much in need of concretizing and specification as it

---

[22] Pp. 113–114.
[23] See particularly Talcott Parsons, "An Outline of the Social System," in Parsons et al., *Theories of Society*, vol. I, pp. 30–79. See also Neil J. Smelser, *The Theory of Collective Behavior* (New York: The Free Press, 1963), ch. 2.
[24] *The Theory of Collective Behavior*, p. 25.

is worked out (or "down") in an economic system as is "democracy" when that is worked out in a political framework.

There is at least one other abstractable sense or aspect of micro-macro relations. This has to do with outcomes of individual actions (whether by individual persons or by larger but still quite limited "units") that raise an analytical problem of "aggregation." Many persons act in society with their particular purposes or ends in view, but those actions aggregate or come out to something that may or may not coincide with those purposes or may even run counter to them. This is the old phenomenon, on which keen speculation runs back to at least the eighteenth century, often now referred to as the unintended or unanticipated consequences of purposive social action. Small driblets of human purpose ("micro" level) run into great streams of results of those purposes as carried out by particular units. The actions of the particular units may be "connected" in the most complex ways, or interplay elaborately, before certain "precipitations" (at the "macro" level) are brought about that catch the interest of the social scientist.

Problems in this sense or aspect of micro-macro particularly catch Boulding's attention. One of his sentences,[25] though taken out of its context, carries its present relevance on the face of it: "The perception that the actual quantities of product produced, consumed, invested, and so on were not the result of the decisions of individual households, businesses, or even governments, but were *the result of the interaction of the decisions of all the parties to the system,* is perhaps one of the most profound insights to come out of economics" (My italics.)

This sort of perception leads Boulding to observations about what he calls macro-economic paradoxes, which feature discrepancies between what individuals intend by particular actions and what results from their actions in the aggregate, in the large, at the macro level, at the system level—however one wishes to put it. Boulding writes[26] of "systems in which the sum of individual decisions produces results which are quite contrary to the intentions and expectations of any of the individual decision-makers"; and the meaning of his reference to "counter-intuitive-results" is quite clear.

In all senses or aspects reviewed, "micro-macro" issues run across the concerns of the several social sciences, plainly going beyond any one. Whether our focus is on "personality-culture" or "culture-congruity-incongruity" and "hierarchy" or "unintended or unanticipated consequences," we deal with matters that might as easily come up in sociology or anthropology or history or even economics (though here with some distinctive reservations perhaps particularly with regard to "personality-culture," if we consider the preoccupations at the center of traditional economic analysis). But if we are to advance cultural analysis and make more potent

[25] P. 62.
[26] P. 63.

"the idea of culture" in the social sciences, it seems well to make some such differentiation of senses or aspects of micro-macro relations as is here suggested. Strictly cultural matters are most to the fore in the culture-congruity-incongruity and hierarchy aspects, but obviously "culture" is also very much involved in "personality-culture;" and, in the unintended-unanticipated aspect, we *can* be concerned with cultural phenomena proper and in the strictest sense one could wish. Also, I would urge (and the point will recur) that the notion of hierarchy is in particular need of further development for those interested in an overall cultural theory. Finally, the unintended-unanticipated aspect will come in for special stress when we come to the terminal portion of these observations, on misplaced humanism.

History. Berkhofer does not concern himself with elaborating a refined conception of culture for the field of history. He does not draw on cultural theory to try to rear a structure of thought that might in some sense order historical data better than they are now ordered. In a relatively short article, he may well be wise to hold back from such enormously ambitious tasks, *assuming* that there could be any profit in them.

It was remarked above that Berkhofer tends to associate the idea or concept of culture with broad theories of history and society and that this tendency is challengeable. One not versed in American historiography may be quite willing to believe Berkhofer when he suggests[27] that under the influence of something like an excessive stress on ideas (supposedly brought about by certain notions of culture), a number of American historians came to hold that "people voted for Jackson not on the basis of their sectional and economic alignment but because he symbolized their fears for traditional ideals in a time of apparent rapid change or because of their ethico-cultural and religious prejudices." Berkhofer's characterization of the relevant historical work may well be correct: so too the evident implication that the historians who so construed things unduly slighted or mistakenly pushed aside "sectional and economic alignment." It may even be that such errors *were* due precisely to an excessive stress on ideas deriving from particular views of culture. Quite possibly, too, the sheer central thrust of the idea of culture, insofar as it stresses symbols, values, beliefs, myths may constrain historians or others affected by this thrust to pay too much attention or attribute too much significance to—symbols, values, beliefs, myths. And again errors may thus arise as, for instance, "for the conflict of economic and class interests" historians unduly substitute "symbolic tensions and cultural antinomies."

But there is nothing necessary about such errors. One might define culture more or less in the Tylor or the Kroeber-Kluckhohn sense and then decide with regard to various areas of historical concern (sectional interests, economic alignments) that an approach to them in the mode of cultural analysis would give results of only quite limited value. The con-

27 P. 88.

cept of culture as such does not prejudge, say, an "economic interpretation of history," although in such an interpretation cultural analysis might not be very important. "Culture" is not the only concept in the social sciences nor does it involve all the "conceptions" that the social sciences have at their disposal. It is freely granted that any concept—or conception—may in a sense mislead because of its intrinsic character, because it is what it is and directs thought as it does. But, even if historians have in fact been misled by various notions pertaining to "culture," it seems clear that in principle the central concept as such should not be made to bear the burden of a theory of history or society. To wish to throw it out because it cannot bear such a burden would surely also be mistaken. Once more, it may conceivably not be very helpful in various areas of historical concern. But that, again, is another matter.

Geography. Sopher, too, is not concerned with any precise articulation of the concept of culture for the uses of geography. He presents, to be sure, a convincing case for the view that "cultural" notions in a broad sense have provided geography with important descriptive material and research tasks. But his terminal comments perhaps suggest the need for further theoretical work on the concept of culture itself. He observes that the concept, in its geographical application, has never been more elusive than it is today and wonders[28] whether cultural geography "can still use the concept of culture successfully in elucidating man's present and future, as it has his past." As becomes a geographer, Sopher gives a "down-to-earth" sense of cultural realities. It may be that geographers need to move more into the upper air, where some "theory" or a bit of frankly high-flown speculation about culture may be appropriate.

The most ambitious current attempt to analyze culture in its *general social-science significance* may well be that of Parsons, sketched in his paper in this symposium but much more extensively developed elsewhere. Anthropology of course has a considerable heritage of its own in the way of developing notions about culture. The other social sciences have been attracted by the general culture concept, have made some shrewd applications of it to their own areas, and have used it for descriptive enrichment, but have tended to take it over without special concern for how it might be "integrated" into them, given their peculiar theoretical preoccupations. The clearest hint of such concern in these papers perhaps comes from Boulding's discussion of cultural evolution. On the other hand, the sheer broad "relevance" of the idea or concept of culture across the social sciences seems fairly evident and is at points made quite plain.

Because Boon's paper has its particular concerns and because Parsons could present some of his ideas most relevant for present purposes only briefly, there is a residue of largely older ideas (although also to some

[28] P. 117.

extent newer ones, as in Parsons' own case) that one would have liked to see given consideration in the above papers, but that have been largely omitted. They strike me as indispensable for what I have casually referred to as "cultural theory." Some of them are presented under the next heading by way of supplementation to matters taken up in the papers.

NOTIONS RELATING TO CULTURE IN NEED OF FURTHER DEVELOPMENT

There is actually some overlap between the notions considered in this section and what the contributors to the symposium have written, particularly with respect to the notion of hierarchy. But I submit that "cultural theory" also needs the sustenance that comes from the ideas now to be reviewed.

The notion of cultural "autonomization" is an old and familiar one. But it has lost none of its cogency. Culture has a way of taking off and going "into orbit" on its own. It is subject to development more or less on its own terms. A primitive geometry arises, say, out of practical needs for spatial orientation or parcelling of land. But geometry in time goes off into independent elaboration. It leaves the practical sphere. Mathematics is notoriously prone to this sort of secondary elaboration, if one may use a suggestive Freudian term. Mathematics also has the disconcerting quality of sometimes coming out with results from its elaborate flights from the practical sphere that have an amazing relevance to the latter and enable men to perform practical wonders that would otherwise not have been possible. The same mechanism of course holds for music, for example, although it does not work in "reverse" in the fashion true for mathematics. The arts and sciences generally have cultures of their own that powerfully suggest the presence of autonomization. Hauser puts the point well for the arts when he comments in his provocative book on mannerist art:

> The unnaturalistic peculiarity of mannerism also appears in the fact that the origin of artistic creation is not nature, but something already fashioned out of it. In other words, the mannerists were inspired less by nature than by works of art, and as artists they were not so much under the influence of natural phenomena as of artistic creations. Wölfflin's remark that a picture owes more to other pictures than to the painter's observation is nowhere better justified than by them. They also provide corroboration for Malraux's dictum that the painter is in love, not with landscape, but with pictures, that the poet cares nothing for the beauty of the sunset, but so much the more for the beauty of the verse, and that the musician is interested, not in the nightingale but in music.[29]

Here culture, then, is already clearly "in orbit" and developing out of itself. The mannerist painter (if Hauser is right), in particular, tends to respond not to aboriginal stimuli from nature but to responses to such

[29] Arnold Hauser, *Mannerism* (New York: Alfred A. Knopf, 1965), vol. 1, pp. 29–30.

stimuli made by other painters—and even this statement of the matter may put him closer to nature than he should be put. The point is stated in this way to allow the hint that, depending on just how we approach autonomization, one way of stating its presence or operation may be more suggestive than another. At times, "response to response" seems quite appropriate. A group may "respond" with a primitive weapon to the presence in its environs of consumable animals, and then show a response to the weapon itself, as in its artistic elaboration in a context without reference to game.

Given the point of view of social scientists there has been constant interest in cultural autonomization in regard to the extent to which it is feasible in various cultural fields. There is a cultural strain toward freedom, toward autonomy, toward independence of the matrices in which culture has its sources. But, we may ask, how many degrees of freedom from what may conveniently be called extra-cultural constraints are feasible? Kroeber notes: "Since human culture cannot be wholly concerned with values, having also to adapt to social (interpersonal relations) and to reality (survival situations), the totality of a culture can scarcely be considered outright as a sort of expanded style."[30] A clear example of the kind of constraint or limitation on degrees of cultural freedom alluded to is provided by architecture. Munro observes pertinently:

> The arts have never, in advanced cultures, followed any one stylistic trend in the same way or to an equal extent. This is impossible because of their increasingly different materials, forms, and functions. In the romantic period, garden and landscape design accepted and fulfilled the prevailing trend much more than architecture did, partly because architecture is forced by human requirements to be largely geometrical. Its floors and ceilings must be mostly flat and horizontal, its walls mostly vertical, or people will be dizzy and uncomfortable with it. (Minor exceptions are in amusement parks where houses are deliberately put askew or upside down for the fun of temporary visitors. Thatched roofs and neo-gothic details are also minor concessions to romanticism.) Architecture tended in its main concerns to resist and oppose the romantic movement, or at least to lag behind other arts in following it. . . . In being essentially "frozen," so that men can move about in it securely, architecture cannot follow very far a trend toward instability and evanescence.[31]

Numerous other arts are clearly less bound than architecture. Their strain toward freedom is more successful. The dadaist poet, Tristan Tzara, who invented the "accidental" poem (made by arranging words in the order in which they come from a bag of words individually cut from newspapers) seems rather removed from various primitive functions of poetry,

[30] A. L. Kroeber, *Style and Civilization* (Ithaca: Cornell University Press, 1957), p. 152.
[31] Thomas Munro, *Evolution in the Arts* (Cleveland Museum of Art, distributed by Harry N. Abrams, Inc., 1963), p. 510.

assuming that the accidental poem is still legitimately called a poem.[32] One scarcely knows what to say in this context about the art of the Swiss, Jean Tinguely, whose machines made out of junk include items that "commit suicide." Egbert notes an expectable artistic pedigree for Tinguely, who derives "from futurism, from the nihilistic side of dada, and from surrealism."[33] The strain toward freedom can clearly go a long way. But there are still the broad, general constraints Kroeber referred to, constraints imposed as by sheer social necessities (an unrestricted, pure cultural enthusiasm for woman-stealing would encounter certain obstacles) or by biological necessities.

Kroeber's statement also implicitly postulates a hierarchy in its references to "value" and "style," to "social (interpersonal relations)" and to "reality (survival situations)." We accordingly return to the notion of hierarchy. As a general notion (often rather crudely conceived), it is quite old. We may refer to intra-cultural hierarchy or to hierarchy involving culture but also extending to extra-cultural phenomena. With regard to the latter, one thinks readily of the hoary hierarchical conception of inorganic-organic-superorganic levels. With regard to intra-cultural hierarchy, one thinks readily of Parsons' treatment of values, norms, collectivities, roles (involving analysis of collectivities and roles on their cultural side). Values are at the "top" of a normative hierarchy and exercise influence downward.[34] But Parsons also allows a more extensive kind of hierarchy, ranging from cultural system downward through social system, personality system, and behavioral organism. And there is not only, for him, a control hierarchy from the top downward but also a conditioning hierarchy from the bottom upward, as limits or constraints are imposed by the "low"-level hierarchical elements.

Again, this is not the place to attempt criticism of Parsons' ideas. But we have now deliberately touched on hierarchy twice, in the present context and previously in regard to micro-macro relations. We have just noted that the general notion of hierarchy is an old one in cultural theory. Parsons has afforded refinements and extensions of it which constitute some new features. In anthropologists like Kroeber and sociologists like the Sorokin of *Social and Cultural Dynamics*, similar ideas are unquestionably present if in more embryonic form. This all suggests the considerable importance for cultural theory of the idea of hierarchy. It may not be too outrageous to guess that no theory of culture serviceable for the social sciences is likely to develop without strong concern with this idea. Yet the idea is one that still stands in need of much exploration.

I would like further to reinforce the suggestions that the idea of hierarchy is an old one in social science and that even some of Parsons'

[32] See Donald D. Egbert, *Social Radicalism and the Arts* (New York: Alfred A. Knopf, 1970), p. 295.
[33] *Social Radicalism and the Arts*, p. 366.
[34] See also above, p. 43.

relatively new notions have had their adumbrations. Reverberations from "top" to "bottom" have long posed intriguing problems, although these have not, indeed, been represented in the terms of Parsons' special theoretical apparatus. An Oriental poet avers, "If that unkindly Turkish girl would take my heart within her hand, for the birthmark on her cheek I'd give Bukhara and Samarkand." An exquisite cultural flower, if one will, yet no matter how refined and lovely such expressions may be they would clearly make no "sense" to creatures not sexed as men and women are. The "bottom" of a hierarchy thrusts into the "top" and the poetry of love has a secure foundation in the animality of man. On the other hand, it has long since been pointed out—and constitutes a bit of elementary anthropology—that our appetites are culturally shaped. We become hungry and want, not "food," but steak and potatoes. We become sexually aroused and yearn for sexual objects bedizened, painted and shaped in very particular ways. The cultural "top" reaches down and forms the biological "bottom." Reverberations, then, run through the hierarchy both ways.

There is surely nothing novel about this. Yet, too, how little social scientists know about such things is witnessed in the considerable stimulation one can still find in the old, engagingly pertinent book by the humorist Clarence Day, entitled *This Simian World*.[35] And when we come to strictly intra-cultural hierarchies, there is clearly a tremendous amount of work that should ideally be done.

If we turn back, now, to autonomization, it is easy to see that it ties in with mechanisms of alienation. The first volume of Marx's *Capital* presents an unforgettable treatment of the fetishism of commodities.[36] Workers, it will be recalled, produce commodities that "get away" from them and seem to act on their own accord and their own volition, exhibiting ostensibly mysterious relations to one another that man does not know actually result from his social work-relations to his fellow-man. The whole effect is that of an alienated economic world which constrains and oppresses man. Georg Simmel wrote a famous essay entitled "The Tragedy of Culture" in which the Marxian view is in a way extended to cover larger cultural fields. Marx may well have exaggerated his point and the particular essay of Simmel's referred to may reflect some of his more dubiously romantic dispositions. Yet the theme of alienation is certainly a significant one for cultural analysis. The theme must interest virtually all social scientists.

Whether Marx exaggerated or not, economic phenomena do often give an impression of things being in the saddle and riding mankind—and an accompanying feeling of impotence and being at the mercy of impersonal forces. The impersonal forces, notoriously, are often personalized. Complex results of economic, social and cultural activity are conceived in such terms that it seems "reasonable" to say that the Jews did it, or the Communist

[35] Clarence Day, *This Simian World* (New York: Alfred A. Knopf, 1920).
[36] Karl Marx, *Capital* (New York: Modern Library, 1936), vol. 1, pp. 81–96.

opposition is totally responsible. And this sort of personalization clearly carries the advantage of what might be called spurious actionability. One may be able to go ahead and kill or maim or repress the guilty devils, while there is little one can immediately do about numerous acknowledgedly complex economic, social and cultural processes that happen to be humanly uncomfortable. There is a large playground here for social psychologists, sociologists, political scientists, and historians.

But it is not difficult to stay close to the heart of culture here. Part of the current and older romanticism about alienation may well arise because certain elementary distinctions are not made in connection with it. There is a quite ineluctable human condition, a condition of man under culture and especially under the circumstances of highly developed culture, which need not bring with it that dissatisfaction or distress or mitigation of humanity that seems so often to be imputed to alienation. Herder described this condition eloquently nearly two centuries ago in a book of great sweep and power.

> Vain . . . is the boast of so many Europeans, when they set themselves above the people of all other quarters of the Globe, in what they call arts, sciences and cultivation, and, as the madman by the ships in the port of Piraeus, deem all the inventions of Europe their own, for no other reason but because they were born amid the confluence of these inventions and traditions. Poor creature! Hast thou invented any of these arts? have thy own thoughts anything to do in all the traditions thou hast sucked in? Thy having learned to use them is the work of a machine. Thy having imbibed the waters of science is the merit of a sponge that has grown on the humid soil. Steer they frigate to Otaheite, bid thy cannon roar along the shores of the New Hebrides, still thou art not superior in skill or ability to the inhabitant of the South Sea Islands, who guides with art the boat which he has constructed with his own hand. Even the savages themselves have had an obscure perception of this, as soon as they become more distinctly acquainted with Europeans . . . . No one will deny Europe to be the repository of art and of the inventive understanding of man. The destiny of ages has deposited its treasures there. They are augmented and employed in it. But everyone who makes use of them has not therefore the understanding of the inventors.[37]

Some may think Herder too ethnocentric still, even with his astonishingly modern view of things. The point need not be argued. He saw clearly that culture is indeed a social heritage, but that men who are beneficiaries of a rich heritage neither need have any special native talents nor need, in numerous particular cases, have internalized, or possessed themselves of, much of the heritage in order to profit vastly from it. This is something that has often been pointed to by students of culture. It would seem arbitrary to insist that it constitutes "alienation." True, it may evoke con-

[37] Johann Gottfried von Herder, *Outlines of a Philosophy of the History of Man* (New York: Bergman Publishers, 1966), pp. 241–242. (First edition published in 1784.) I have changed punctuation slightly.

templation about a world one never made—a world of science or philosophy or art of which one's knowledge is slight, as one may be aware, and to which one's own sensibilities are hardly alert, as one may also be aware. One can regret that one is not more than one is. But there the matter may end. Yet it is also true that this can build a foundation for what is with greater warrant called alienation. The world of culture of which one is not "possessed" may come to be sensed as strange, hostile and oppressive. Personalization and reification might then add to the flavor of alienation. Once the necessity of certain distinctions is acknowledged and some perverse constructions have been avoided, I, for one, cannot see how cultural analysis could renounce a large concern with alienation, granted all the distinctively psychological considerations the term suggests.

It is also well to call attention to something I may be allowed to label cultural alternation. This, too, is a slightly new name for some long known things, but I intend to suggest by it a bit more than is usually suggested by some of the older labels that are applied, such as "functional alternatives." What has previously been set out in this section consists in a number of statements about matters that are closely coherent. Cultural alternation gets us somewhat away from these matters, but it strikes one sociologist, at least, as something that also requires the closest consideration by analysts of culture who are ambitious to make the idea more useful in the social sciences.

The citation from Herder that has been made may serve to remind us how often modern anthropological and sociological insights appear in eighteenth-century writers, who can state them with just as much cogency as any contemporary and who may therefore be quoted with a minimum of pedantry while we are chastened by the reflection that in numerous respects our advances in social sciences have been decidedly modest. Adam Ferguson observes:

> It is the form of respect in Europe to uncover the head. In Japan, we are told, the corresponding form is to drop the slipper, or to uncover the foot. The physical action in these instances is different, *but the moral action is the same*. It is an act of attention and respect; dispositions equally acceptable, whether expressed in words, gestures, or signs of any other sort.
>
> Persons, unacquainted with any language but their own, are apt to think the words they use natural and fixed expressions of things; while the words of a different language they consider mere jargon or the result of caprice. In the same manner, forms of behavior, different from their own, appear offensive or irrational, or a perverse substitution of absurd for reasonable manners.[38]

Ferguson correctly saw the phenomena he pointed to as cultural alternatives or matters of cultural alternation. Only a mindless anthropology, with a sensationalist tinge at that, would at once exclaim at the first

---

[38] Adam Ferguson, *Principles of Moral and Political Science* (Edinburgh: W. Creech, 1792), vol. 2, p. 142; italics supplied.

sight of a few salient differences between Flatbush Avenue and the Fiji Islands, "Ah! how *different* they are!" "Different" they undoubtedly are, but it is also beyond doubt that many "differences" are scarcely differences at all. Yet it requires some courage and obstinacy to pursue this.

It is still instructive to have rather easy starting points.[39] The members of one group say, "The grass is always greener in the other fellow's field." Those of another complain, "Other men's women are always the prettiest ones." But still a third group comes out with a really gifted generalization of the reflections of the other two; and we now encounter, "There it is good where we are not." The "meaning" is the same from case to case. These are plain cultural alternatives, granted the impressive talent for generalization exhibited in the last statement. But there *are* cases in which we are more easily fooled. Time was when a pious man might (and did) call sweetheart or wife "a handmaiden of the Lord." But the woman was due to become "a very fine girl," and even before very long "quite a kid." In a "religious age," one says many things religiously. But pious language should not obscure important similarities (which is not to claim that there are "no differences" at all). The man who spoke of a handmaiden of the Lord meant much the same thing as later speakers who referred to fine girls and enticing kids. We encounter culturally alternative ways of saying things. Perhaps in a "political age," if that is what ours is, we are easily deceived into thinking of certain ideologies as considerably less "religious" than they actually are, since, in a political age, theology, demonism and the like express themselves in "political" form.

We may "miss" cultural alternatives in numerous areas and thereby corrupt cultural analysis or fail to make it better than it is. The references just made to religion suggest a number of such possibilities. A fairly obvious yet not uninstructive instance is afforded by studies in the history of antinomianism, the old doctrine that faith frees one from obligation to the moral law. A recent student of Catharist morality touches upon the notion of liberation from this evil world and observes that one could scorn the flesh in libertinism or punish and repress it in asceticism. That the soul is untouched by what the body does is a common antinomian idea. If one indulges one's self sensually to the utmost, of what importance is that? One is only indulging this utterly insignificant flesh. For a really sturdy asceticism, too, the flesh is of no importance whatever. Koch accordingly observes, "The origins as well as the goals of libertinism were the same as those of asceticism. The two orientations were but two poles of a fundamental disposition, which proposed disdain for matter."[40] In a crucial respect, then—the radical devaluation of matter, including flesh—

---

[39] The next two paragraphs draw on the writer's paper, "The Sociology of Religion: Some Areas of Theoretical Potential," *Sociological Analysis*, 31 (Fall, 1970), pp. 131–144.

[40] Gottfried Koch, *Frauenfrage und Ketzertum im Mittelalter* (Berlin: Akademie Verlag, 1962), p. 116.

libertinism and ascetism are cultural alternatives. One may note in passing that political extremists of the right and of the left may be united in a fundamental rejection of the notion that some social order is susceptible of any considerable reform. Admittedly, we are now launched into spheres in which differences may be just as significant as similarities, but then it is extremely important to discern the similarities amidst the differences.

If notions like those of autonomization, constraints on autonomization, hierarchy, alienation and alternation, as I contend, press for inclusion in a cultural theory that should be genuinely "useful" for social science purposes and there is a valuable heritage of ideas already available in these premises, there are also, I believe, current tendencies in social science that might mitigate the advantages some of these notions might conceivably bring us. I refer particularly to a certain disposition to shy away from cultural analysis when it ceases to remain close to human beings. It will be noted that I refer carefully to "a certain disposition." It is certainly not universally shared among, say, anthropologists, sociologists or historians. It is often qualified by those who do manifest it. But it can constitute an authentic intellectual mischief and I believe it warrants some discussion before I bring these observations to a close.

MISPLACED HUMANISM

It is certainly possible to consider culture as abstracted from social systems and persons. Kroeber, Sorokin, Parsons and numerous others have had occasion to consider culture in such abstracted terms. In these terms, one may give a description and analysis of, say, "Greek culture," "modern Western culture," and the like; and one develops a vocabulary adapted to the abstraction made.

One is then under no compulsion to "reify" culture. One realizes its various important connections with human beings and social arrangements. One merely approaches it as a product that has a structure of its own, like a poem or a piece of architecture or a mathematical or philosophical system or, for that matter, an anthropological or sociological theory. There is now a social science bias that turns away from this older abstracting approach or is at least very hesitant about it. It seems to want to stay very close to human consciousness, human appreciations, human action. It seems rather averse toward the intellectual twist needed to get away (temporarily but, it may be argued, very helpfully) from human beings altogether and to scrutinize such things as their cultural products in their own right.

Anthropologists among others have worked and continue to work with abstracted or "objective" culture. But unless I am much mistaken, there is among anthropologists of the newer "emic" persuasion a strong reluctance to get away from culture as anchored in the human consciousness. It may be helpful to have Harris's indication of the meaning of "emic statements" before us. "Emic statements," he writes, "refer to logico-empirical systems whose phenomenal distinctions or 'things' are built up out of contrasts and discriminations significant, meaningful, real, accurate for, or in some other fashion regarded as appropriate by, the actors themselves."[41] When one analyzes culture in "objective" terms (or, for that matter, when one writes of social structures and functions) one is on the other hand very likely to employ categories that in varying degree depart from what is in the apprehension of the actor. One is quite willing, whenever it seems necessary, to relinquish the actor's point of view or terms of discourse that rest on that point of view.

In noting a certain current reluctance to get away from culture as anchored in consciousness, I am aware that qualifications have to be made. Tyler writes:

> Each individual . . . may have a unique, unitary model of his culture, but it is not necessarily cognizant of all the unique, unitary models held by other members of his culture [sic]. He will be aware of and use some, but it is only the anthropologist who completely transcends these particular models and constructs a single, unitary model. The cognitive organization exists solely in the mind of the anthropologist. Yet to the extent that it will generate conceptual models used by the people of a particular culture [sic] it is a model of their cognitive systems.[42]

This is a significant reservation if I understand it correctly, but there remains the powerful thrust toward preoccupation with the "emic." I want to support the view, quite unoriginally but emphatically, that too much insistence on this sort of emic approach to culture is a handicap to cultural analysis. What is humanly insulting or "immoral" about pointing out that there are aspects of human cultural and social life that go beyond anything contained in the subjective apprehensions of human agents and that may call for analysis on "objective" terms quite removed from those apprehensions and not even "resting" on them or necessarily building from their base in the fashion the above quotation from Tyler suggests?

All this may recall the previous observations on micro-macro relations as they bear on unintended or unanticipated consequences. Beyond men's intentions or anticipations their aggregated performances amount to a "Protestant Reformation" or an "Industrial Revolution" or the like. Or "structures" are precipitated that were never contemplated and have little to do with contemplation or the subjective life of actors in any sense. The whole matter goes beyond culture as such, but it certainly has to do with culture. At the same time, given the significance and scope of the problems presented, some more general considerations will not be amiss.

[41] Marvin Harris, *The Rise of Anthropological Theory* (New York: Crowell, 1968), p. 571. I have taken some very slight liberties with Harris's statement. My quotation is not entirely faithful to the original, but by adding the word "for" and two commas that do not appear in Harris's text I think I have clarified his meaning.
[42] Tyler, *Cognitive Anthropology*, p. 5. This is also quoted by Berkhofer, above, p. 93.

Thus, there is a variety of social precipitants that can be expressed as rates—suicide rates, crime rates, rates of mental illness. It is currently very fashionable in some social science quarters to seek to "reduce" such rates, to make it appear that they are merely artifacts of particular modes of recording, influenced by particular "interpretations." What is counted as suicide in the city may not be counted as such in rural areas, and to aggregate differently grounded counts and speak of an overall suicide rate, as if the cases counted in were uniformly determined and all had the same meaning, is arbitrary procedure. There is without doubt a point here. But it seems idle to overlook the further point that beyond all arbitrary modes of reckoning there is something at work in these rates which one might speak of as the overall effect of the carrying out of many particular wills (expressed however badly in official statistics) which is not traceable to anyone's will in particular.[43] So, too, psychiatrists may help to "produce" rates for mental illness, as by approving and treating well patients who show the "right" syndromes and allow themselves to be "properly" classified. But there is still presumably an aggregated incidence of authentic mental difficulty that is not eliminable, no matter how subtly one analyzes the dubious nosological endeavors of psychiatrists and no matter how poorly available data may measure the incidence.[44] In the case of suicide again, this whole phenomenon of precipitation of a resultant (the rate) out of individual actions and orientations may be argued to require an analysis heavily depending on extra-subjective categories.

Consider now the specifically cultural phenomenon of style, which was so important to Spengler and to an anthropologist like Kroeber and which plays so crucial a part in art history. Hauser writes: "The concept of style derives from the paradoxical fact that the endeavors of several artists working separately and often independently are found to exhibit a common direction, that their individual aims are unconsciously subordinated to an impersonal, superindividual trend, and—seemingly insoluble contradiction of art history—that an artist, by giving free rein to his own impulses, produces something that goes beyond what he actually intended." And Hauser adds later: "A style is no more than the result of

---

[43] This is of course designed to be a quick, succinct formulation. I recognize that there may be need for very careful language in these premises and I do not pretend that it would always be satisfactory to refer simply to individual "purposes" and their overall effects. One area in which the need for care about these matters is at once obvious is that of mental illness. It would be impossible to derive such illness from simple presumptions about "purposive" action. I have neither the space nor the competence to discuss seriously questions about the sheer "reality" or character of mental illness itself, although I do think that it has a "reality" independent of psychiatric constructions of it.

[44] See, in connection with this paragraph, Jack D. Douglas, *The Social Meanings of Suicide* (Princeton: Princeton University Press, 1969); Thomas Scheff, *Being Mentally Ill* (Chicago: Aldine, 1966); Aaron V. Cicourel, *The Social Organization of Juvenile Justice* (New York: Wiley, 1967).

many conscious and purposive achievements; it cannot itself be said to have been consciously or deliberately originated; it is not part of the consciousness for any of the individuals whose products are the substrata of its being."[45]

Once more, consider the entirely familiar idea of function as it has been used in anthropology and sociology. There is no need on this occasion to go into the various sophistications that have been built into the idea nor is there any need to go into present-day criticisms of structural-functional analysis. What I need stress is only that the idea of function makes room for the view that, say, various human actions can contribute to the maintenance of a larger system of social relations, without any awareness on the part of any involved actors that this is so.[46] If I sense some current tendencies correctly, such a view now can arouse a sort of violent "humanistic" reaction. Again, insulting; immoral. Maybe this sort of thing should be legislated out of the social sciences. Something decidedly milder yet perhaps not so very different appears in the recent able study of Herbert Spencer by J.D.Y. Peel. Peel writes:

> Some change, it is true, does happen without men either willing it or being aware of it except as *faits accomplis* (the economic history of the classical world is full of examples), and the unintended consequences of deliberate action ("latent functions," in the patchwork terminology of modern functionalism) are extremely significant, as Spencer reiterates. But as Max Weber spelled out for us, social action, *qua* the doings of men, only becomes meaningful and specially comprehensible to us when it is made to make sense in terms of the purposes of its agents. In the first instance, it is these, rather than its consequences for adaptation, which provide the explanation of behavior, and so must be central to sociology. The permanent debts which we owe to Spencer for the theory of evolution are considerable, but in this vital respect it must be judged a failure.[47]

But others have contended that the very heart of the preoccupation of the sociologist is with unintended or unanticipated consequences.[48] If one

[45] Arnold Hauser, *The Philosophy of Art History* (New York: Alfred A. Knopf, 1959), pp. 208, 209–210. From this point on I shall not argue explicitly, as I might, that social or cultural precipitants out of individual actions might in case after case be analyzed in terms that do not build on or synthesize the contents of subjective apprehension.

[46] Malinowski long ago made a simple distinction between "cultural need" and "individual motives" that bear upon the need and inadvertently contribute to it. "The cultural need is the body of conditions which must be fulfilled if the community is to survive and its culture to continue. The individual motives, on the other hand, have nothing to do with such postulates as the continuity of race or the continuity of culture or even the need of nutrition. Few people . . . realize that such general necessities exist." B. Malinowski, "Culture," in *Selections from the Encyclopedia of the Social Sciences* (New York: Macmillan, 1948), p. 629.

[47] J. D. Y. Peel, *Herbert Spencer: The Evolution of a Sociologist* (New York: Basic Books, 1971), p. 165.

[48] Note the statement by Barnes, "Sociology has sometimes been described as the study of the unintended consequences of social action. . . ." John A. Barnes, *Sociology in Cambridge* (Cambridge: Cambridge University Press, 1970), p. 19.

wants to argue that Spencer might well have given much more serious attention than he did to human subjectivity, there is little to quarrel about. There are, of course, those who would share Peel's view. Charles Horton Cooley, for one, contended in a paper of 1920 that Spencer was not really a sociologist at all on much the same ground as that on which Peel here criticizes him.[49] But for Peel to refer himself to the authority of Max Weber in particular in this connection is in a way rather strange.

Weber did certainly argue that we must figure to ourselves the meaning of the behavior of others, get "inside" their subjectivity as it were. Action, he wrote, is social "insofar as its subjective meaning takes account of the behavior of others and is thereby oriented in its course."[50] But this is the same Weber who also put what one can only describe as enormous emphasis on unintended or unanticipated consequences of purposive social action. Who can go through the vast body of Weber's work without seeing that this is the case? It is one of the most familiar of Weber's statements that "the cultural consequences of the Reformation were to a great extent . . . unforeseen and perhaps even unwished-for results of the labors of the reformers."[51] Some of the silliest misunderstandings of Weber have come from historians who are enamored of the point that the Protestant reformers themselves cared not about economic matters but only to save souls from hell, as if Weber did not know full well that their primary concern was with salvation. He was talking about effects that transcended their intentions. As if to reinforce the point beyond doubt, Weber remarked in his study of Chinese religion that Puritanism created an intermediate link between a religious ethic and "a civic and methodical way of life," adding that Puritanism did so "unintentionally"; and we are thus instructed in "the paradox of unintended consequences, in the discrepancy between what men actually want and what comes out of their action."[52]

The same sort of point comes up repeatedly in Weber's work. When he discusses formal and substantive rationality in the economic realm, for

[49] See C. H. Cooley, "Reflections upon the Sociology of Herbert Spencer," in Cooley, *Sociological Theory and Social Research* (New York: Augustus M. Kelley, 1969), chap. 7.

[50] Max Weber, *Economy and Society* (New York: Bedminster Press, 1968), vol. 1, p. 4. I do not think I misunderstand Weber. Mühlmann writes relevantly, "Max Weber, in his day, formulated the program of an *understanding sociology* ("einer *verstehenden Soziologie*") in that he started from the view that in social events there exist non-understandable regularities aside from the understandable ones. But the understandable ones *specifically define* the object of the field. This may simply be extended and interpreted in the sense that for the scientific consideration of man in the sphere of humanistic anthropology the ascertainment of non-understandable regularities is not really specific, however important such regularities may otherwise be." Wilhelm E. Mühlmann, *Geschichte der Anthropologie* (Frankfurt am Main-Bonn: Athenaum Verlag), 2nd ed., 1968, p. 159. I would certainly grant what might loosely be called the "methodological" point. The great *actual* emphasis on unintended ("non-understandable") consequences in Weber's sociology, that I indicate, remains.

[51] Max Weber, *The Protestant Ethic* (London: Allen and Unwin, 1930), p. 90.

[52] Max Weber, *The Religion of China* (Glencoe: The Free Press, 1951), p. 238.

example, it is quite evident that his economic agents, operating, we may say, in a formally rational way, do not seek deliberately to fall short of some welfare standard projected by substantive rationality. Individual business firms seek their profits, but if the aggregate effect of this activity as such is not to attain some welfare standard, some substantive ideal proposed for the economy, this is surely no part of their intention and presumably also often enough no part of their anticipation.

Berkhofer has devoted a portion of his paper to the "fundamental dichotomy" that Peel suggests, the split between orientations to the subjectivity of the actor and to the outcomes of his actions that elude the grasp or exceed the scope of the subjective. But Berkhofer[53] appears to think that compromise in or combination of these orientations is, though "desirable," yet "analytically unattainable so far in historical analysis." Perhaps I do not quite understand him, but I do not readily see why this should be the case. Certainly Max Weber made do with both orientations. Berkhofer may have in mind some really profound interplay and analytical fusion which have not been attained up to now. But I cannot see why this sort of thing should not be possible at least in principle.

To return to Peel for a moment: his statement almost suggests that a sociology solely oriented to the study of unintended consequences and "latent functions" might be said to fail of being "human." But a sociology inattentive to such consequences and functions might *in some senses* be said to fail of being "social" or even "cultural." After all, if there are aspects of man's whole life that lend themselves to objectivistic handling, it may be the part of an ultimate greater "humanistic" wisdom to recognize these as involved in his humanity too.

I have, to say it in effect once again, conceived my polemical task broadly here, and have referred to such data as suicide rates, which in and of themselves are not "cultural." But it would have been easy enough to confine one's self to rather strictly cultural matters, such as styles. The broader range of reference has seemed desirable. Economists and historians, as well as anthropologists, sociologists and political scientists, constantly must deal with unintended or unanticipated consequences of action. Fueter's classic outline of modern historiography makes it clear that a well founded modern discipline of history could not arise except by transcending narrow "pragmatistic" views of historical agents (attributing far too considerable rationality and insight to such agents) and limited "catastrophist" outlooks, precisely in the way of recognizing the importance of the unintended and unanticipated.[54] Economics, so far as I can see, rests heavily on a base of close consideration of precipitations of market action, very often without any special concern for subjectivity. The misplaced humanism I have referred to would by too much turn our attention away

[53] P. 99.
[54] See Edouard Fueter, *Geschichte der Neueren Historiographie* (Munich and Berlin: R. Oldenbourg, 1936), esp. pp. 344–345.

from the unintended and the social and cultural precipitations that arise therefrom. While acknowledging that *both* subjectivistic and objectivistic orientations are, broadly, indispensable in the social sciences and certainly in the study of culture, I see the misplaced humanism I have been commenting on as a source of what I have already made bold to call authentic intellectual mischief.

As Boulding expresses cautious hope for a cultural economics, a cautious hope may here be expressed for the future of the idea of culture in the social sciences. But it does indeed seem well to be cautious. There appears to be no royal road or unequivocally fair prospect ahead for such social scientists as may be interested in seeking to enhance the services that the idea of culture and the analysis that has appeared in connection with it may perform for the social sciences. Yet there are some hints of heartening things here and there. Not the least heartening, in my view, is the willingness to grapple with pertinent issues shown in these essays. In ending, after all, on this "positive" note, I realize I run the risk of seeming as presumptuous as I already may have in the statement of the various disgruntlements I have expressed above. So be it.

Boon is seeking to articulate a set of intellectual dispositions with genuine flair, with erudition, and with an engaging willingness to have others witness what one suspects is a rather passionate groping for high-level understanding of culture. Boulding's effort is the more impressive as coming from a man who can hardly be accused of inadequate understanding of the core of economic analysis. One suspects, with him, that the activities of Federal Reserve officials could indeed, with some profit, be looked upon as tribal, ceremonial work. Parsons' summary of his thought on culture and social systems may in its very conciseness serve to remind readers how extensive the larger body of relevant work he has accomplished actually is. (It does no harm whatever to emphasize his scope— and his acumen—in a time when he is often perversely misunderstood and supposedly "explained" and disposed of on the grounds of a shoddy "sociological analysis" of his sociology.) Berkhofer's obvious desire and ability to acquaint himself with large areas of scholarship outside of history allow the hope that there will be more of this sort of thing and that wide-ranging social scientists will grapple with problems that call, precisely, for far-flung interests and for courage in pursuing them. Pye and Sopher exhibit a sheer consciousness of and sensitivity to cultural dimensions in their fields that also convey their measure of encouragement. The social sciences notoriously are not the highly impressive intellectual structures they might ideally be, and this is as true of cultural theory as of anything else in them; but, whatever the reasons for this, it is not obvious that lack of talent or of shrewd diligence on the part of the men devoted to them is a major cause for the situation.

INDEX